C000129854

An Introduction to the Ei
International Relations

AN INTRODUCTION TO THE ENGLISH SCHOOL OF INTERNATIONAL RELATIONS

The Societal Approach

BARRY BUZAN

polity

First published in 2014 by Polity Press

Polity Press
65 Bridge Street
Cambridge CB2 1UR, UK

Polity Press
350 Main Street
Malden, MA 02148, USA

ISBN-13: 978-0-7456-5314-3
ISBN-13: 978-0-7456-5315-0 (pb)

A catalogue record for this book is available from the British Library.

Typeset in 10.5 on 12 pt Times
by Toppan Best-set Premedia Limited
Printed and bound in Great Britain by Clays Ltd, St Ives PLC

CONTENTS

FOREWORD

Louise Knight at Polity had the original idea for this book, which she put to me in January 2010. It was conceived as a teaching text, but it has become more than that. It explains not only what the English School is, where it came from and how it is placed in the wider canon of IR, but also what its key concepts and ideas are and what is distinctive about them. It examines the English School's standing as theory, and it provides a guide to the main branches of work and their principal authors in the literature. It does not introduce many new concepts or arguments not already in the literature, though it does call for some obscure ones to be given more attention and in places goes into considerable depth to clarify complex issues and debates. It picks out the main trends, identifies places where further work is necessary, and sets out the ongoing research programme. The aim of the book is to makes sense of the existing literature rather than to try to extend it, as I did in my previous English School book (Buzan 2004).

The book speaks to three audiences. It provides a comprehensive guide to the English School's approach to international society that will serve the needs of beginners, whether at undergraduate or postgraduate level. For those with partial knowledge of the English School, it will both round out the picture and put what they know into context. For those already very familiar with the English School, I hope that the concentrated and comprehensive overview will provide them with new insights and new questions, as the process of writing this book has done for me. I hope that all readers will get a sense of where good research opportunities lie and that they will feel invited to join the English School's conversation.

Since part of the aim is to introduce readers to the literature, the bibliography and referencing are fairly extensive, though going for general representation rather than trying to be exhaustive. The book thus has a bibliographical essay woven throughout, which links to the more complete annually updated bibliography on the English School website: www.leeds.ac.uk/polis/englishschool/. To avoid obstructing the flow of reading, any reference containing more than three sources has been put into the endnotes. The book covers a very wide range of topics, from war to environment and from nationalism to the market, many of which have extensive literatures of their own. My strategy is to focus almost exclusively on the English School output on these topics and not to reference the wider literatures, except where they are sensitive to English School ideas.

The English School is taught mainly as part of omnibus courses at both undergraduate and postgraduate level that cover IR theory as a whole. The book will be of use in such courses, and, like similar volumes on realism and other IR theories, also to those individuals who want to pursue the ideas further.

Since I am a part of the story here, and since this book is in part intended to be a guide to the literature, I have referred to myself and my work in the third person, trying to locate my own contributions in the same way that I have done for other authors. My aim is to provide an evenly balanced description and assessment of the English School. I have tried to avoid making it merely an extension of my own lines of argument, which, while part of the English School's conversation, are not representative of the mainstream.

Several people across the range of the English School have been of invaluable assistance in helping me to shape and execute this project. Alex Bellamy and Molly Cochran commented on the original proposal. Will Bain, Tim Dunne, Andrew Hurrell, Andrew Linklater, Richard Little, Cornelia Navari and John Williams commented both on the proposal and on the first draft of the full manuscript. Robert Falkner, Rita Floyd and Nick Wheeler commented on the first draft, and Cornelia Navari, Brunello Vigezzi, Peter Wilson and Yongjin Zhang commented on the penultimate version. Lene Hansen, George Lawson and Iver Neumann helped me on particular points. The thoughtful, constructive and often very detailed inputs of this group represent collegiality of the highest order. They had a considerable impact both on the ultimate design of the book and on too many of the points made along the way to allow for more than occasional individual acknowledgment. I thank them deeply both for helping me to find a fair balance and for embodying the collaborative spirit of the English School's 'great conversation'.

I would also like to thank the anonymous reviewers for Polity for helpful comments on the proposal and the manuscript.

The text of chapter V draws heavily on Barry Buzan and Richard Little, 'The Historical Expansion of International Society', in Navari and Green, 2014.

Part I gives a general overview of the English School's history, main ideas, methodology and placement in the wider canon of IR theory. Part II gives a detailed look at the historical, regional and social structural strands of English School work. Part III explores the normative side of the English School through an in-depth account and analysis of pluralist and solidarist orientations towards order and justice, and how these play out in the evolution of primary institutions over the last half millennium. The concluding chapter looks at ongoing debates and at how the English School research programme is unfolding.

Barry Buzan
London, September 2013

PART I   BACKGROUND AND CONTEXT

INTRODUCTION

The three short chapters in this part set the context for the longer looks at the main lines of work in the English School in parts II and III. Chapter 1 gives a brief history of the English School, and chapter 2 sets out the key concepts, distinctions and understandings used in its literature. Chapter 3 addresses its methodology and theoretical standing, and surveys how it stands in relation to other mainstream approaches to thinking about international relations.

1 THE EVOLUTION OF THE ENGLISH SCHOOL

A reasonable date for the beginning of the English School is 1959, when the British Committee on the Theory of International Politics (hereafter, the British Committee) first met. But, like the association between 1648 and the sovereign state, any such date marks a fairly arbitrary median point in a longer process. In organizational terms, the origins of the British Committee can be traced back to the mid-1950s (Vigezzi 2005: 109–16; Epp 2010). In conceptual terms, the idea of 'international society', often seen as the flagship concept of the English School, is not original to it. The German historian Heeren's (1834) discussion of states-systems was influential on early English School thinking (Keene 2002; Little 2008b), and the term has been intrinsic to international law since at least the nineteenth century (Schwarzenberger 1951).

The name 'English School' was not coined until Roy Jones (1981) used it in calling for its closure. In a sweet irony, it became a label accepted both by those within and those outside the School (Suganami 2003: 253–7). Like many such labels, including 'realism' and indeed 'international relations' itself, 'English School' is a poor fit with what it represents. Some of its founding figures were not English – Hedley Bull was Australian, Charles Manning South African – and its focus has always been on history and theory for the global level of international relations. It never had any particular interest in British foreign policy. More arguably, there is nothing particularly English about its ideas, which might better be understood as a European amalgam of history, law, sociology and political theory. The key classical theorist with whom the English School is most closely associated is Grotius, a Dutchman. Somewhat embarrassingly, its initial funding came from American foundations (initially Rockefeller, later Ford). But

'English School' has now become an established brand name, pushing alternatives ('British School', 'classical approach', 'international society school') to the margins.

Why 'School'? Dunne (1998: 1–22) sets out the various criteria of self-identification, external recognition and shared intellectual foundations that justify the use of the term in this case. More abstractly, Suganami (2010) offers a helpful way of thinking about the ontology of the English School by distinguishing between a club and a network, and between a grouping and a succession of scholars. How did this 'School' unfold?

Initially, there was just the idea of a society of states/international society. This was a more historical, legal, philosophical and, up to a point, sociological way of thinking about international relations than the more mechanistic idea of international system that was becoming dominant in the field of International Relations (IR) in the US after the Second World War. As Wight (1991) sets out in detail, the idea of international society offered a kind of middle ground, or what later became labelled the *via media*, between the extremes of liberal, or revolutionist, and realist views of international relations. The English School conception of IR had, as Epp (2010) puts it, right from the beginning 'seen a somewhat different subject all along'. Robert Jackson (1992: 271) nicely sums up this conception of the subject of IR as:

> a variety of theoretical inquiries which conceive of international relations as a world not merely of power or prudence or wealth or capability or domination but also one of recognition, association, membership, equality, equity, legitimate interests, rights, reciprocity, customs and conventions, agreements and disagreements, disputes, offenses, injuries, damages, reparations, and the rest: the normative vocabulary of human conduct.

Thinking along these lines was developing inside several heads well before the first meeting of the British Committee, not just Schwarzenberger's but also those of Martin Wight and Charles Manning, both teaching at the London School of Economics (LSE) during the 1950s (Manning since 1930). De Almeida (2003: 277–9) goes so far as to argue that the British Committee was not just constructing a *via media* between realism and liberalism. Under Wight's leadership it was recovering a fully fledged third position of thinking about IR – *rationalism* – with its roots in the works of Grotius, Locke, Hume, Burke and de Tocqueville, that had got lost during the great world wars of the twentieth century.

Following on from the idea of international society came that most English of things, a club. The British Committee was a self-selected group of scholars and practitioners mixing academics from History, Philosophy,

IR and Theology with practitioners from the Foreign Office and the Treasury.[1] The British Committee eschewed current affairs and policy questions and focused on developing a general understanding of international relations around the concept of international society. It was perhaps more successful as a discussion group, sharpening up and pushing forward the thinking of its individual members, than it was as a project group generating publications. One cannot divorce the outstanding individual works of those who participated in it from the deliberations of the British Committee.[2] It did, however, produce two landmark edited volumes in its own right: *Diplomatic Investigations* (1966), edited by Butterfield and Wight, and *The Expansion of International Society* (1984), edited by Bull and Watson. The British Committee also inspired independent but linked projects. Porter (1972) has a strong English School content, and a parallel project group based at the LSE published three edited volumes picking up and extending on many of the themes within the British Committee's work on the idea of international society.[3]

Being a club with a clear set of participants, the British Committee generated unhelpful disputes about the membership of the wider School: who was in and who was not, as members of the English School network more broadly (Dunne 1998; Linklater and Suganami 2006: 12–42; Suganami 2010). The participants in the British Committee are on record (Vigezzi 2005), and there is no question that Herbert Butterfield,[4] Hedley Bull,[5] Adam Watson[6] and Martin Wight[7] were the key players. The principal exclusions from this club were Charles Manning[8] and E. H. Carr, both of whom have their backers as foundational figures for the English School. Manning was an influential thinker who did much not just to establish IR as a distinct field of study in Britain but also to embed a sociological, constructivist way of thinking about 'international society' as a 'double abstraction', with imagined states imagining themselves to be members of an international society. His idea that international society is a game of 'let's-play-states' (1962: 165) is one that might well resonate with contemporary poststructuralists, as might his use of extravagant metaphors. Since, in Manning's view, both states and international society are social constructions, they are, in contrast to realist conceptions, malleable.

Carr's most influential work for IR (Carr 1946) had no obvious sympathy for the idea of international society. In it he argued against harmony of interest liberalism and saw international society largely as an artefact of the dominant powers, whom he described as 'masters in the art of concealing their selfish national interests in the guise of the general good' (ibid.: 79, 95–7, 167). Yet he did allow for something like international society to exist, albeit with its terms very much set down and manipulated by the dominant powers rather than being in some sense independent of them (ibid.: 143). His dialectical critique of both utopianism (as dangerously divorced from the nature of things) and realism (as politically sterile and fatalistic), and his argument for the necessity of blending power and morality in international relations, seemed to leave room precisely for a *via media* of the type offered by the English School's idea of international society (Dunne 1998: 23–46). At the same time, however, the oppositional tensions between realism and idealism tended to diminish the space for thinking about international society. It was not uncommon for the founding writers of the English School to think that the extremes of Cold War politics were squeezing out international society (e.g., Wight 1991: 259–68).

Two others, also not part of the British Committee, John Burton (1972) and Evan Luard (1976, 1990; Roberts 1992), worked on similar themes around this time. Luard wrote about international society, and Burton, prefiguring what would later become the debates about transnationalism and the transcendence of the state system, about world society. They worked in Britain, but are not generally considered to be part of the English School because, despite some commonality of terms, they did not relate to its concepts and discussions. Indeed, Burton and the English School rather saw each other as enemies (Brown 2001: 429–32).

Following Suganami's lead, one can see that by the 1970s, and certainly during the 1980s, the English School was becoming more of a network of scholars than a specific club, and increasingly a succession of scholars across generations rather than a particular grouping in place and time. The club element faded away during the 1980s and was replaced by a looser and more global network and generational succession of scholars during the 1990s. Among other things, this made debates about who was in or out much less relevant. In this book, I take a broad view – the English School is a 'great conversation' comprised of anyone who wants to talk about the concepts of international and world society and who relates in some substantive way to the foundational literature on those topics. It is not a School in the narrow sense of representing a specific line of thought on which all adherents are agreed.

Thanks in no small part to the impact of Bull's (1977) *The Anarchical Society*, the main elements, or themes, of this 'great conversation' were already pretty well worked out by the end of the 1980s and set the template for much of the English School literature that would follow during the 1990s and beyond. There were two reasonably distinct historical projects. One, mainly comparative, was initiated by Martin Wight and carried forward by Adam Watson. This project, discussed in chapter 4, looked back into history to find other cases of international society that could be compared with each other and with the European case (Wight 1977; Watson

1992). The other, mainly in the form of developmental history (set out in chapter 5), was to look more specifically at the formation of the European ('Westphalian') international society. Here the key theme was, from the late fifteenth century, the expansion of European international society beyond its cultural home base to dominate the whole planet, together with the problems that arose as a result (Wight 1977; Bull and Watson 1984a; Gong 1984a). As Epp (1998: 49) notes, this project sustained a specific English School interest in the consequences of decolonization and a more general one in the role of culture in world politics, even when these topics, and the School itself, were unfashionable.

The expansion story gave rise to a number of more conceptual and normative themes. Considerable attention was given to the five institutions of the classical Westphalian international society: war, diplomacy, the balance of power, international law, and great power management.[9] How had these institutions evolved in Europe, and what kind of order did they produce, both there and in the global international society that Europe imposed on the rest of the world? These classical five institutions did not satisfy everyone as a complete set, and other candidates for this status were also put into play: sovereignty (Brewin 1982; James 1986) and nationalism (Porter 1982; Mayall 1990).

Related to this were both more general attempts to theorize international and world society (Butterfield and Wight 1966; Bull 1966a, 1971, 1977) and more practical and normative concerns about the management of contemporary international society. Although the British Committee was famously disinterested in giving policy advice on current affairs (Dunne 1998: 90, 96; Epp 2010), the English School was deeply interested in the questions of order and justice that arose from the highly uneven and inequitable way in which the expansion story had generated the contemporary global-scale international society. What were the proper roles and responsibilities of the state in international society, both in general (Windsor 1978; Navari 1991) and specifically relating to great power responsibilities and the management of international society (Bull 1980, 1982)? How was one to understand the legitimacy of an international society that mixed equality and inequality (Wight 1977; Butler 1978)? In general, how could the sometimes conflicting and sometimes interdependent imperatives for order and justice be met in international society?[10] This order/justice dilemma framed what become known as the pluralist–solidarist debate within the English School, which is covered in depth in Part III. More specifically, given that nonintervention was almost a corollary of sovereignty, what was the role of intervention in international society (Vincent 1974; Little 1975; Bull 1984b)? Linking to the more general order/justice question, this topic became a prominent part of another key branch of the

English School literature, that on human rights and the relationship between the society of states, on the one hand, and the cosmopolitan community of all humankind, on the other (Bull 1984a; Vincent 1986).

Naturally, these various themes, approaches and debates generated controversy and opposition within the English School. But it is important to understand such divisions of approach and analysis as interrelated aspects of a broader attempt to work out the history and nature of international society as a social construction. That done, one might then try to clarify the implications of this way of understanding international relations for the possibilities of public policy.

During the 1990s, the post-club English School network continued to produce work on all of these themes, both collective volumes[11] and significant individual and joint works.[12] Buzan's (2001) 1999 call for a reconvening of the English School failed to re-create any sort of club, but it did succeed in strengthening both the sense of community within the School and the degree of recognition outside it.[13] The English School became a more organized presence at IR conferences, and from 2003 there was an active English School section within the International Studies Association. It became more acknowledged as one of the mainstream IR 'paradigms' and attracted more attention as a subject for PhD work.

Roy Jones's (1981) critique of the English School also inaugurated an ongoing critical discussion and self-assessment, which, depending on one's point of view, can be seen either as a sign of healthy self-reflection or as suggesting a bit of angst and self-obsession.[14] Whichever interpretation one prefers, this literature and the various edited volumes about the English School constitute a useful guide to how the School's understanding of itself has unfolded, and how it sees itself as relating to other Schools of thought in IR. Also notable is the continuing centrality of Bull, who remains the best-known representative of the English School. After his death in 1985, (re)considerations of his work became a significant niche in the English School literature.[15]

In the twenty-first century, the English School both consolidated itself as a network and confirmed itself as an ongoing succession of scholars across generations. The tradition of collective works about the School carried on,[16] and there was an impressive flow of significant individual and joint volumes.[17] The long-neglected subject of international society at the regional level began to receive attention.[18] Both the normative and structural approaches to international society sharpened up their acts, and there was intensifying interest in revisiting the by now dated story told by the British Committee (Bull and Watson 1984a) about the expansion of international society (Keene 2002; Buzan 2010a; and, for a review of the literature, Buzan and Little 2010). Despite some earlier work by Armstrong

(1977, 1993), Fred Halliday (2009) was still rightly of the view that the English School had not paid enough attention to the role of revolutions in the story of international society. For those wanting more detail on sources, a reasonably full bibliography of English School writing can be accessed and searched at www.leeds.ac.uk/polis/englishschool/.

The English School retains a strong but far from dominant position in British IR, with notable concentrations at Aberystwyth, the LSE and Oxford and a presence in most places where IR is taught. As from the beginning, some of this strength comes from Australians and other non-Brits working in the UK. In Europe more widely, there is significant interest in Denmark, Germany and Italy, with outposts in Norway, Turkey and Israel. The English School has a solid presence in the white Commonwealth, mainly Canada and Australia, and some outposts in India. It struggled to get established in the intensely parochial US IR market, despite having a scattering of followers. But, with the establishment of the ISA section, it seems now to have found its feet. As Stephen Krasner (1999: 46) acknowledged, the English School is the 'best known sociological perspective in IR'. More recently, the School has attracted interest in Northeast Asia, particularly in China,[19] and also in Japan (Hosoya 1998; Ikeda 2009) and Korea (Shin 2008, and see other articles in that issue of *Journal of World Politics*),[20] where it resonates with historical approaches to IR and also serves as an antidote to what some see as the excessive influence of American IR theory in their universities (Y. Zhang 2014). Whether appropriately or not, the existence of an 'English' School is taken as justification for developing more national approaches to IR theory, such as the mooted 'Chinese School' (Qin 2005; Wang and Buzan 2014).

2 KEY CONCEPTS

English School thinking is built around a triad of three key concepts: *international system, international society* and *world society* (Cutler 1991; Little 1995: 15–16). Within the English School discourse these are usually codified as *Hobbes* (or sometimes *Machiavelli*), *Grotius* and *Kant*. They stem from Wight's (1991) foundational 'three traditions' of IR theory: *realism, rationalism*[1] and *revolutionism*. Wight's three traditions can themselves be traced back via the work of Hersch Lauterpacht to a parallel debate in International Law among those supporting natural law, positive law and the *via media* of the Grotian view combining elements of both (Simpson 2004; Jeffery 2006). The three traditions idea thus reflects a time when International Law and International Relations were much less separated fields of study than they have now become.

Broadly speaking, these terms are now understood as follows:

- *International system* (Hobbes/Machiavelli/realism) is about power politics among states and puts the structure and process of international anarchy at the centre of IR theory. This position is broadly parallel to mainstream realism and neorealism and is thus well developed and clearly understood outside the English School. It is based on an ontology of states and is generally approached with a positivist epistemology, materialist and rationalist methodologies, and structural theories.
- *International society* (Grotius/rationalism), or sometimes *states-system*, or *interstate society*, or *society of states*, is about the institutionalization of mutual interest and identity among states and puts the creation and maintenance of shared norms, rules and institutions at the centre

of IR theory. The basic idea of international society is quite simple: just as human beings as individuals live in societies which they both shape and are shaped by, so also states live in an international society which they shape and are shaped by. Wight (1991: 137) nicely captures it with the idea that international society is a social contract among societies themselves each constituted by their own social contract.[2] But because states are very different entities from individual human beings, this international society is *not* analogous to domestic society (Bull 1966b, 1966c; Suganami 1989) and has to be studied as a distinct form. This social element has to be put alongside realism's raw logic of anarchy if one is to get a meaningful picture of how systems of states operate. When units are sentient, how they perceive each other is a major determinant of how they interact. If the units share a common identity (a religion, a system of governance, a language) or even just a common set of rules or norms (about how to determine relative status and how to conduct diplomacy), then these intersubjective understandings not only condition their behaviour and identity but also define the boundaries of a social system. This position has some parallels to regime theory, but is much deeper, having constitutive rather than merely instrumental implications (Hurrell 1993; Dunne 1995b: 140–3). International society has been the main focus of English School thinking, and the concept is quite well developed and relatively clear. In parallel with international system, it is also based on an ontology of states, but is generally approached with a constructivist epistemology and historical methods. It can also be approached as a social structure.

- *World society* (Kant/revolutionism) takes individuals, non-state organizations and ultimately the global population as a whole as the focus of global societal identities and arrangements and puts transcendence of the state system at the centre of IR theory. Revolutionism is mostly about forms of universalist cosmopolitanism. It could include communism, but, as Wæver (1992: 98) notes, these days it is usually taken to mean liberalism, an interpretation that underlines Halliday's complaint that the English School pays insufficient attention to revolution. This position has some parallels to transnationalism but carries a much more foundational link to normative political theory. It clearly does not rest on an ontology of states but, given the transnational element, neither does it rest entirely on one of individuals. Critical theory defines some but not all of the approaches to it, and in Wightean mode it is more about historically operating alternative images of the international system as a whole than it is about capturing the non-state aspects of the system.[3]

In typically terse fashion, Bull (1991: xi) sums up Wight's view as Machiavellians being 'the blood and iron and immorality men'; Grotians being 'the law and order and keep your word men' who represent 'the perspective of the international establishment'; and Kantians being 'the subversion and liberation and missionary men'.

Jackson (2000: 169–78) puts an interesting twist on the three traditions by viewing them as defining the diverse values that statespeople have to juggle in the conduct of foreign policy. Realism he sees as giving priority to national responsibilities, rationalism as giving priority to international responsibilities, and revolutionism (which, picking up the now dominant liberal interpretation, he prefers to call cosmopolitanism) as giving priority to humanitarian responsibilities. He adds a fourth, more recent value – stewardship of the planet – in effect giving priority to responsibility for the physical environment.

The classical English School framework is summarized in figure 2.1.

As captured in figure 2.1, the idea is that these three key concepts form a complete and interlinked picture of the IR universe. Although each element is conceptually and methodologically distinct, they blur into each other at the boundaries. In the English School perspective all three elements are in continuous coexistence and interplay, the main question at

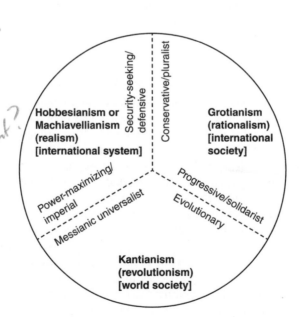

Figure 2.1   The classical 'three traditions' model of English School theory

any given time and place being how strong they are in relation to each other (Bull 1991: xvii–xviii; Dunne 1995b: 134–7). This fluid framework opens up a wide range of scenarios: from hard realist ones in which states compete ruthlessly for power (system dominant); through more ordered ones in which states pursue degrees of coexistence, cooperation, and even convergence (society dominant); to ones in which states are no longer the dominant unit (world society dominant). In Wight's view, 'The greatest political writers in international theory almost all straddle the frontiers dividing two of the traditions' (Roberts 1991: xxv). The distinction between system and society has played a central role in English School thinking, with world society playing more at the margins. Both the system/society distinction and the marginalization of world society have been disputed, on which more below. Yet despite some harsh critiques (Keene 2002: 29–39) this framing remains influential at the core of most English School writing. Since international society is the concept most distinctive to the English School, much of its literature privileges this over the other two parts of the triad.[4]

Within this general framework three other pairs of concepts define the core vocabulary of the English School:

- *First- and second-order societies First-order societies* are those in which the members are individual human beings. Such societies have been the principal subject of Sociology, and much of what falls under *world society* is about first-order societies. *Second-order societies* are those in which the members are not individual human beings but durable collectivities of humans, such as states, which are possessed of identities and actor qualities that are more than the sum of their parts. As noted above, the English School rejects the domestic analogy for international society, seeing it as a distinctive form. The terms first- and second-order society are not (yet) in common use, but the very idea of an international society requires acceptance that such a thing as a second-order society is possible. In the English School perspective, IR is mainly about the study of second-order societies, a subject largely neglected by Sociology (Buzan and Albert 2010).
- *Pluralism and solidarism* Within the idea of international society, and particularly related to the debates about order and justice, human rights and (non)intervention, two positions have emerged which are labelled *pluralist* and *solidarist*. The terms were coined by Bull (1966b) and have remained central structuring concepts for normative debates within the English School (Wheeler 1992; Dunne and Wheeler 1996; Bain 2010). They are quite complex, and I will return to them in more detail in Part III.

o *Pluralism* represents the communitarian disposition towards a state-centric mode of association in which sovereignty and nonintervention serve to contain and sustain cultural and political diversity. It is in this general sense status quo orientated and concerned mainly about maintaining interstate order. As a rule, pluralists, following Bull, will argue that, although a deeply unjust system cannot be stable, order is in important ways a prior condition for justice.

o *Solidarism* represents the disposition either to transcend the states-system with some other mode of association or to develop it beyond a logic of coexistence to one of cooperation on shared projects. In principle solidarism could represent a wide range of possibilities (Buzan 2004: 121, 190–200), but in practice within the English School it has been linked mainly to liberal cosmopolitan perspectives and to concerns about justice. Solidarists typically emphasize that order without justice is undesirable and ultimately unsustainable.

Pluralism and solidarism hinge on the question of the type and extent of norms, rules and institutions that an international society can form without departing from the foundational rules of sovereignty and non-intervention that define it as a system of states. In the English School context it is important to see pluralism and solidarism *not* as opposed and mutually exclusive positions. Their proponents may sometimes think of themselves as opposed, and the language of the debate may sometimes take oppositional form. But, in a detached perspective, their core function is to define the central, permanent tension in the English School's 'great conversation' about how to find the best balance between order and justice in international society. As indicated in figure 2.1, pluralism and solidarism define the boundary zones of rationalism/international society, respectively towards realism and revolutionism, and so play an instrumental role in linking together the English School's triad of concepts.

• *Primary and secondary institutions* This usage is also not (yet) well established, even though the understanding it represents is deeply implicit in the whole idea of international society. It relates to the common usage of 'institution', which can be understood either in quite specific terms, as 'an organisation or establishment founded for a specific purpose', or in more general ones, as 'an established custom, law, or relationship in a society or community' (for detailed discussion, see Holsti 2004; Buzan 2004: 161–204; Schouenborg 2011).

o *Primary institutions* are those talked about by the English School and reflect the second usage of 'institution' above. They are deep and relatively durable social practices in the sense of being evolved more than designed.[5] These practices must not only be shared among the members of international society but also be seen among them as legitimate behaviour. Primary institutions are thus about the shared identity of the members of international society. They are constitutive of both states and international society, in that they define not only the basic character of states but also their patterns of legitimate behaviour in relation to each other, as well as the criteria for membership of international society. The classical 'Westphalian' set consists of sovereignty, territoriality, the balance of power, war, diplomacy, international law and great power management, to which could be added nationalism, human equality and, more recently and controversially, the market. But primary institutions can be found across history wherever states have formed an international society.

○ *Secondary institutions* are those talked about in regime theory and by liberal institutionalists and relate to the organizational usage of the term. They are the products of a certain types of international society (most obviously liberal, but possibly other types as well) and are for the most part intergovernmental arrangements consciously designed by states to serve specific functional purposes. They include the United Nations, the World Bank, the World Trade Organization and the nuclear non-proliferation regime. Secondary institutions are a relatively recent invention, first appearing as part of industrial modernity in the later decades of the nineteenth century.

Also worth highlighting are two other concepts distinctive to the English School. The first is *the 'standard of civilization'*, which will recur frequently throughout the book. This concept was taken from International Law and diplomatic and international legal practice, where it became deeply embedded during the nineteenth century (Kingsbury 1999: 72–7; Fidler 2000; Bowden 2009: locs. 1633–1787), but its contemporary usage in IR is distinctive to the English School. It originates from the nineteenth-century practice of differentiating among states and peoples in hierarchical terms of 'civilized', 'barbarian' and 'savage', and using these classifications to gatekeep on entry to European, and later Western, international society. Since 1945, the blatancy of such designations has more or less disappeared from polite international discourse. But, as Fidler (2000: 388–9) argues, 'the rejection of the "standard of civilization" as a driving force of international law [has] been more apparent than real.' The substance remains very much in terms of conditionality of entry to various clubs, the conduct of the global economy (Bowden and Seabrooke 2006), and much of the discourse around human rights. Bowden (2009: loc. 2589) shows how the discourses around failed states and terrorism have revived the 'standard of civilization' and notes that, 'Like the classical standard, the current measure of civilization revolves around the capacity of Non-western states to govern and conduct themselves in such a manner that they can engage with the West on its terms, whether that be through trade or war.' For the English School this concept provides useful leverage against a too easy assumption that sovereign equality is a simple or uniform practice. I put 'standard of civilization' in inverted commas to signify that it is always the construct of one party in a relationship, usually the dominant one, and not a statement about some essential condition. As Fidler (2000: 389) sums up the idea: 'to engage fully in international relations, your behaviour has to conform fully to expectations, policies, and rules established by the prevailing powers.'

The second concept is *raison de système*, coined by Watson (1992: 14) and defined as 'the belief that it pays to make the system work'. This concept can be seen as a way of encapsulating the English School's core normative debate between pluralism and solidarism. It stands as a counterpoint to the idea of *raison d'état*, which is central explicitly to realism and implicitly to much Western IR theory.[6] *Raison de système* is not widely used in the English School literature but has a good claim for wider deployment. It neatly encapsulates the logic underlying international society, and therefore what differentiates English School thinking from other lines of IR theory.

While these concepts and vocabulary are broadly common to English School thinking, it is nevertheless possible to understand the School's approach to international society in three different, though potentially overlapping, ways:

1 as a set of ideas to be found in the minds and language of those who play the game of states;
2 as a set of ideas to be found in the minds of political theorists;
3 as a set of concepts defining the material and social structures of the international system in terms set by academic analysts.

Manning (1962) is the classical exponent of the first view. For Manning, the idea of international society was just that – an idea. What was important for him was that this was not just any idea, or anyone's idea. It was an idea incorporated into the official thinking of states about their mutual intercourse. It formed part of the assumption that was intersubjectively embedded as orthodoxy among those who talked and acted in the name of states. For Manning, understanding world politics necessarily meant that the analyst should understand the thoughts that underlie the actions of statespeople. Thus, the idea of international society was not an analyst's idea, invented externally to the practice. Rather, the analyst reconstructs the idea of international society already contained in the collective discourse and reproduced in the practice.[7] The central subject of study in this perspective is diplomats and diplomatic practice (see also Osiander 1994: 1–11; Jackson 2000; Wilson 2012).

The second view is most manifest in Wight's (1991) idea of the three traditions, but it is also strongly present in the work of Bull (1966b, 1977), Vincent (1986), and many others who participate in the debates of the English School from the perspective of political theory.[8] Wight's three categories of international thought are extracted from writings by international lawyers, political philosophers, diplomats and statespeople. In this version, English School theory is a set of ideas that fill the minds of people as they think about and/or participate in world politics. The three traditions can be seen as the framing for the English School's 'great conversation', setting out the primary positions that are always in some sense in play in discussions about foreign policy and international relations. The approaches and concerns of political theory and international legal thought are strong in this perspective. They inform not only the influential strand of normative theory in English School thinking but also the disposition to think in terms of both universal principles and a levels of analysis distinction between individuals and the state. By 'universal principles' I mean here those principles whose validity requires that they be applied to all the members of a specified group.

There is some tendency in this political theory understanding to treat English School theory as part of the history of ideas, and therefore as essentially a philosophical debate, as opposed to a discussion about the condition of the real world. The scope for normative positioning within this debate is large. At one end, much of English School writing about pluralist international society could be read from a progressive perspective as justifying the history of imperialism. At the other end, there is a strong and persistent progressive concern to improve the condition of world politics by getting practitioners to change their conceptual maps of world politics towards more enlightened forms. This normative approach to English School theory has been the dominant one, strongly influenced by the core questions of political theory: 'What is the relationship between citizen and state?'; 'How do we lead the good life?'; and 'How is progress possible in international society?'.

The third view sees international system, international society and world society as a set of analytical concepts designed to capture the material and social structures of the international system (Buzan and Little 2000; Buzan 2004). This view is strong in the work of Bull (1977) and even more so in that of James (1978, 1986, 1993). Some inspiration for it might be taken from Manning's (1962) idea to validate the standing of states as collective actors and to understand the games that they play. Thinking along these lines is analogous to the structural approaches taken by non-English School IR theorists such as Waltz (1979), who is interested only in material structures, and Wendt (1999), who sets up a social structural approach. This approach does not have any necessary normative content in the sense of promoting preferred values (though that is not excluded). Norms and ideas play their role here as different forms of social structure: not normative theory, but theory about norms. It is about finding sets of analytical constructs with which to describe and theorize about what goes on in the world, and in that sense it is a positivist approach, though not a materialist one. One illustration of its potential strengths is shown by Little's (2000: 404–8; 2007) discussion of how English School theory leads to a much different understanding of the balance of power than one finds in the purely mechanical idea of it in neorealism.

This, then, is the key vocabulary and set of distinctions that both mark out English School theory from other approaches to IR and structure its societal approach to the subject. Unless otherwise specified, the definitions set out here will apply to all that follows.

3 THEORIES AND METHODOLOGIES

Given the demand for methodological precision and theoretical rigour led since the 1950s mainly by American IR, there have been longstanding questions put to the English School about its methods, theoretical standing and place in the discipline of IR. Is the English School a theory? Does it have any methodology? Is it methodologically eclectic? Are its terms specified rigorously enough? Is it a distinctive position within IR, or just some kind of soft version of realism, or an early (and by implication primitive) version of constructivism? Does it represent some kind of Atlantic divide between an American IR that strives to reduce the subject to a branch of physics amenable to the cause–effect logic of positivist analysis and a European IR that takes a more contingent, historical and sociological view of the subject?

Questioning the English School's methodology and theoretical standing

These kinds of questions were given a particular edge early on by the robust stance taken by Hedley Bull (1966a), already a leading figure in the English School, against the 'scientific' (positivist) approaches and methods that, under the label *behaviouralism*, were coming to dominate American IR during the 1950s and 1960s. Bull defended a so-called classical approach to the subject based more on history, law and political theory and, for some (not Bull: most clearly Wight, Butterfield and Mackinnon), also resting on more than a touch of Christian theology. This 'classical' approach carries with it a clear and coherent method that has been most clearly articulated by Jackson (2000). It aims to combine the normative and the analytical, and it is most clearly represented in the work of Jackson (1992, 1996a, 2000, 2009) and Hurrell (2001, 2007b). Bull's view was fairly representative of the attitude in the British Committee (Dunne 1998: 117–24; Linklater and Suganami 2006: 97–108; Navari 2009: 5–14), and so from an early point both set the English School apart from mainstream American IR theory and marginalized it within the American-dominated IR discourse. From a behaviouralist perspective, the English School represented the traditional thinking, with its soft logic, fuzzy methodology and confusion of the normative and empirical, that they were trying to move away from (Copeland 2003). As Finnemore (2001) notes, the English School did not generate much traction in American IR debates because it did not do enough to specify either its methods or its aims and did not sharpen up its own understanding by engaging with other theories. She (2001: 509, 513) puts the pointed questions: 'How do you know an international society (or international system, or world society) when you see one?' and 'How is it, exactly, that politics moves from an international system to an international society, or from an international society to a world society?'

As Navari (2009: 39–57) argues it, English School scholars were not closed-minded about materialist factors and causal hypotheses: e.g., Wight's (1977: 174–200) look at polarity; Watson's pendulum theory (1990, 1992: 13–18, 120–32; see also Buzan and Little 1996; Wæver 1996: 223–5); and, even more clearly, Holsti's approach to institutions (2004, 2009). In both its comparative and developmental historical work, the English School was certainly interested in finding general patterns and making structural comparisons across space and time. But English School scholars were generally much more interested in analysing the social dynamics: the ideational forces, the rules of conduct, the intentionality of the actors, and the normative tensions and problems generated by the interplay of these factors. They were specifically interested in sustaining the normative engagement with the study of IR that materialist, 'scientific' approaches tended to marginalize, and this commitment explains their methodological choices and priorities. Whereas material causality was appropriate to the study of *systems*, *societies* could only be understood through the consciousness and moral character of the actors within them. Not until the rise of constructivism to respectability in American IR made intersubjective understanding fashionable, and stood mutual constitution against cause–effect logic, did the English School and its approach achieve real recognition in the US as a respectable approach to the subject.

As a result of the pressure arising from this epistemological divide, and from critics such as Finnemore and Copeland, there is now a substantial literature on English School methodology.[1] The earlier indifference of the School to methodological specification has given way to a greater awareness of the need to position oneself in the epistemological debates. Although there are now at least some answers to Finnemore's questions,[2] more remains to be done. Finnemore's questions can also be put to the concept of primary institutions, and here too there are some answers,[3] though again more needs to be done.

Perhaps the most common depiction of the English School in these terms is that it is theoretically and methodologically eclectic or 'pluralist'.[4] This understanding has been developed most prominently by Linklater (1990) and Little (1995, 1998, 2000, 2009). It is closely linked to the triad of international system, international society and world society, which requires the School to address the ontologically distinct aspects that compose the international whole (Buzan 2004: 6–10, 22–4). Linklater and Suganami (2006: 81–4), no doubt correctly, argue that theoretical/methodological eclecticism was an accidental development in English School thinking rather than one that was consciously planned. Little (2009), building on his earlier work, and particularly his critique of Linklater's (1990) attempt to link the pillars of the triad to different methodological approaches, defends his broad view of the English School and the necessity within that breadth for the School to be methodologically eclectic. Linklater associates international system/realism with positivism, international society/rationalism with hermeneutics, and world society/revolutionism with critical theory. Little agrees on positivism and international systems, but he assigns hermeneutics to both international society and world society (see also Epp 1998). For Little, as for Linklater, methodological eclecticism is a necessary consequence of the English School's basic triad and, more broadly, its ambition to take a holistic approach to the study of international relations. Indeed, Dunne (2008: 271) goes so far as to argue that this holistic approach is the key defining feature of the English School, more so than its flagship concept of international society.

The English School never accepted the argument about incommensurable paradigms that for a time separated liberal, realist and Marxian approaches to IR. In its search for *raison de système*, it always retained its potential as a site for synthesizing grand theory. Little (2008a: 682–3) compares the English School's holistic approach to knowledge creation with the 'fragmented' approach dominant in the US. Dunne (2008: 280) similarly contrasts the English School with the 'metatheoretical exclusionism' practised in the US. He sees it as avoiding the conflictual 'either/or' choices of realism versus idealism and explaining versus understanding by offering an approach that combines agency and structure, theory and history, and morality and power (ibid.: 268, 271).

This debate about how to integrate and understand the English School's triad clearly reflects back on the point made above about materialist theories being appropriate for the study of international systems, while international society (and world society) requires an understanding of the intentions of the actors and the shared rules of conduct. It also reflects the English School's views on international law (see Wilson 2009), with pluralists leaning towards positive international law and solidarists towards natural law and progressive international law. This methods debate blends into the longstanding tension between the normative (pursuit of progressive values) and the structural (objective, empirical) approaches in the British Committee and the English School more broadly (Dunne 1998: 99–104; Linklater and Suganami 2006: 108–13; see also Jackson 2009: 22–8). Within the British Committee there was general agreement to keep normative arguments separate from empirical ones. Hedley Bull and Alan James were notable sceptics about normative promotionalism, but John Vincent[5] and Nicholas Wheeler aimed to transcend mere empiricism. Bull remained suspicious of normative positioning, though his later work (1984b) revealed his own liberal stance. Perhaps in more recent times the mainstream view is that the normative and structural sides of the argument should not, and cannot, be separated (Cochran 2009: 221).

Whether or not one can talk about 'English School theory' depends somewhat on where this question is asked. Many Europeans use the term 'theory' for anything that organizes a field systematically, structures questions and establishes a coherent and rigorous set of interrelated concepts and categories. Many Americans, however, demand that a theory strictly *explains*, and that it contains – or is able to generate – testable hypotheses of a causal nature. English School theory clearly qualifies on the first (European) account but mainly not on the second (for an exception, see Mendelsohn 2009). And in its constructivist and normative theory aspects it cannot (and does not want to) meet the criteria for 'hard' (mainly positivist) theory. Given its necessary theoretical and methodological eclecticism, the English School cannot meet a requirement of theory that is linked to a single epistemology.

Nevertheless, the English School's ideas do have some interesting and important theoretical qualities. Most obviously, it sets out a distinctive taxonomy of what it is that IR should be taking as its principal objects of study: the triad of international system, international society and world society; first- and second-order societies; and primary and secondary institutions. Taxonomy has not been fashionable in IR theory but, because it identifies what it is that is to be theorized about, it is absolutely foundational to any theoretical enterprise. To the extent that a taxonomy is flawed, the whole foundation of theory is weakened. In my view, the English

School deserves more theoretical credit for its distinctive taxonomy than it gets, and I will try to show why in the discussion below about how the English School compares and contrasts with other mainstream IR theories. That said, however, the English School certainly deserves the brickbats it has received for not having been rigorous enough in defining its terms (Finnemore 2001; Buzan 2004; Navari 2009: 14–18; 2010), especially international and world society, and in Buzan's (2004) view also primary institutions and solidarism. This is, however, improving. Holsti (2004) has led the way on giving greater specificity to institutions (see also Buzan 2004: 161–204, and, for a dissenting view, Wilson 2012). There is now also more debate, building on James's (1993) critique of Bull, about whether or not the distinction between international system and international society is necessary, or whether a typology of international societies, such as Buzan's (2004: 190–5) power political, coexistence, cooperative, convergence, can capture both (Dunne 2008: 276–9; Little 2009: 81–7; Williams 2010a). I return to these debates in chapter 10.

Placing the English School in IR's theoretical canon

Given these general features, what is the English School's place in the wider field of International Relations? More specifically, how does it relate to the other main strands of IR theory? This latter question is particularly interesting given that the English School has been variously classified as a mere offshoot of realism, or a part of the idealist enterprise, or an early form of constructivism. The initial focus of English School work, particularly during the British Committee phase, centred on opening up space for the rationalist, international society, position between the longer-established realist and idealist (whether liberal or socialist) positions. By introducing international society as a third element, not only as a *via media* between realism and liberalism/cosmopolitanism but also as the keystone to an interdependent set of concepts, English School theory offered a way of transcending the binary opposition between them that formed the essence of the supposed first great debate about IR theory. As Wæver (1992: 99–100, 121) puts it, the English School has the ability to

> combine traditions and theories normally not able to relate to each other. . . . It promises to integrate essential liberal concerns with a respect for a fair amount of realist prudence; it promises to locate structural pressures in specific historical contexts and to open up for a structural study of international history.

IR theory in brief

All general theories of international relations identify some basic mechanism or driving force that explains how and why things work the way they do. For realism, this is power politics and relative gains. For liberalism, it is rational choice and absolute gains. For Marxism, it is the materialist dialectics of class struggle. For poststructuralists and constructivists, it is discursive process and the creation of intersubjective meaning. For the English School, it is the social dialectics of the desire to create a modicum of both order and justice beyond the level of the state. Some IR theories also offer a general picture of what the international system looks like and might look like. Realism sees a world of states and balance of power. It does not offer a vision of improvement, but it does show how things change with different distributions of power (polarity). Liberalism too sees a world of states, but also a variety of non-state actors, especially transnational firms and intergovernmental organizations (IGOs). It offers a vision of improvement in the form of ever more agreement around regimes and IGOs to regulate both specific areas of behaviour and the general pattern of relations among states and non-state actors. Marxism sees a world defined by a capitalist political economy, stratified by class structures and working through a system of states differentiated into core and periphery. It offers a vision of struggle to create more equality both socially and among states. Most poststructural theories offer only a process and not a picture of international relations, though critical theorists, of course, will offer both a clear picture of what they think is wrong with the world and prescriptions about what needs to be done to fix it.

The English School's picture of international relations is both more complicated and less determinate. Like that of realists and liberals, it starts with the state but, through its concepts of international and world society, primary institutions, and *raison de système*, it has a deeper and more social vision of international order than either. The idea of primary institutions makes it considerably more than just a *via media* between them. Because international societies can come in a great variety of forms, the English School can offer various visions of the future and contains no teleological assumptions about how things will unfold. The balance between the provision of order and justice could get better or it could get worse, and deciding in which direction it is going will very much depend on the normative stance of the observer.

In more detail, the English School can be positioned in relation to other mainstream IR theories as follows.

Realism

The English School's focus on international society shares state-centrism with realists. But power, while certainly a key feature in English School thinking, is not necessarily dominant, as it is for realists. The taxonomical difference between *society* and *system* as the central focus is a big one: the English School's struggle against realism was to pose the more social concept of international society against, or alongside, the more mechanical idea of international system. While realists looked only for a balance of power, the English School looked for *raison de système*. The English School position interleaves the logic of more material theories of the international system, driven by billiard ball metaphors, with the view that sentience makes a difference and that social systems cannot be understood in the same way as physical ones. When the billiard balls can sense and think, their behaviour becomes considerably less predictable: they acquire independent agency. As Williams (2010a) notes, realists see states as given and anarchy as an essentially material condition, whereas the English School sees states and anarchy as social constructions. In the realist view, anarchy has one major outcome – the balance of power – whereas for the English School international anarchy can support a wide variety of social forms.

The actual debate about how the English School and realism stand in relation to each other is quite diverse, though it is generally true that similarities are easier to find between classical realism and the English School and differences more obvious in relation to neorealism. A few people argue for a close link. Molloy (2003) makes the case that Wight's thinking, and by extension that of the English School, was so underpinned by realist assumptions as to make it more a modification of realism than an alternative to it. Griffiths (1992) argues that the English School's triad is very close to an understanding of political realism that he derives from the work of Berki. But since his general aim is to question the meaning of realism in IR, and he sees Morgenthau and Waltz as idealists, his view deconstructs much of the mainstream understanding of what realism is. The strongest alignments of the English School with realism come from Halliday (1994: 97–9), who thought of the English School as 'British realism' on the grounds that its concept of society was state-centric rather than cosmopolitan or counterposed to the state, and Brown (2001: 423–6), who sees Bull and Wight as part of the same group as Morgenthau, Kennan and Wolfers and, on that basis, argues that 'the work of the ES cannot be easily distinguished from [classical] realism'.

More common is a middle view featuring both shared ground and significant differences. Buzan (1993) is keen to link neorealism to international society using their common roots in state-centrism and anarchic structure. He uses a neorealist-type logic of anarchy to argue that structural forces should produce not just a balance of power but also international societies, because having an international society gives a survival and power advantage to those states that have it as opposed to those who don't.

If mutual recognition of sovereign equality is the foundation of international society, then this extends the meaning of 'like units' found in neorealism. But, although he argues for a shared structural root between international societies and neorealist logic, he does not thereby identify the English School as realist. He also ties it into liberal thinking about regime theory and keeps a sharp distinction between the realist idea of international systems and the English School ones of international and world society. Little (2003) sees the English School as having quite a lot in common with classical realism but very little with neorealism. The English School makes explicit many things that are implicit in classical realism and focuses them in the idea of international society. It problematizes anarchy, while realism just assumes it (Little 2003: 459). Classical realism and the English School are also linked by Spegele (2005: 98–9), who perceives both as being marginalized as methodologically traditionalist by the turn to 'scientific' causalism and as suffering a similar loss of standing within IR because of their 'methodological quietism', and Wæver (1999: 10–11), who sees similarities in their sense of tragedy in IR.

At the other end of the spectrum are those emphasizing the differences between the English School and realism. Copeland (2003) contrasts the methodological softness of the English School with the rigour of realism, and rightly sees the English School's agenda as ranging much more widely than realism into neoliberal and regime theory concerns about cooperation. Here too he sees regime theory as methodologically much more rigorous in identifying the causes and conditions of cooperation. Mearsheimer (2005: 144–5) goes further, characterizing the entire English School, and indeed the whole of British IR, as essentially idealist because they want to improve the world rather than study the realities of power politics. People writing more from the English School side also emphasize difference, seeing the School as having being set up as an explicit challenge to realism. De Almeida (2003) argues this case strongly, demonstrating that the British Committee specifically set itself to challenge the dominance of realism in IR by recovering the rationalist position. Although the British Committee's work was mostly state-centric, it differed fundamentally from realism in its interpretation of Hobbes and the consequences of anarchic structure. In the English School tradition, international anarchy was always differentiated from domestic anarchy on the grounds that there are big basic differences between states and people as the constituent units, and therefore the analogy is false.[6] Linklater and Suganami (2006: 44) also note how the English School approach set up international social structure as an alternative reading to the neorealist idea of structure as polarity. Reversing Molloy's (2003) view about Wight, noted above, Jeffery (2006) argues that, inasmuch as the English School's three traditions idea was drawn by Wight from the work of the international lawyer Hersch Lauter-pacht, it was specifically opposed to realism. Lauterpacht argued against E. H. Carr's denial of morality in the workings of international relations and, like the English School, set Grotius up as a *via media* between the extremes of utopianism and realism.

One can conclude that the English School is not just a soft form of realism but differs from it on some quite basic issues. Realists take the international system as their main, perhaps only, object of study, whereas for the English School the international system is just one of the things taken into account, with the main focus being on international society. For realists, international society either doesn't exist or is merely an epiphe-nomenon of calculated great power foreign policy – in Carr's (1946: 167) cynical words: 'every doctrine of a natural harmony of interests, identifies the good of the whole with the security of those in possession.'[7] This disparity in the principle object of study generates deep epistemological differences. International systems are amenable to positivist approaches and mechanistic theories, whereas international societies lend themselves more to historical, legal and constructivist approaches. Realists abstract themselves out of history by assuming both the permanent domination of power and survival motives and the timeless universality of anarchic struc-ture and the balance of power as a 'hidden hand' mechanism. By contrast, the English School is always concerned about historical contingency and has a wider vision of both state motivations (which includes the realist one) and international system structures. Where it comes closest to realism is in its primary institutions of the balance of power and great power man-agement (on which more in Part III). Yet, for the English School, the balance of power is a social contract, not a mechanistic property of the system system, which is a profoundly different understanding. Great power management is perhaps the closest point of contact between the two, espe-cially regarding the need to accommodate changes in the distribution of power (Ayson 2012). But again there is a significant difference, with real-ists such as Carr emphasizing the self-interest of great powers in 'manag-ing' the international society, and the English School emphasizing *raison de système*. Mearsheimer is wrong that the English School is utopian, but its abiding concern with society as opposed to system, with the dialectics of order and justice, and with pluralism and solidarism, does put a lot of blue water between it and the pure power politics of realism.

Liberalism

With the exception of regime theory, there has not been as much discussion about drawing parallels between the English School and liberal approaches

to IR, let alone seeing it as a subset of liberalism in the same way as some
want to make it a subset of realism. As noted above, Mearsheimer lumps
the English School with all other kinds of idealist, but few others would
take so stark a view. The English School is broadly meliorist, thinking that
an imperfect world can be made better by human effort, rather than idealist
or utopian.[8] It mainly opposes radical reform as either impossible or undesirable, or both. And while there are some cosmopolitan elements in
English School thinking, there is not much of the liberal enthusiasm for
giving practical priority to global civil society, and much more commitment to working through states. The English School focuses mainly on
primary institutions, which are by definition difficult to manipulate or
reform, whereas liberals focus mainly on secondary institutions, which
they see, like domestic institutions, as specific instruments of functional
reform. For the English School, secondary institutions are reflective and
supportive of primary ones, and their possibilities are constrained by the
broader framing of primary institutions within which they necessarily
operate. While the English School has concerns about justice, these are
balanced by its concerns about international order and stability. As
Linklater and Suganami (2006: 108–13) point out, there is a considerable
ambivalence within the English School about making normative claims,
more so than among liberals. That said, some English School solidarist
writers, whose concerns lie mainly in the area of human rights, do go down
the progressive line,[9] and there are others, such as Cronin (1999, 2003),
who operate between the liberal and English School traditions.

The main discussions linking the English School and liberalism are
found in the middle ground, particularly in regime theory, where there are
some parallels between the solidarist wing of the English School and the
kind of normative aspiration to identify structures that promote cooperation and to improve the peacefulness and justice of the human condition
that are generally associated with liberal IR perspectives. Quite a bit has
been written about the similarities and differences between the English
School approach to institutions and that of regime theory.[10] There is general
agreement that these two bodies of literature overlap at several points, and
that there is significant complementarity between them. But there are also
significant differences:

1 Regime theory is focused more on contemporary events, while the
English School has a mainly historical perspective;
2 Regime theory is concerned primarily with 'particular human-
constructed arrangements, formally or informally organised' (Keohane
1988: 383), whereas the English School is concerned primarily with

'historically constructed normative structures' (Alderson and Hurrell 2000: 27) – the shared cultural elements that precede rational coopera- tion, or what Keohane (1988: 385) calls enduring 'fundamental prac- tices' which shape and constrain the formation, evolution and demise of the more specific institutions. Onuf (2002) labels this distinction as 'evolved' versus 'designed' institutions, or what above were termed *primary* and *secondary* institutions.

3 Closely tied to the previous point is that the English School has placed a lot of emphasis on the way in which the institutions of international society and its members are mutually constitutive. To pick up Manning's metaphor of the game of states, for the English School the primary institutions define both the rules of the game and what the pieces are. Both of these can change over time as primary institutions evolve and sometimes become obsolete (e.g., colonialism) as new institutions arise (e.g., nationalism). Regime theory tends to take both actors and their preferences as given and to define the game as cooperation under anarchy. This difference is complemented and reinforced by one of method, with regime theory largely wedded to rational choice (Kratochwil and Ruggie 1986; Wæver 1998: 89–92) and the English School resting on history, normative political theory and international legal theory (Hurrell 2001).

4 Regime theory has applied itself intensively to institutionalization around economic and technological issues, both of which have been neglected by the English School, which has concentrated mainly on the politico-military sector and human rights.

5 Regime theory has proceeded with its analysis mainly in terms of actors pursuing self-interest using the mechanisms of rational choice, while the English School has focused mainly on common interests and shared values among actors and the mechanisms of international order (Evans and Wilson 1992: 337–9; Buzan 1993; Hurrell 1993; Dunne 1995b: 140–3). In a sense, the English School is concentrating on the social conditions that underlie the processes that interest regime theorists, which is what Copeland (2003) sees as methodological softness versus rigour.

6 *De facto*, but not in principle, regime theory has examined mainly sub- global phenomena. Its stock-in-trade is studies of specific regimes, which usually embody a subset of states negotiating rules about some specific issue (fishing, pollution, shipping, arms control, trade, etc.). The English School has subordinated the subglobal to the systemic level, talking mainly about the character and operation of international society as a whole.

More broadly, while the English School has a liberal cosmopolitan element within it, its main concern is to differentiate the idea that there could be a society of states from the cosmopolitan practice of thinking in universalist moral terms about the great society of humankind as a whole. While humankind remains a key moral reference point for English School thinkers, it was the society of states that provided most of the practical possibilities for realizing idealist objectives or, if mismanaged, for providing many of the main obstacles. Here the English School was, like liberals, against the realist view that international society could not be more than a self-interested epiphenomenon of great power foreign policies. But it was more in line with Carr (1946) than with the liberals in arguing that there was no automatic or easy harmony of interests, and in general it remained more state-centric than liberals who tended to emphasize the roles of global civil society and non-state actors. The English School also largely lacks the mainstream crusading element found in offensive liberalism. It would be difficult to imagine an idea such as the 'concert of democracies' (Ikenberry and Slaughter 2006) coming out of the pragmatic and pluralist traditions of English School thinking, although it might just about be found as an extreme form of 'offensive solidarism'.

Constructivism

Is the English School just a precursor to constructivism, and therefore now outdated? Or does it share some key features with constructivism, inasmuch as both focus on the social structure of international relations, while at the same time retaining some important and useful features of its own that differentiate it from constructivism? The bottom-line similarity is that any study of society is necessarily constructivist in some central way, because society cannot be understood as anything other than a social construction. As Reus-Smit (2005: 83) puts it, the English School and constructivism 'are engaged in a similar, if not common, project – to understand the social bases of international relations.' In that sense, the English School was 'constructivist' before constructivism became mainstream (Dunne 1998: 187–90). And, although difficult to prove, it is almost certainly the case that the arrival of constructivism into mainstream IR in the US during the 1990s made the English School more accessible to American IR. Via a constructivism that had achieved some methodological respectability in the US, the English School's concerns about international society became themselves more respectable and comprehensible to American IR. Before that time, the latter's obsession with international system and positivist epistemology, and its commitment to leaving behind the classical methods of political theory, law and history, meant that the English School and international society had only a marginal position on the fringes of American IR.

There was therefore a happy synergy between the rise of constructivism in IR and the resurgence of the English School during the late 1990s. Each drew some support from the other, the most obvious traffic from the English School to constructivism being the conspicuous influence of the three traditions on Wendt's Hobbesian, Lockean and Kantian types of international society. Partly as a result of this, Reus-Smit (2005: 82–4) justly complains that the English School gives too much weight to Wendt in its engagement with constructivism, ignoring the other, mostly more radical, strands that make up constructivism overall. Dunne (1995a), for example, sees quite close parallels between the English School and Wendtian constructivism in their adherence to intersubjective construction of social structure. But he views constructivists as more open to change in the social structure, at least compared with the more conservative position of classical English School writers such as Bull and Wight. Suganami (2001b) also perceives many parallels between the English School and Wendt's constructivism, including state-centrism, a bottom-up theory of society and a macro-sociological approach. But he sees differences most starkly both in the historicism of the English School versus Wendt's ahistoricism and in the different conceptions of anarchy, with American writers generally starting from Hobbesian assumptions and the English School assuming that anarchy is always a social condition. Buzan (2004) also favours Wendt, using his ideas to reformulate the English School's triad.

The general view in the literature follows the line of some shared features but some key differences, many of which relate to the general difference of approach to the study of IR in Britain and the US (Zhang Zhenjian 2004). The English School has its main roots in the study of history, political theory and international law, whereas constructivism grew out of debates about epistemology and method. As Reus-Smit notes, the normative side of the English School, especially the pluralist/solidarist debates about order and justice and the willingness to take explicit normative positions, is largely absent from constructivism.[11] Cochran (2008; 2009: 221) takes this further, arguing that the normative and structural should not, and cannot, be separated, but should go hand in hand, and that this linkage gives the English School a position distinctive from, and superior to, constructivism.

In the other direction, constructivists see the English School as methodologically challenged. Finnemore (2001: 510) makes the point that 'Arguments that how things are constituted makes possible other things (and in that sense causes them) are a large part of American constructivist IR, yet the English School has not emphasized constitutive causality.' She argues that the English School could pursue causality in relation to how primary institutions are constitutive of, and therefore cause, international order, and that doing so would make the English School more acceptable within American IR. Reus-Smit (2002: 502–5; 2009: 69–72) maintains that constructivists would question the separability of the society of states from world society because world society significantly influences the norms of the society of states. Within the English School he sees this separation as largely analytical, the main question being to what extent the needs and imperatives of the two levels are necessarily conflictual or potentially and actually reconcilable. These kinds of challenges have found replies. Navari (2009, 2010) clarifies the English School position on methodology. Clark's (2007) empirical work demonstrates clearly that world society does shape some of the norms and institutions of the society of states (see also Mitrani 2013).

Wæver (1998: 93–8) rejects the idea that the English School is simply an early form of constructivism. He sees constructivists as having more detailed concerns about types of rules (regulatory versus constitutive – for discussion, see also Buzan 2004: 176–82) and about how and by whom and how well social constructions are built. This leads constructivists to a more questioning view of statehood than that generally taken within the English School, not to mention realism and liberalism. Wæver (1999) argues that constructivism and the English School are alike in:

1 accepting a mix of material and social structures (and therefore occupying the middle ground between the all-material world of neorealism/neoliberalism, on one end, and the all-ideas world of poststructuralism, on the other); and
2 their positions on the role of ideas and identity.

He sees two advantages of the English School over constructivism (and therefore reasons not to conflate them):

1 the openness of the interplay among the three traditions; and
2 the ability of the English School to handle open ethical debates of a non-resolvable kind.

Aside from their different origins, approaches, methods and attitudes to normative debates, perhaps the other key distinction between constructivism and the English School is the way they approach the institutions of international society. A key strength of the English School is in 'ascertaining the institutional framework of historical and existing international societies' (Linklater and Suganami 2006: 115). Wendt's view of social structure is coarse-grained in terms of simple Hobbesian, Lockean and Kantian models and enemies', rivals' or friends' relationships, while other constructivists focus more on detailed particularities of international/world society. The English School's concept of primary institutions, by contrast, gives a much more fine-grained picture of interstate society than Wendt's (Bull 1977; Buzan 2004; Holsti 2004).

Where the English School and constructivism run most closely in parallel regarding the conceptualization of international society is in the work of Reus-Smit, who conceives 'fundamental institutions' as '"generic" structural elements of international societies' (Reus-Smit 1999: 4). They are authoritative because they embody 'sets of prescriptive norms, rules, and principles that specify how legitimate states "ought" to resolve their conflicts, coordinate their relations, and facilitate co-existence' (ibid.: 34). What is perhaps most insightful is Reus-Smit's argument that these fundamental institutions are shaped by 'higher order values', which he calls 'constitutional structures' of international societies, meta-values that define legitimate statehood and rightful state action. 'Constitutional structures', in his words, 'are coherent ensembles of intersubjective beliefs, principles, and norms that perform two functions in ordering international societies: they define what constitutes a legitimate actor, entitled to all the rights and privileges of statehood; and they define the basic parameters of rightful state action' (ibid.: 30). Reus-Smit's term 'fundamental institutions' feels close to the English School's 'primary institutions' and his 'constitutional structures' close to Clark (2005: 245), who argues that 'the evolution of specific legitimacy formations forms the essential history of international society', where legitimacy is defined in terms of rightful membership and rightful conduct (ibid.: 2, 9). Reflecting on the history of European international societies, Reus-Smit further posits that three normative elements are constitutive of such constitutional structures: a hegemonic belief about the moral purpose of the state, an organizing principle of sovereignty, and a norm of pure procedural justice. It follows that, as the emergence of international societies is contingent on different historical and cultural contexts, international societies vary in their constitutional structures, which informs the establishment of different fundamental institutions (Reus-Smit 1999: 27–31).

Perhaps another parallel between them hinges on the system/society distinction. As noted above, the English School is divided on this, with some defending Bull's distinction between the two and others arguing that, both empirically and theoretically, there is a stronger case for seeing degrees of society all the way down, with no asocial systems. Constructivists seem similarly divided, with some (Wendt 1999) preserving a rump materialism and others wanting social construction all the way down.

There is much to be observed about synergies and complementarities between the English School and constructivism and a good case for promoting cross-fertilization between them. Henderson (2001: 423) notes that 'The constructivists probably owe a greater debt to the English School than they have acknowledged and could enrich their more developed approach with a careful study of the considerable body of literature that amounts to the English School approach.' But Wæver is right that they should be kept distinct. Although they do share some key things, their differences are also important, and strengths would be lost by trying to conflate them.

Critical theory and poststructuralism

There is much less discussion of the English School in relation to critical theory and poststructural approaches than there is of its relation to the other three mainstream approaches. One extreme view from the pluralist side of the English School is that of Robert Jackson (2000: 51–5), who denounces the moral posturing of critical theory and 'postmodernists' in vituperative terms – a position, it has to be said, matched by his equally damning fusillades against the shortcomings of systems theory and positivism. Jackson perhaps sees himself following on from Bull's robust defence of the classical approach against behaviouralism.

From the other side, Andrew Linklater (1990, 1996a, 1998) has led the way in bringing critical theory to the English School, and Williams (2004) has also called for this link to be strengthened. The postmodernist work of James Der Derian (1988, 1992, 1994, 1996) clearly shows English School influence imparted by his supervisor at Oxford, Hedley Bull. Ole Wæver is a complex figure, sometimes described as a poststructural realist, but sympathetic to the English School. He sees the work of Manning (1962), especially his interest in the grammar of international society, as displaying poststructural elements which he is keen to preserve against any attempt to try to reduce the English School to the terms of mainstream American IR theory (Wæver 1998: 117–22, 129–32). Waever (1999: 9–13) recognizes the English School as being in some respects close to poststructuralists, both in its sense of language and the elements of discourse method in its study of practice and on account of the self-conception of IR scholars in relation to their subject matter. Ironically, this does not sound far removed from Jackson's (2000: 55–101) call for the study of human conduct in IR by situating diplomatic discourse within the general frame of the situations, the social ethics, and the self-understanding of the actors themselves of the events within which they were operating.

Wæver (1998: 98–101) also argues that, for the poststructuralists, international society as understood by the English School offers a way out of Walker's (1993), and also Wight's (1966a), inside–outside problem. Inside the state there is relative order and the possibility of progress. Outside it there is anarchy and disorder and no possibility of progress. By rejecting the domestic analogy, the English School constructs an alternative to both the domestic (as hierarchy/order) and the international (as anarchy/disorder).

As with constructivism, the English School clearly runs parallel to poststructuralism in some respects. That said, poststructuralists, like constructivists, proceed with a much higher level of methodological and epistemological self-consciousness than most who work in the English School tradition.

The capacity of the English School to connect, and sometimes be confused, with most of the main branches of IR theory is a reflection of its holistic approach stemming back to Wight's three traditions. Realism/Hobbes, rationalism/Grotius and revolutionism/Kant quite naturally create links in many directions. This explains both how and why it shares features with many other IR theories, and why it stands outside the game of playing these theories off against each other as being somehow mutually exclusive positions. Holism by definition necessitates taking a wide range of variables into account, so this disposition also explains both its theoretical and methodological eclecticism.

Others

The absences are also interesting. So far there is relatively little interplay between the English School and feminism. True (2005) charts some of the reasons for this, while Towns (2009) and Blanchard (2011) show some of the ways in which the two agendas might be fruitfully combined. Blanchard offers the intriguing suggestion that gender be considered a master institution of international society and patriarchy a derivative one. The same neglect is true for international political economy (IPE), International Security Studies and European Studies, though for all of these a strong case can be, and has been, made that there should be such links (Buzan 1996, 2005, 2010b; Diez and Whitman 2002; Riemer and Stivachtis 2002). There are obvious synergies between the English School's expansion story and the interests of International Historical Sociology, though so far these have run in parallel more than interacted. As various writers have pointed out (Brown 2001: 432–7; Buzan 2004: 72–4), there are also interesting but largely unexplored synergies between the English School and both the Stanford School and Wallerstein's World System Theory.

A more recent development, with roots in both constructivist and post-structural thinking, is the call for a turn to *practice theory*, both for IR generally (Neumann 2002; Adler 2008; Pouliot 2008) and for the English

School in particular (Navari 2011). Practice theory looks for a logic of action below the levels of rational choice, conscious belief or discourses of argument into the realm of *doxa* and 'background knowledge' (Pouliot 2008). Neumann (2002: 629–31) defines practice as 'patterns of action that are organized around the common implicit understanding of the actors', or 'socialized patterns of action' that are 'nested phenomena'. The point of interest here is that this approach seems to cut very close to the English School's core concept of primary institutions. This link is reinforced by most of the authors just cited focusing on diplomacy as a key illustration of what they mean by practice. Although not keen on the poststructural link, Navari (2011) has laid the groundwork for bringing this way of thinking into the English School. She charts how the work of Manning (1962), Keens-Soper (1978), Jackson (2000) and Bain (2003) all run close to practice theory, and how this opens up a new way of understanding the primary institutions of international society. The empirical approach to the study of institutions proposed by Wilson (2012), based on Manning, also lies close to practice theory. Although not specifically linked to the English School, Adler's (2008) highlighting of self-restraint within communities of practice is very close to the foundational English School understandings of *raison de système*.

Since primary institutions remain rather weakly theorized within the English School, there is perhaps a fruitful synergy to be harvested here.

CONCLUSIONS TO PART I

The English School is now a well-established approach to the study of international relations. It has generated distinctive concepts and literatures and has a firm claim to theoretical standing. Unlike realism, liberalism and constructivism, each of which claims a certain sector of the subject, the English School is not so much part of a division of labour within IR as a way of approaching the subject as a whole. Seeing it as 'the international society' approach could suggest that it claims only part of the subject. But more important is its many overlaps with other approaches to IR. It is this holism and methodological eclecticism which position it better to integrate IR than to add to the differentiations that divide it. Keeping this background in mind, we can now turn to examine the substantive work of the English School.

PART II   THE HISTORICAL/
STRUCTURAL
ORIENTATION

_____

INTRODUCTION

One of the attractive features of the English School's societal approach is that, much more so than either realism or liberalism, it opens the door to studying international and world history in terms of the social structures of international orders. The presence of several influential historians in the British Committee (Herbert Butterfield, Martin Wight – himself much influenced by Arnold Toynbee – and Michael Howard) and the sympathy towards a historical perspective of other key figures (Hedley Bull, Adam Watson) ensured that this orientation would be prominent in its attempt to understand and develop the concept of international society. As Bain (2007b, 2009) argues, the English School makes something of a fetish of the importance of history to IR, generally taking the view that knowledge of history is useful and necessary to understanding international relations.[1] But the English School generally rejects the view that history can predict or explain, or that it has any kind of mechanical relationship with, the present. Rather, history gives a perspective helpful to informed speculation about present and future events and processes and roles. And, as in their different ways both Weber (1998) and Keene (2008) point out, the English School's engagement with history was with the more traditional, constitutional and diplomatic approaches to that subject. Butterfield and Wight were particularly opposed to the more social and structural (and Marxist) approaches taken by the new historians in Britain during the time the British Committee was doing its foundational work (Hall 2002: 727–34; Keene 2008: 388–91). That said, the Toynbee connection meant that the British Committee was open to world history as well as to the more parochial sort.

At some risk of oversimplifying, the broad differences between the English School and other theoretical approaches to IR in relation to history might be characterized as follows. Realists are backward looking in terms of the narrow criteria of polarity and the balance of power (the future will be similar to the past). But, because they see history mainly as recurrent validations of power politics, they are not much interested in its details except to confirm the validity and longevity of their general ideas about power politics. Liberals tend to be forward looking. They have difficulty looking back more than two centuries, before which most of their main ideas did not exist in comparable form.[2] They focus mainly on the dynamics of and possibilities for change and progress that are inherent in modernity. Thus they seldom venture back more than a century or two, and sometimes incline towards a teleological view of history as progress. Marxists have a well-known historical story to tell, also based on a teleology of progress, but it is one that tends either to marginalize the state or to see it mainly in the context of class struggle rooted in the structure of the international political economy. Postcolonialism focuses on the relationships of imperialism itself and their downstream consequences. Some constructivists, most notably Wendt (1999), have a framing that could be used to inform a historical approach in terms of movements from one type of international social system to another: Hobbesian (enemies), Lockean (rivals), Kantian (friends). But this framing has not yet been much used in that way, and in general constructivists focus on the role of ideas and do not attempt to generate portraits of how the international system is, or should be.

Some more recent English School work (e.g., Keene 2002; Keal 2003) links to postcolonial concerns, but most of the classical writers took little interest in the relationships of imperialism as such. They were concerned more with the 'standard of civilization' and the consequences of decolonization. Even though, as we shall see, Wight and Watson were drawn to looking for larger patterns in their historical studies, the English School shares with constructivism the lack of a determinist approach to history. It is not wedded to the necessity of repetition, or progress, or the particular working out of dialectics. It lets the historical record speak for itself, and is concerned with working out what that record tells us about how international societies have evolved, and how they could and should evolve. For most English School writers, international society is an element that is always present in international relations, but whose depth, character, and influence all fluctuate with historical contingency.

The historical wing of the English School pursues two projects. The more general one is comparing how different international societies have evolved in different times and places (Wight 1977; Watson 1992) – the varieties, as it were, of *raison de système*. Its main focus is on premodern cases stretching back to the earliest history of civilization. This work provides a broad sense that international relations is partly a social order or structure, not just a mechanical system, and that the specific nature and dynamics of this social order are the key objects of study. The more specific project focuses on how the contemporary global international society came about as a result of the expansion to planetary scale of what was originally a novel type of international society that emerged in early modern Europe (Bull and Watson 1984a). Here the focus is on the world after 1500. Baldly put, this expansion story is told mainly as one of how colonization and decolonization remade the world (often badly) in the political image of Europe. It is partly a story of power and imposition and partly one of the successful spread and internalization beyond the West of Western ideas such as sovereignty and nationalism. It is also a story about what happens when international society expands beyond the cultural heartland that gave birth to it. How does international society function when it contains many cultural traditions rather than one? These two projects overlap during the early phase of the rise of the West (1500–1800) and merge into one when the West becomes globally dominant during the nineteenth century.

In the context of this part, it might be argued that the comparative project shows something about what forms of international society other than the Westphalian one can look like and that the expansion project shows how we got to the particular social and material structures we are now in, and why the legacy of a core–periphery formation makes some of the politics of it take the form that they do. *Inter alia*, a knowledge of their history is necessary to grasp the normative dynamics of international societies and the roles that humans play in making and maintaining them.

One must, however, exercise caution before accepting the differentiation between an *evolution* story and an *expansion* one implied by the titles of Watson (1992) and Bull and Watson (1984a). The premodern stories told in the comparative project are as much about developments that were largely separated from each other by time and place, with relatively limited passage of learning among them, as about 'evolution' in any sense. The 'expansion' story is about both expansion and evolution and how they played and still play into each other, even though the expansion side ceased to be active once international society reached global scale. The comparative story told in chapter 4 is thus focused mainly on world history before the rise of the West, and the expansion story told in chapter 5 is largely about the rise of the West and its creation of a global-level international society. The expansion story, however, also reaches back into premodern history. And there is a possibility that, as the revolutions of modernity continue to spread from the narrow initial core within the West to most other cultures and peoples, the comparative story will become relevant again in the form of multiple modernities and regionally differentiated international societies.

There is an important link between the English School's historical projects and the development of its thinking about the institutions of international society as a way of understanding international social structure. Thus chapters 4 and 5 look at the English School's two main historical projects, while the Conclusion to Part II takes up the idea of primary institutions as a way of understanding the social structures of international societies.

4 INTERNATIONAL SOCIETY IN WORLD HISTORY

Compared to the large and diverse body of writing in the expansion project, the English School literature on comparative international societies in a world historical context is relatively small. It consists mainly of two classical works by Wight (1977) and Watson (1992). Where it talks about non-European, premodern international societies, this literature has attracted relatively little criticism or comment. Perhaps the most active ongoing area of this part of the project is now centred on China and the attempt to recover and develop in English School terms the story of the classical Sinocentric international society in East Asia (aka 'the tribute system': Y. Zhang 2001; F. Zhang 2009, 2014; Y. Zhang and Buzan 2012). Most of the criticism and commentary addressed to the two classical works relates to where the comparative history project overlaps with the expansion one around the story of the rise of European international society. I will deal with this in the next chapter. This chapter reviews the main content and ideas of Wight (1977) and Watson (1992) and, more briefly, the related work of Buzan and Little, Linklater and Clark. In addition, it surveys the contemporary English School literature on regional international societies, which is also in comparative mode. This regional literature might be seen as reflecting a kind of resurfacing of the classical world as the period of Western dominance and hegemony begins to draw to a close. What Fareed Zakaria (2009) labels 'the rise of the rest' can be understood as a more diffuse distribution of power and the reassertion of non-Western cultures acting once again to differentiate regional international societies from a Western-dominated global one (Buzan 2010a, 2011).

Martin Wight's *Systems of States*

Barry Gills (1989: 105) sees Martin Wight as 'the interpreter of the Toynbean research project to the field of International Relations', and Wight was undoubtedly the progenitor of the comparative history project within the English School. His book *Systems of States* (1977), published five years after his death, was based on papers he wrote for the British Committee. It was not designed by the author as a coherent work, and the papers to the British Committee that compose it are of a very preliminary and exploratory character, albeit based on a very wide and deep historical knowledge. Wight takes the key idea of 'systems of states' or 'states-systems' from the earlier work of Pufendorf and Heeren, and he understands it as a group of independent sovereign states in regular interaction with each other, sharing some form of recognition and diplomacy as institutions, and also trade. This concept did not yet make the distinction between international system and international society that Bull (1977) brought into play, but rather bundled both into the same term. Wight (1977: 39) accepted states-systems as 'constituting a valid society of mutual rights and obligations', so his position was more than just a realist, system one. The book contains both the theoretical and empirical beginnings of a comparative historical project. His method was to construct an analytical scheme with a taxonomy of types and then to pursue a comparative analysis via case studies. The empirical chapters cover in some detail classical Greece; the wider classical Mediterranean system, including Greece, Persia, and Carthage; and the creation of the modern European states-system out of the hierarchical mediaeval order. Alongside these quite developed case studies are briefer forays into several other classical states-systems.

The analytical scheme is set up mainly in the first chapter, in which Wight puzzles his way through four questions about states-systems. How should 'states' be understood as the members of the system? What kind of interactions and institutions give meaning to 'system'? How does cultural identity play into states-systems? And what kind of political questions should one ask about states-systems in terms of numbers of members, coherence (or not) of political type, phases of structure and eventual fate? Some of these questions are explored in a bit of depth, others just sketchily drawn. There are two key distinctions in Wight's (1977: 21–45) taxonomy of states-systems, the first between *international* and *suzerain states-systems* and the second between *primary* and *secondary states-systems*.

- *International states-systems* approximate to what mainstream IR theory thinks of as anarchic systems/societies, in which the units relate to each other as sovereign equals and cultivate the balance of power as an organizing principle. Wight's examples are Europe and the classical Greek and Hellenistic systems, which form his main case studies, and China between 771 and 221 BC.

- *Suzerain state-systems* are where states relate to each other on a basis of sovereign inequality, with one state in some sense dominating the system in core–periphery fashion, both claiming, and having recognized by others, a higher status. Here the organizing principle is divide and rule. Wight (1977: 24) insists on the singular 'state-system' for this type because of its hierarchical structure. His examples are the Byzantine Empire, China and the Abbasid Caliphate. He muses about whether the mediaeval system in Europe was not a states-system, but perhaps 'a double-headed suzerain state-system' (ibid.: 26–9). Interestingly, he also mentions the British Raj in India, with its suzerainty over the princely states, as the most recent case of this form (ibid.: 23). This is a rare exception to the general reticence of first-generation English School writers to think about the European colonial era in terms of international society.
- *Primary states-systems* are where the units are states, and again the obvious examples are Europe and the classical Greek and Hellenistic systems.
- *Secondary states-systems* are systems of systems, where the units are primary states-systems. Somewhat confusingly, Wight starts by confining the membership of secondary states-systems to suzerain state-systems, and his example of this form is the Middle Eastern Armana system during second half of the second millennium BC (see also Cohen and Westbrook 2000). He goes on to muse about the Mediterranean system during the twelfth and thirteenth centuries AD, but gets lost in the messy multiplicity of the types of actors in that system. It is then not entirely clear whether a secondary states-system could include not just suzerain state-systems but also primary states-systems and, indeed, individual states. Along this line, Gills (1989: 108–9) makes the interesting suggestion that, up until the nineteenth century, the relatively equal relations among the states-systems of Eurasia could be classified as a secondary states-system in Wight's terms. But with the huge relative power advantage that developed in Europe's favour during the nineteenth century this was 'transformed into a primary state system on a global scale'.

Wight also touches on the idea of open versus closed states-systems, the relationship between core and periphery in a system, whether or not states-systems had characteristic phases of development, and what, in contemporary IR, would count as polarity theory. He made a quite extensive study of tripolar systems (Wight 1977: 174–200) and speculated in relation to international society that low number systems such as Rome–Parthia don't generate strong rules (ibid.: 25). Along with many others in IR (Gilpin 1981; Modelski 1987; Kennedy 1989), Wight (1977: 42–4) was attracted by the question of whether states-systems were fated always to end in a 'succession of hegemonies', being finally submerged into some type of unified entity – traditionally an empire (see also Gills 1989: 105–6).

On the basis of his historical studies, Wight (1977: 33) also concluded with his much-cited observation that 'We must assume that a states-system will not come into being without a degree of cultural unity among its members.' This put a pre-existing culture at the heart of both the formation and the stability (or not) of international societies. This thought was, as I will show in the next chapter, influential in the English School's pessimism about the loss of cultural coherence contingent on the great round of decolonization following the Second World War. It implied that international societies that expanded beyond their cultural base would necessarily be weakened.

Apart from this one point, however, Wight's interesting, if very preliminary schema for comparative international society has not yet been followed up. Linklater and Suganami (2006: 74–80) observe that neither Watson (1992) nor Buzan and Little (2000) make any serious use of Wight's typology of states-systems. The potentially useful idea of secondary states-systems continues to lie fallow in terms of both needed conceptual development and application. The idea of suzerain state-systems is partly, though mainly implicitly, carried forward in the English School literature on hegemony, on which more below. Interest in suzerainty might also be in for a revival in the context of the new research into the Chinese tribute system mentioned above. The classical Sinocentric international society in East Asia was certainly not an international states-system, but neither was it exactly suzerain as that term is understood in the context of Western history. One possibility is that the study of this case will generate new categories of international society.

Adam Watson's *The Evolution of International Society*[1]

Watson's book, by contrast, was a consciously designed attempt to deliver the comparative history project started by Wight. This was done by compiling a complete history of all major international societies from the beginning of civilization to the modern day. The rationale for Watson's project was his recognition that it was not possible to understand the contemporary global international society without having some sense of how international societies developed and operated in the past. In a reflection on the British Committee's discussions, Watson (2001: 467–8) notes that they focused almost exclusively on the European model of anarchical society and 'did not get around to serious study of hegemonial and suzerain systems'. He elaborates:

> Wight and I were the unhappiest about this limitation. We felt that in our search for a theory we needed also to study systems where some or most of the political entities were in varying degrees dependent. He and I wanted especially to discuss hegemonies and suzerain systems, where partially dependent states retained nominal independence and a high degree of autonomy in practice.

Watson's book aimed to remedy this gap in the British Committee's work in two ways. First, it provided sketches of international societies from ancient Sumer and Assyria, through classical Greece, Rome, India and China, to Byzantium and the Islamic system, ending up with a detailed look at the emergence of the European system, from mediaeval and local to modern and global. Despite the book's title, this aspect of the study is more about comparing different forms of international society than it is about evolution.

Second, Watson also had theoretical ambitions. Based on the comparative method made possible by his wide range of historical cases, he wanted to investigate the structure of international societies across a spectrum ranging from highly decentralized at one end (the anarchy model) to highly centralized at the other (something close to empire). This aspect of his study aimed particularly at the British Committee's neglect of international societies outside the Eurocentric Westphalian model of anarchy/sovereign equality. Based on his historical survey, Watson's (1992: 120–32) key conclusions were that:

- the extremes of the spectrum (anarchy and empire) are unstable, meaning that the equilibrium position on the spectrum lies towards the middle (hegemony);
- there is often a significant difference between the formal principle about the degree of integration in an international society and the actual practice, that this can vary in either direction, and that it creates problems of legitimacy for the formal principle;
- both legitimacy and power are crucial to stability, with the former explaining the propensity for empires to be tolerant of diversity.

Watson's theory comes in the form of a pendulum metaphor in which the condition of an international society can swing between the extremes of anarchy and empire.[2] His first move is to deconstruct the binary distinction that Waltz (1979) famously established between anarchic and hierarchic systems. His starting position is that it is not possible to investigate world history without having a reasonably robust model for comprehending empires, which across time have been a very significant feature of world politics. Although the conventional view of empires fits neatly within Waltz's hierarchic system, from Watson's perspective this assessment considerably oversimplifies how most empires in world history have been structured. He argues that it is more appropriate to model empires in terms of a series of concentric circles, with the power of the empire weakening as the circles extend outwards. According to this model, although there is an imperial core that can be characterized in terms of hierarchy, most long-lasting empires have survived because they have been willing to tolerate different degrees of independence with the various political communities that fall within their sphere. Watson identifies as *dominions* political communities whose external and, to some extent, domestic policies are regulated by the imperial authority. When the imperial authority is weaker and extends only to recognition of political overlordship of one state over others, he talks of *suzerainty*. When one or more powers are able in some sense to 'lay down the law' about the operation of a system of independent states, he labels this *hegemony* (Watson, 1992: 14–16; see figure 4.1).

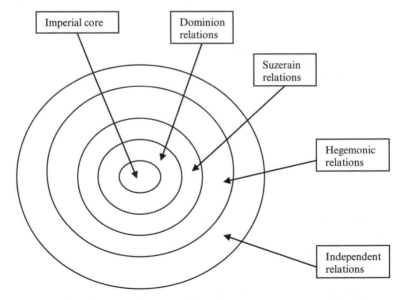

Figure 4.1   Watson's model of an imperial system

This model is an ideal type, and in practice power relations with the imperial core do not diminish in this tidy spatial fashion. Moreover, this view of empire is not particularly original or very controversial. However, by scaling this thinking about degrees of integration upwards to encompass international societies in general, Watson opens up the anarchy–hierarchy spectrum by inserting hegemony, suzerainty and dominion into it. The full spectrum of Watson's pendulum theory of international societies is thus: anarchy, hegemony, suzerainty, dominion, empire. Again, Watson is thinking in ideal-type terms, and so in this model the empire would directly administer all of the political communities in the system, and the other end of the spectrum would be made up of societies of completely independent states. The most interesting aspect of this move is when Watson opens up the spectrum to look at the intermediate positions. In practice, however, he focuses only on the middle position of hegemony, which he came to think of as the most important and enduring feature of international order. One key point he makes is that in an international system there can be more than one hegemon (multiple or collective hegemonies). So, for example, when he comes to look at the Greek city-states he identifies both Athens and Sparta as hegemonic powers. He also saw the contemporary international society as one of collective hegemony (Watson 2001: 470). Having established the idea of a spectrum of international societies that are distinguished in terms of the degrees of authority that some political communities exercise over others, Watson then goes on to make the very bold hypothesis that, because of the instability of the extremes (too much disorder and conflict in anarchies; too much domination and exploitation in empires), there is a natural tendency in international relations for international societies to find greatest stability in some degree of hegemonic relations (see figure 4.2).

Watson's hypothesis does not presuppose that the metaphorical swing has any literal implications. There is no assumption that if an empire disintegrates it will give way to a hegemonic system. It is just as likely to give way to an anarchy. What the hypothesis suggests is that, across world history, hegemonic-type systems will tend to be the norm.[3]

Watson (1992: 14) argues that political communities experience a constant tension between the desire, on the one hand, for order, which he argues can be most effectively achieved under the umbrella of empire, and, on the other hand, independence, which can be most effectively achieved under the umbrella of anarchy. It is this systemic tension that provides the motor for the pendulum. There is a constant tendency at the empire end of the spectrum for the imperial authority to take actions that drive political communities towards the anarchic end of the spectrum. By the same token, the chronic insecurity and competition experienced under conditions of

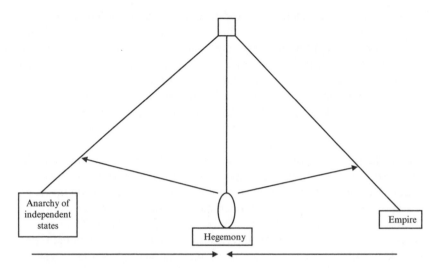

Figure 4.2   A simplified version of Watson's metaphorical pendulum (from Buzan and Little 2009)[4]

anarchy drive states towards the empire end of the spectrum. This is a powerful and compelling dynamic deserving further exploration and development. Buzan and Little (1996: 420–3) for example, have argued that there exists a parallel version of Watson's spectrum, emphasizing consent rather than coercion, and stretching from anarchy, through common market and union, to federation. Although Watson's pendulum theory allows for legitimacy as well as coercion, it is still based essentially on the equation of hierarchy with empire, which necessarily places coercion above legitimacy. With cases in mind such as the EU, and up to a point the US, one can envisage a consent-led version of the pendulum in which coercion might play a subordinate role, and in which the logic of unstable extremes pushing towards a hegemonic middle might change. Simpson (2004) is notably interesting on the role of consent in the emergence of a legitimized form of hegemony in Western international society.

Even with this limitation, Watson's pendulum theory not only offers a major alternative to neorealism but also challenges the general linkage between anarchy and international society in much of English School writing. By extending the idea of international society away from the assumption of anarchy and into the spectrum of his pendulum theory, Watson delivers on his and Wight's sense that there was more to the game of international society than just the British Committee's obsession with the Westphalian model. By moving international society into the hegemony part of the spectrum, and possibly beyond, Watson exposed the tension in post-1945 international society arising from the fact that the principle of legitimacy lies with sovereign equality and nationalism, but much of the practice is hegemonic (Watson 1992: 299–309, 319–25). This problem of how to legitimize *de facto* hegemony in the face of the strong postcolonial normative commitment to sovereign equality still echoes on. Clark (2005: 227–43, 254) notes the contemporary problem of US dominance in 'the absence of a satisfactory principle of hegemony – rooted in a plausibly wide consensus – in which that actuality would be enshrined.' This disjuncture between hegemony and sovereign equality preoccupied Watson's thinking to the end of his life and formed the central theme of his last two books (Watson 1997, 2007).

Watson's second and in some ways more daring move is to endeavour to link the pendulum model to the distinction articulated by the British Committee between an international system and an international society. To make this move, he argues in language that is very similar to that later used by Jackson (2000: 113–16), who accepts that the two terms point up a useful distinction, but argues that it is better captured by distinguishing between instrumental and non-instrumental behaviour. Instrumental behaviour is based on strategic conceptions of self-interest that necessarily take the actions of other actors into consideration. Failure to take account of others will all too easily give rise to self-defeating strategies – like playing chess without paying attention to your opponent's moves. By contrast, non-instrumental behaviour is based on legal and moral obligations that necessarily embrace the legitimate interests of others who will be affected by it. Jackson accepts that both forms of behaviour need to be accommodated in any analysis of international society. This formulation corresponds closely to that drawn by March and Olsen (1998) between the logic of consequences and the logic of appropriateness. It also plays into the debate about whether the system/society distinction is necessary, or whether it is better to think only in terms of types of society (more on this in chapter 10).

Buzan and Little (2009: x, xxx) argue, contra Vigezzi, that, by making these major advances over his and Bull's earlier *Expansion of International Society* (1984), Watson's *The Evolution of International Society* deserves to be seen as the culmination of the work of the British Committee. Watson's work was the precursor of two contemporary English School debates about hegemony and legitimacy (on which more in Part III). One key lesson from Watson's work was that even in the Westphalian system hegemony was a significant factor, and that this disjuncture between the *de jure* position of sovereign equality and the *de facto* one of partial hegemony created problems of legitimacy for international society. The pendulum theory incorporated, or perhaps replaced, Wight's idea of suzerain state-systems and extended the possibility of types of international society. It fits with, and partially fed into, Simpson's (2004) story of the tension between sovereign equality and legalized hegemony from 1815. And its scale and ambition inspired, and fed into, the work of subsequent authors such as Buzan and Little (2000) and Clark (2005, 2011).

Other works

While there has been no obvious successor to the pioneering works of Wight and Watson, a few other authors deserve mention in relation to their project: Buzan and Little, Linklater, and Clark.

In a series of works starting in the mid-1990s, Buzan and Little (1994, 1996, 2000) opened an enquiry into the nature of international systems. This work was inspired in part by Wight and Watson and concluded very much in favour of an English School approach to the study of international relations. But it neither specifically pursued an international society framework nor operated at the level of specific cases. While the more generalized survey of eras was broadly framed along the lines of the English School's triad, Suganami (2003: 257) is correct to argue that Buzan and Little's *International Systems in World History* (2000) was aimed more as a corrective to neorealism than as a conscious extension of the English School's comparative international society project. Even so, Watson (2001: 468–9) said that it brings out 'the major role played by economic and cultural exchanges in knitting the world together', and that the concluding chapters 'seem to me the fulfilment of what Wight and I had in mind as a necessary basis for further study.' Like Wight and Watson, Buzan and Little argue that IR needs to pay more attention to empires both as actors within international society and as forms of international system/society in themselves.

Andrew Linklater (Linklater and Suganami, 2006: 189–222) sees himself as building on the comparative history approach to international society pioneered by Wight and Watson to pursue his own project on cosmopolitan thinking and the harm principle in international relations (on which more in chapter 8). In a first volume he has already set out the theoretical framework for reviving Wight's sociology of states-systems project (Linklater 2011b) and linking it more firmly to the sociological literature, particularly Elias's process sociology. At the time of writing, he is well advanced on a second volume applying this comparative framework across the history of the West, from classical Greece, through the Hellenistic system and Rome, to mediaeval and modern Europe.

Ian Clark's work on legitimacy in international society (2005, 2007, 2011) might also be seen as associated with this project. Clark shares the comparative historical method with Wight and Watson, but he applies it largely within the confines of European history since 1648 and the global level international society that was created by European expansion. His concern with legitimacy and *raison de système* echoes Watson's, focusing more on the evolution of international society, and the forces that drive it, than on the comparative side of the equation.

Regional international society

Until recently, the English School showed little interest in the idea of regional international societies. There is some acknowledgement that Europe did not expand into a social vacuum, and Watson (1992) gives a lot of coverage to premodern international societies. But these were not strictly speaking regional because there was as yet no global international society for them to be subsystems within. Rather, they were, like Europe, quasi-autonomous subglobal societies, for the most part thinly connected to each other, with each thinking of itself in universalist terms. As with international systems, only when there was a global international society could regional international societies exist within it. The expansion story largely took over the English School's perspective on world history, fixing its focus firmly on the global level. Given that the School grew up during the depths of the Cold War, regional international societies might also have seemed necessarily divisive and conflictual. The Cold War, after all, is easy to construct as a zero-sum competition between two subglobal international societies competing with each other to see which would dominate. In that perspective, any regional developments might easily have been seen as dividing and weakening international society at the global level. The classical English School's disposition to focus on the global level was also reinforced by the normative commitments of its liberal solidarist wing (on which more in chapter 8) to view things through the lens of universal principles such as human rights. A good example of the English School's neglect of international society at the regional level was Hurrell (1995), who, when writing on theoretical perspectives on regionalism, did not mention the English School (see also Vincent 1986: 101, 105; Bull 1977: 279–81). Hurrell corrected this in later work on 'one world and many worlds' (Hurrell 2007a, 2007b: 239–61).

As Buzan (2004: 205–27) argues, this leaves out regional developments and, in so doing, contributes to the general gloom of pluralists about contemporary international society. Regional developments *may* lead to conflict over who dominates at the global level, but there is nothing determined about this. Regional international societies may equally well evolve in relative harmony with the global level. In this context, the English School's neglect of the EU as a highly solidarist regional international society embedded quite comfortably in the global one (Diez and Whitman 2002: 45) is nothing short of astonishing. The EU is an ongoing experiment in the difficulties and limits of constructing advanced solidarism across a substantial group of states and societies. More generally, other authors argue that the expansion of European international society beyond its home culture to global scale almost necessarily generated regional international societies with greater cultural homogeneity than the global level (Riemer and Stivachtis 2002: 21–2). There is growing interest (especially in East Asia) not only in recovering the regional level stories[5] but also in the prospect of a more region-centric structure for international society as the likely future (Kupchan 1998, 2002, 2012; Buzan 2010a). Others, using both historical and contemporary cases, argue for the regional distinctiveness and differentiation of international society even if they do not necessarily see higher solidarity in the regions than in the core (Hurrell 2007a, 2007b; Wang 2007; Stivachtis 2010; Merke 2011; Schouenborg 2012). Jackson also supports the view that the English School should take a more regionally differentiated view of contemporary international society, seeing it as 'of mixed character and uneven depth from one global region to the next' and as more solidarist in Europe/the West than elsewhere (Jackson 2000: 128).

There are two reasons for including regional international society as a topic within this chapter. First, in a historical sense, this emergent literature is in some ways a continuation of Wight and Watson's project of looking at different premodern international societies around the world, but now doing so in the context of the expansion story. The idea is that culture still matters, and that regional differentiation within a globalized international society is hardly surprising. As the period of intense Western hegemony begins to draw to a close, one might reasonably expect the regional level to become more prominent and more differentiated, perhaps making connections to some of the international societies studied by Watson that were submerged and transformed, but by no means completely destroyed, by the Western expansion and overlay. The second reason is that this perspective reopens the comparative possibilities of the Wight and Watson project that became submerged by the expansion story which subordinated all to the military might and cultural hegemony of a West empowered by the revolutions of modernity (Buzan 2010a, 2011). Regional international societies can be compared with each other, and with the Western one, across both time and space.

Bringing regional international society back into the picture also raises interesting and important questions about to what, exactly, the term 'global level international society' refers. Is it correct to think of a global international society in the coherent, uniform sense that this phrasing implies? Or is it better to think about it as a kind of conglomerate, more core–periphery in form, with a dominant West and a variety of regional international societies in varying degrees of concordance with and alienation from each other and the core? For that view the term *Western-global international society* might be appropriate, and I will use it in that sense in the remainder of this book. The orthodox conceptualization of international society does not capture either of these differentiations at all well, suggesting that there might be a need to take up Thomas's (2000: 829–31) suggestion of revisiting Wight's neglected concepts of suzerain and secondary states-systems. These might provide a useful way of thinking about culturally diverse international societies. Although Wight developed these concepts more for looking at the ancient and classical world, the disjunctures between the principles and the practices of contemporary international society make them relevant in ways he did not foresee.

At this point it becomes impossible to separate the comparative and expansion projects. In the story of contemporary international society, evolution and expansion merge.

5 THE EXPANSION OF EUROPEAN INTERNATIONAL SOCIETY

Introduction

It is worth noting from the start that the particular historical framing of this story often skews it in Eurocentric ways. The main aim of the story is to cast light on the contemporary global international society within which we all live. The very fact of its globality makes this international society unique, not just because of its scale and cultural diversity, but also because it is geographically closed. In principle, a global international society could have come about in one of two basic ways. One way would have been for the various civilizational cores of the ancient and classical world to have expanded into increased contact with each other, so requiring that they develop rules of the game to mediate their relations: a *polycentric* system of systems. In such a case, global international society would have developed on the basis of cultural diversity and fusion. The other way is closer to what actually happened – namely, the takeover of the whole system by one of the civilizational cores and the absorption of all the others into its particular rules, norms and institutions. This *monocentric* model necessarily starts from relations of inequality and highlights 'the standard of civilization' as the key criterion for non-Western societies to gain membership (Buzan 2010a). This model sets up tensions over how such a society is now to evolve, as the distribution of power reverts from the extreme concentration that allowed its creation in the first place to something of the more even distribution (the rise of China, India and other non-Western powers) that marked the ancient and classical world. Thus, although there are even and uneven routes to a global international society, and they end up in the same place, the monocentric model ends up there with a very different set of dynamics and problems than would have been the case had we arrived here by the polycentric route. As already noted, it is a theme of English School writing that, although the legitimacy of contemporary international society is based on the sovereign equality of states and, up to a point, the equality of people and nations, it is still riddled with hegemonic/hierarchical practices and inequalities of status. Contemporary international society is thus still a long way from resolving the inequalities that marked its founding, and it remains culturally and politically insecure.

In a strictly geographical sense, the main expansion story is finished. Barring remaining uncertainties over the deep seabed, expansion is closed until humankind colonizes space. But it is more useful to see the current period not as the end of expansion, but as a merger of the specific expansion story with the more general evolution one. International society is now global in scale, meaning that the only story to follow is about how this global society is and should be evolving. Is it getting deeper, more homogeneous and more universal, or, as raised in chapter 4, is it better understood in more differentiated terms as Western core plus global periphery or Western core plus a variety of regional international societies with varying degrees of similarity and difference from the core?

The next section sketches out the classical expansion story in English School literature and is followed by a section reviewing the main critiques and extensions of this story. There is some unavoidable arbitrariness in how one draws the line between the classical story and the critiques/extensions because the two are in reality fairly seamlessly interwoven. The final section looks at how the expansion literature is evolving.

The classical 'expansion' story in the English School literature

Like much else in the English School canon, the expansion story first comes to life in Bull's classic work *The Anarchical Society*. Although it is mainly a theoretical work, Bull (1977: 27–40) does set out the basic story of the emergence of a Christian international society in early modern Europe and how this evolved from natural to positive law, from dynasticism to popular sovereignty, and from Christian to European civilization (on the early phase, see also Wight 1977: 110–52). Bull looks at how the expansion of this society from European to global scale has weakened its common culture and strengthened Hobbesian (the world wars of the twentieth century) and Kantian (the UN) elements at the expense of Grotian ones. Bull devotes the last five chapters to thinking about how this global international society might evolve, both as a variant on the states-system and as an alternative to it. His outlook is pessimistic, seeing international society as weakened both by its expansion to global scale and by the central conflict among the great powers represented by the Cold War. He is conscious of the problems of inequality created by the expansion of a Western international society to global scale, and he opts for reforming the states-system by emphasizing common interests and adapting international society to bring in non-Western cultures (Bull 1977: 315–17). He is concerned about the tension between, on the one hand, state-centric international society as the main and possibly only provider of world order and, on the other, world society (the collectivity of humankind), which he sees as the basis of moral claims (ibid.: 20–2) and the essential framing for the problem of reconciling order and justice (ibid.: 77–98). *The Anarchical Society* thus put on the table many of the themes and issues taken up by subsequent 'expansion' literature.

Three other landmark books in this literature were Bull and Watson's (1984a) *The Expansion of International Society*, Gong's (1984a) *The Standard of 'Civilization' in International Society*, and Watson's (1992) *The Evolution of International Society*. Vigezzi (2005) lauds Bull and Watson (1984a) as the culminating and most important work of the British Committee, and it is generally accepted as the principal English School account of the expansion. Arguably, however, the expansion story is told with more depth, detail and coherence in the books of Gong and Watson. Many other authors have also contributed to the classical expansion literature, and the most efficient way to set this out is in terms of the themes and issues first raised by Bull. At some risk of oversimplification, the basic pattern of the classical expansion story can be rendered as:

1 the emergence and consolidation of a distinctive anarchical international society in Europe built around the Westphalian institutions of sovereignty/nonintervention, territoriality, the balance of power, war, international law, diplomacy and great power management;
2 the transfer of this society to the rest of the world on the back of expanding European economic and military power, mainly in colonial form but also in encounters with non-Western societies that escaped colonization;
3 decolonization, the bringing in of the Third World to equal membership of global international society, and the subsequent problems.

This is presented mainly as a historical story of what happened and with what consequences, rather than as an attempt to explain why expansion occurred.

Emergence

The story of how a Westphalian international society developed out of mediaeval Europe was sketched by Bull (1977: 27–40) and is told by several others. As noted in chapter 4, Wight (1977: 110–73) examines the mediaeval-to-modern emergence of international society in Europe, including looking in detail at the changing foundations of political legitimacy within it, from dynasticism to popular sovereignty, and highlighting the importance of shared cultural foundations. This cultural angle applies not just to the emergence of European international society but also to the multicultural global one that resulted from its expansion. Jackson (2000: 156–67), too, looks at the transition from mediaeval to Westphalian international society. Watson (1992: 138–262) gives probably the most detailed telling of the story around the ideas of diplomacy, anti-hegemonialism (the precursor to balance of power), territoriality, dynasticism, international law and, after the French revolution, nationalism and collective hegemony (Concert), seen as a synthesis of balance of power and hegemony. This literature basically sets out what it was that expanded and how it came to be, and provides the background to the expansion story.

Transfer

The expansion part of the classical story is about how Europe imposed a global international society on a previously existing 'system' of several regional international societies each reflecting a local culture (Bull and Watson 1984b: 1; Watson 1992: 265–76). Vigezzi (2005: 106) is critical of Bull and Watson's (1984a) under-exploration of the subglobal international societies that the European expansion overrode. This defect was, however, partially remedied by Watson (1992: 214–27), who looks at the systems/societies it displaced. Europeans played into these local systems (trade, alliance) long before taking them over. Watson (1984c: 17–19, 24–32) notes how the initial expansion by Spain and Portugal was a continuation of their reconquest of the Iberian peninsula from Islam, and how expansion was in part about managing conflict among European powers. He tracks the general shift from trade to administration as European power increased versus the rest of world, especially by the nineteenth century. Reus-Smit (2011a: 207–15) identifies five waves of expansion of what was initially a European international society, each contingent on the disintegration of empires: 1648 (Holy Roman Empire), 1808–25 (Spanish Empire in the Americas), 1919 (Austro-Hungarian and Ottoman Empires), 1945 (beginning of the general decolonization by Britain,

France, the US and other lesser imperial states) and 1991 (the Soviet Union).

In some ways, this expansion story is rather oddly told in the classical account. It puts much more emphasis on the relatively small number of encounters between the expanding West and societies that it failed to colonize than it does on the wholesale colonization of much of the world by Europeans. The reason for this is easy to see. Colonized territories and peoples were the possessions of the metropolitan powers and so did not register much, if at all, in thinking about a society of states. It was easy to suppose that colonization simply expanded European international society to global scale without centrally affecting the international society of Europe itself, other than making it a society of empires outside Europe. But this assessment is increasingly challenged. Benton (2002), for example, rejects the idea of colonial institutions being imposed from the imperial hub, because, although imperial powers may frequently have wished to establish a common institutional structure across their colonies, they were, in practice, often unable to overcome the complex and competing forces that they encountered on the ground. What tended to prevail, therefore, was a form of 'legal pluralism' – where the state was only one among many legal authorities. Up until the nineteenth century, both the great varieties of peoples and cultures that fell under European administration and the severe limits on European capacity to extend detailed control over the distances involved meant that empires became quite politically diverse. This was particularly true of the British Empire (Darwin 2012). For several centuries, this diversity of order in Christian and Islamic colonies was the dominant form because it generally proved to be the most effective structure for dealing with the social differences that existed in all colonies across the globe.

It was only in the middle of the nineteenth century that the European states began to remake the colonies in their own image. McKeown (2003) argues that the emergence of this new colonial regime is associated with the contemporaneous move from universal natural law to the adoption of positivist law, which was seen to be a feature of more advanced civilizations. Members of the English School were familiar with this line of argument through the work of Alexandrowicz (1967).

This elevated view of themselves adopted by the Europeans was also closely linked to the general take-off of modernity, centred in Europe during the nineteenth century, of which the shift towards positive law was just one part (Buzan and Lawson forthcoming). Modernity opened up a huge power gap between a mainly European core and a mainly non-Western periphery and transformed the *raison de système*. It inevitably raised questions about the terms and conditions under which premodern polities could become members of the now global, but still European-dominated, international society – the so-called standard of civilization. Then as now, the 'standard of civilization' was linked to modernity through the ever unfolding criteria that defined 'progress'. Then as now, the 'standard' was not fixed, but evolved with the development of the leading-edge powers who were strong enough to define their own model as the universal standard and force others to comply with it (Bowden 2009: locs. 1424–787). The 'standard of civilization' also, and prior to later concerns arising with decolonization, opened up Wight's question about the relationship between an underlying common culture and the ability to form and maintain an international society.

The key works on the standard of civilization are by Gong (1984a) and Bowden (2009). Gong argues that the expansion of European international society required changes of identity, starting with 'Christendom' in the emergence phase, then moving to 'European culture' (to bring in the Americas and other European offshoots during the decolonization of settler states in the Americas during the nineteenth century; see also Watson 1984b; Clark 2005: 35–50, 48) and finally to the 'standard of civilization' in the late nineteenth century, when non-Western powers began to qualify for entry (Gong 1984a: 4–6). These changes reflected a mix of cultural arrogance towards other cultures (comparable to similar Islamic and Chinese attitudes of cultural superiority) and the necessities of interaction among equals, which required certain standards of effective government, particularly the ability to meet 'reciprocal obligations' in law (ibid.: 64–93). The 'standard of civilization' supported a partly racist taxonomy of 'savage, barbarian and civilized' as a way of classifying the non-European world in relation to Europe (see also Louis 1984; Bowden 2009: locs. 755–848). The expansion of international society was thus achieved on unequal terms in two ways: by the imperial absorption of much of the non-West into European empires and by the phased admission of a few non-colonized states into international society once they were deemed 'civilized'. As Wight (1991: 50–82) revealingly observes, realist logic allowed conquest, exploitation and even extermination of barbarians, whereas rationalist logic pointed to a paternalistic obligation of the 'civilized' to tutor the barbarians up to the 'standard of civilization', giving them only the partial rights of a ward along the way.

Gong explores the nature and operation of the 'standard of civilization' in some depth. He notes the clash of civilizations explicit in the expansion, and how the 'standard of civilization' created a pressure for conformity with Western values and practices which posed a demanding cultural challenge to the non-West, much of which had to go against its own cultural grain in order to gain entry. This left an ongoing legacy of problems for the legitimacy of international law, still seen by some as reflecting imperial Western values (Gong 1984a: 7–21). Gong notes how the European need for access (trade, proselytizing, travel) was what drove the functional aspects of the 'standard of civilization' (to protect life, liberty and property) and therefore the demand for extraterritoriality and unequal relations where the locals could not or would not provide these (ibid.: 24–53). Decolonization put an end to the 'standard of civilization'. With the right of independence and sovereign equality becoming almost unconditional (see also Watson 1992: 296), the dismantling of the Western empires did not really confront the question of conditions of entry in anything like the same way as the earlier encounters had done. Gong (1984a: 90–3) does, however, make an interesting point, subsequently taken up by several others, that the conditionality of Western demands for human rights, with its concerns about life, liberty and property, is the successor to the 'standard of civilization'.

De facto, then, the classical English School's version of the encounter, and the whole 'standard of civilization' question, is confined mainly to a small number of cases. The early decolonization of the Americas created few problems because the new settler states were offshoots of European culture and therefore easy to accept as 'civilized'. Four cases attracted the most attention – Russia, the Ottoman Empire, China and Japan – although some others (Siam, Iran) get passing mention. Other encounter and entry stories are still being written (Stivachtis 1998, 2010). Interestingly, little is written about India, despite its being one of the major centres of classical civilization, because it was colonized and therefore did not pose the 'standard of civilization' question. Russia was half European anyway, and had made it into European international society by the early eighteenth century (Watson 1984a; Gong 1984a: 100–6; Neumann 2011). The Ottoman Empire served as Europe's alien Other for many centuries (Neuman and Welsh 1991; Yurdusev 2009), but it was also in close interaction with the European balance of power during much of that time. This meant that the Ottoman encounter story has a different quality from the later ones involving European expansion. For the Ottoman Empire, the question was about joining (or not) *Europe's* international society, not the later Western-global version of it. It has inspired an ongoing debate about how to understand the difference between just being part of the European international system and meeting enough of the 'standard of civilization' to become a member of its international society. There is still no consensus about when (or if) the Ottoman Empire became part of European international society,[1] and this whole debate gives useful depth to the current debates about the EU and Turkey.

Japan provides the model case for a rapid and successful adaptation by a non-Western power to the 'standard of civilization', with its acceptance into international society by 1899 and as a great power shortly thereafter

(Suganami 1984; Gong 1984a: 164–200). But there are interesting twists to this story, such as Japan's failure in 1919 at Versailles to get Western recognition of racial equality (Clark 2007: 83–106). China's struggle with the 'standard of civilization' was much more protracted and is, indeed, like Turkey's, still ongoing (X. Zhang 2011a). There are, in a sense, two rounds, one classical and one modern, to China's encounter story. In the classical round, as with the Ottoman Empire, there is a debate about when China gained entry – possibly not until during the Second World War with the final removal of extraterritoriality.[2] In the modern round, there is the story of communist China's encounter. Yongjin Zhang (1998) tells this story in detail, seeing communist China as alienated from international society (both excluded and self-excluding), but increasingly becoming more integrated with it in terms of sovereignty, nonintervention, diplomacy (rising participation in IGOs and global economy), international law, and suchlike. China has successfully adapted to Westphalian international society, yet it remains alienated from the human rights and democracy elements that have come more to the fore in Western practice since the end of the Cold War (Foot 2006; see also chapter 9).

Decolonization

These encounter stories, and the issues raised by the 'standard of civilization', are mainly specific to the colonial world before 1945. With decolonization, we move to the third part of the classical story, in which the whole of the non-Western world is given largely unconditional membership of international society. During the expansion phase, the story was one of insiders (Europe and the West) and outsiders wanting to get in (the encounter stories), with not much being said about those who were colonized – inside in one sense, but very much in the third-class carriages. With decolonization, almost everyone becomes an insider, and the distinction among 'civilized', 'barbarian' and 'savage' has to be abandoned.

The focus then turns to the consequences of this rapid move to universal membership, the problems it raises for the cohesion of international society, and what, if anything, might be done about them. The general drift of the classical story for this phase is pessimistic. Decolonization triples the membership of international society and brings into it many postcolonial states that are both politically weak as states and economically poor and underdeveloped. It also weakens the cultural foundations of international society by diluting the previously dominant European cohesion. Now all the world's cultures, both great and small, are inside, and this moves Wight's question about the relationship between cultural cohesion and international society to centre stage. As Riemer and Stivachtis (2002: 27) argue, 'the logic of anarchy, operating in the international system, has brought states into international society; once in, the logic of culture has determined their degree of integration into international society.' On this logic, if culture was diverse, then international society could be only weakly integrated. On top of all this was the Cold War, which along with decolonization defined the post-1945 era, and which meant that the great powers were at loggerheads, weakening international society still further (Bull 1980).

The pessimistic view of the post-1945 expansion belongs mainly to the pluralist wing of the English School (see chapter 6) and is clearly evident in some of the chapters in Bull and Watson's book (1984a). Kedourie (1984) sees Marxism (class struggle) and nationalism (self-determination) as undermining the old order of balance of power and concert, which had itself failed in the two world wars. The spread of these ideas by the USSR, and in the Third World, meant that the machineries of chaos were dominant and international society was in deep decline (see also Watson 1992: 277–98). Even further towards what at times reads like nostalgia for the European colonial system is Bozeman (1984: 387–406), who saw international society as having peaked in the nineteenth century, with the height of European power, and the reassertion of non-Western cultures as dragging the international order towards conflict since then.

Even Bull and Watson (1984c) were drawn into this feeling that decolonization had been a great blow to international society. They accepted the negatives of weak states and cultural fragmentation, but tried to balance them with the positive development of the general acceptance by Third World elites of some of the key institutions of international society, sovereignty and juridical equality, and, up to a point, also of Western norms. They read the Third World as wanting more to improve its position than to overthrow the system. Bull (1977: 315–17) argued that, in order to strengthen a declining international society by building up shared values, there was a need to extend and deepen the cosmopolitan elite culture beyond the West. Dore (1984) also found glimmers of hope in the existence of a global elite sharing a Westernized culture as a bulwark against disintegrative multiculturalism, and Watson (1992: 307–8) mooted the possibility of a new cultural synthesis. There is here a distinct absence of celebration about the liberation of hundreds of millions of people from colonial rule and the creation for the first time of a global international society based formally on sovereign equality (as opposed to a Western-global imperial order). The view from the other side was equally gloomy: Mazrui (1984) argues that the legacy of the West for Africa is two contradictory and counterproductive 'prison houses': the state and capitalism.

In his solo work, Watson tried to bring to the post-1945 problem insights from his historical investigations of international society across the whole sweep of world history. He questioned both the empirical and the normative validity of anarchy as the dominant way of framing international society, offering instead Europe–Ottoman relations as the model for overcoming cultural diversity in the expansion of international society (Watson 1990: 100–2). His spectrum of forms of international society, ranging from anarchy to empire, was a way of looking at the expansion story, both early (imperial) and contemporary. Watson (1992: 14) focused on *raison de système* and on tension in post-1945 international society, because the principles of legitimacy lie with sovereign equality and nationalism, but much of the practice is hegemonic (Watson 1992: 299–309, 319–25; 1997). Following Watson's line, Rana (1993: 133) argues for the necessity of a 'pax collaborata' to bring together the hegemonic North and the sovereigntist South in recognition of *de facto* hegemony. As already noted, this problem of how to legitimize *de facto* hegemony in the face of the strong postcolonial normative commitment to sovereign equality still echoes on.[3]

Coming at the problems of postcolonial international society from the bottom up, rather than from the top down, Bull's solo work (1984a: 217–28; 1984b) was dominated by the problem of inequality in the new global international society and the revolt against the West by Westernized Third World elites using Western ideas. Bull used the tensions between order and justice in international society to develop a strong sense of the revolt of the former colonial world against Western dominance. He acknowledged the considerable success of their struggle to regain equality notwithstanding the many moral shortcomings and hypocrisies within Third World positions. The problem, to which he never found the answer, was how to deal with the political, economic and social consequences of inequality seeded by the monocentric creation of Western-global international society.

O'Neill and Vincent (1990: 283–5) also note the unequal relations between the West and the Third World and the consequent regional diversity of international society, with some Third World unity around nonalignment, development, and the elimination of colonialism and racism. Vincent added to the 'revolt against the West' theme by exploring the role of racism in European expansion. Racism became prominent in European thinking about colonialism during the later nineteenth century (Buzan and Lawson forthcoming: ch. 4) and was not rejected in the West until after the Second World War (Vincent 1982: 663), and then more as a reaction against Nazism than against colonial racism (Vincent 1984b). The idea that rulers and ruled should be of broadly similar racial stock was important in anticolonial and anti-apartheid movements. Racism played a role in the formation of nationalisms in the non-Western world, and, although abolished after 1945, the substance of racism was broadly upheld by the strong correlation between white and developed and non-white and underdeveloped in the subsequent half century (ibid.). Along parallel lines, Thomas (2000) argues that religious difference underlies a culturally pluralist international society, not least because the settlement of religion in the evolution of the European state did not happen elsewhere. Religion has become part of the political identity of the 'revolt against the West', sometimes being preferred to development.

The pluralist emphasis on the revolt against the West makes its interpretation of decolonization into one of the creation of a house divided: a coherent global imperial order of insiders and outsiders deteriorates into an incoherent global disorder where everyone is inside but their differences and squabbles are bringing the house down.

Critiques and extensions of the classical story

This section follows the same general framing as the previous one, looking at the expansion story in the three phases of emergence, transfer/encounter and decolonization. The literature here belongs mainly to the solidarist wing of the English School (on which more in chapter 8).

Emergence

The emergence story has been questioned mainly on the grounds that the classical story is too Eurocentric, and underplays the fact that European international society did not emerge fully formed in Europe and then spread from there to the rest of the world. Rather, it developed as it did substantially because it was already spreading as it emerged, and was thus in its own way shaped as much by the encounter as was the non-European world. Alexandrowicz (1967, 1973) provides the most radical challenge to the conventional English School account and is based on a close reading of the treaties that the Europeans signed between the sixteenth and eighteenth centuries with a range of states in Asia. When they moved into the East Indies, the Europeans found a well-developed international society in place. Alexandrowicz shows that, when Grotius argued in the seventeenth century that Europeans should accept the principle that the high seas constituted international territory, the Indian Ocean provided the leading precedent for this principle. Alexandrowicz identifies the existence by the end of the eighteenth century of a global international society that rested on the foundations of natural law. But by that time, the Europeans were beginning to move away from natural law towards positivist law. In the process, they constituted a purely European legal system based on the principle of mutual consent. As a consequence, non-European states that in the past had been acknowledged as fully sovereign states were now viewed only as potential candidates for admission into a European international society. Relations with the non-European world were redefined in a very fundamental way, with the Europeans viewing themselves as 'civilized' top dogs (see also Simpson 2004).

The first generation of English School theorists was well aware of this 'two-way encounter' view of international society as an evolving phenomenon, and indeed Wight (1977) was favorably disposed towards it (Little 2013). By the same token, Bull and Watson (1984a) were mindful that there were anomalies in their conventional expansionist story. Nevertheless, it is only relatively recently that the conventional story has come under systematic scrutiny. Yurdusev (2009), for example, shows how some of the classical institutions of Westphalian international society developed out of modern Europe's oldest encounter, that with the Ottoman Empire. By the same token, there is a growing recognition that European colonization needs to be examined in close conjunction with Islamic colonization (Benton 2002; Abulafia 2008).

Buzan (2010a) pushes this critique of Eurocentrism by setting up a *syncretist* account of the expansion story to incorporate both the Eurasian dimension and the two-way formative interaction between Europe and non-Western international societies. The syncretist account is based on the idea that it is the normal condition of human affairs for cultural ideas to flow between areas of civilization. Cultures thus evolve not only in response to their own internal dynamics but also because of encounters with other cultures, even remote ones. Obviously there has to be some contact in order for syncretism to function, but the interaction capacity requirements for the transmission of ideas are low, which makes such transmission the normal expectation.[4] Both Hobson (2004) and Hui (2005), for example, point out how small numbers of Europeans visiting China from the thirteenth century onwards brought back crucial information about Chinese technology and politics. Bentley (1993) and Lach (1965, 1970, 1993) show how even the fairly thin trading systems of the ancient and classical world served as cross-cultural transmission belts for religions. Buddhism was carried from India to East Asia, and Islam from the Arab World to Africa and Asia. Where contact was closer and interaction capacity higher, as between Europe and the Islamic world and within the trading system of the Indian Ocean, there was a lot of movement of ideas.

While the syncretist account does not equate to the polycentric model of how global international society formed, it does lean in that direction. Parts of the syncretist account, such as the long encounter between Europe and Islamic civilization, look very much like how the polycentric model would have worked. Wight (1977: 34) provocatively speculates that mediaeval Europe picked up the idea of crusade from the Islamic practice of *jihad*. He notes that, during the twelfth and thirteenth centuries, the Crusades brought Europe into close contact with the Islamic world, adding to the contact already created by the earlier Islamic occupation of Spain, which together served as 'the channel for the acculturation of mediaeval Christendom' (Wight 1991: 52). This longstanding blending of cultures goes some way towards addressing contemporary concerns over the lack of cultural cohesion, and so perhaps points towards a less pessimistic view of international society post-decolonization. The syncretist position has also been encapsulated in the idea of 'reciprocal socialization' (Terhalle 2011).

Transfer

In relation to the expansion phase, more work has been done to bring out what the encounter looked like from the other side. Onuma (2000) looks at the imposition of Western international law during the later nineteenth century fulfilling its earlier false pretentions to universalism. Kayaoglu (2010) explores the rise and fall of the extraterritorial jurisdiction established by Western states in Africa, Asia and the Middle East in the nineteenth century, but also demonstrates how the practice helped to consolidate a conception of sovereignty in Europe that continues to hold sway in the twenty-first century. Roberson (2009) shows how Egyptian elites adapted to the financial 'standard of civilization' set by Britain, and Englehart (2010) how the Thai elite played to British cultural norms in order to gain recognition as 'civilized'. Neumann (2011) explores how the cultural memory of being subordinated within a suzerain system affected Russia's encounter with European international society. He sets up the interesting argument that all such encounters have been with polities coming from hegemonic/suzerain systems having to come to terms with the anarchic qualities of European/Western international society. Zarakol (2011) surveys the ongoing impact of the encounter experiences on Turkey, Japan and Russia. Reus-Smit (2011a) sees a recurrent theme in which domestic struggles for individual rights link into anti-imperial struggles and the pursuit of sovereign equality within international society. The humiliations of having to conform to alien standards, and the condescending and often racist attitudes of the Europeans towards those who tried, were important components of the revolt against the West.

A related line of critique, which moves more into the spread/encounter phase of the story, is that of Keene (2002) and others (Holsti 2004: 239–74), who point out the conspicuous and Eurocentric failure of the classical story to feature the fact that colonialism was a core institution of European international society. Hobson (2012: locs. 5247–519, 7574) sees English School pluralism as infused with Eurocentrism and as 'a retrospective justification of pre-1945 imperialism as a benign process that diffused civilization across the world'. In this vein, Gills (1989: 110) suggestively ties Bull and Watson's expansion story during the nineteenth century to core–periphery analysis, considering the rejection of hegemony in the core and the assertion of it over the periphery as linked phenomena. Keene (2002) highlights colonialism and imperialism pre-1945 as emblematic of divided sovereignty in which the core develops a Westphalian principle of sovereign equality and tolerance within itself, but practices divided sovereignty and the 'standard of civilization' against the periphery. Decolonization and Western reactions against the apogee of racism in Nazi Germany appear to eliminate this division, but don't, and Keene (echoing Gong as noted above) understands human rights as a key contemporary extension of this two-worlds character of international society (ibid.: 122–3, 147–8), which continues to play strongly in international society despite the notional uniformity of sovereign equality.

Related critiques point to other areas in which the classical account underplays important elements, most notably the economic side of the expansion story and the extent to which the expansion was conducted by coercion. The classical account has relatively little to say on economics. O'Brien (1984) just refutes the idea that European development depended on overseas trade, and leaves it at that. Neither the economic dynamics of European imperialism (with the notable exception of Roberson 2009) nor the trading systems and international societies of the ancient and classical world into which Europe expanded get much attention. This neglect gives the classical story a rather one-dimensional character, as if European international society was expanding into (and filling) a vacuum. Such a view underplays the existence not just of Eurasia-wide trade routes that existed for millennia before the European expansion but also of extensive non-European international societies (Buzan and Little 1996, 2000). Little (2005) is concerned to recover the pre-nineteenth-century story of multiple international societies encountering one another, and the extent to which European international society overlaid existing international societies rather than expanding its own international society into empty space. This makes the expansion story into more of a two-way encounter. Suzuki,

Zhang and Quirk (2013) examine instances of these international societies during the early modern era in some depth. They also raise analytical questions about how to frame this two-way encounter: as system versus society or as different types or levels of international society? Reinterpreting the expansion and encounter story in this way opens again the question of what 'global international society' actually means as the outcome of the expansion/encounter story. To what extent does it still remain a core–periphery structure with the regional international societies discussed in chapter 4 echoing earlier international societies? Or is it the fairly homogeneous entity implied by the application of sovereign equality on a global scale?

The classical story notes European military superiority as a factor in the expansion (Howard 1984), and coercion certainly appears in the encounter stories, but coercion is never really placed at the heart of the expansion story, as some critics think it should be (Keene 2002: 3–4; Buzan 2004: 222–7; Halliday 2009). Röling (1990) gives perhaps the strongest critique on this score, arguing that Grotius's ideas basically set a law for the rich and powerful to exploit the weak and so underpin the coercive expansion of Europe. This contrasts with Bull (1990), who lauds Grotius as providing the basis not only for international (interstate) society but also for world society (through Grotius's natural law elements underpinning solidarism). Suzuki (2005, 2009) picks up a different aspect of this theme in his reconsideration of Japan's encounter. He complements Keene (2002) by looking at the two faces of international society via how Japan was socialized into wanting to be, and becoming, both an equal to the other great powers and an imperial power itself. He argues that the English School puts too much emphasis on the order side of the expansion story and not enough on the inequality and coercion one, which is its dark side, creating a normative imbalance in its perspective.

This perspective fits nicely with Armstrong's (1998) idea of the 'social state', seeing the dynamics of international society in constructivist terms of mutual identity-shaping between states and international society. The tendency to underplay the dark side of European colonialism, and to view the nineteenth century as the high point of international society, reinforces the suspicions already noted that at least some elements of the classical English School were influenced by a nostalgia for the nineteenth-century colonial order, setting concerns for the cultural coherence of international society above concerns about the inequalities of empires (Buzan 2007 [1991]: 142–7). While it is doubtless true that the role of coercion has been seriously underplayed in the classical English School accounts, one should not go too far in the other direction. Western coercion was not always just about gaining economic and political advantage. A considerable amount of trade was consensual, and Britain's use of force to suppress the slave trade was not to its commercial advantage.

Much of this critique of the expansion/encounter part of the classical story aims to bring out not just the coercive and unequal character of the monocentric creation of global international society but also the Eurocentric telling of the story, which constructs it too much as a one-way street. These critiques are mainly in line with the postcolonial critique of IR generally. Seth (2011) notes a particular disappointment with the English School for being the only mainstream approach to IR that features a historical orientation, but then fails to give anything like a balanced account of how international society was made.

Decolonization

At this point it becomes difficult to separate the critiques and extension of the expansion story from the broader discussion of contemporary international society within the English School. It blends into the debates about how international society can handle the contradiction of its *de facto* hegemonic practices set against sovereign equality and nationalism as its legitimizing principles. That broader discussion is set out in Part III. There is, however, one line of critique that bridges between transfer and decolonization, and that is about the failure to consider what happened to indigenous peoples. In some ways echoing Röling, Keal (1995) uses a legal approach to show how the shift from natural to positive law reduced the rights of native peoples in international society and increased outright territorial seizure by the Europeans. Dunne (1997) looks at colonial practice regarding Australian Aboriginals through the three traditions, and perceives the treatment as largely reflecting a realist right of the civilized to conquer the barbarian and savage. Keal (2003) develops a fuller account, bringing in the impact of expansion on indigenous peoples as the most excluded victims, both in the sense of being badly treated during the expansion (massacred, displaced, enslaved, subordinated) and after decolonization, when they often remained as minorities within hostile states. Like Keene, he sees strong carry-overs to the postcolonial period from the colonial era of expansion, which he characterizes as 'a society of empires' (ibid.: 21). He considers the fate of indigenous peoples as a moral blight on international society and argues the case for a right of self-determination (not necessarily sovereign independence) for such peoples.

Conclusions

The expansion story covers a great deal of ground and has sustained a large and lively literature across several generations of English School writers. Given the immensity of this world historical story, there will always be critiques that some things have been under-recognized or left out of its telling. But, on a deeper level, there are also critiques about how the story has been told.

The list of things that are not yet covered well enough is potentially very long. In general terms, the expansion story still suffers from the English School's neglect of the whole economic dimension. Clark (2007) makes the case that more needs to be done to insert into the history of international society the story of world society, and how it shaped the norms of states. More specifically, there is room for argument about the emergence part of the story, and whether the emergence was largely a European event or a more global one that co-evolved in interaction with non-European societies. For the expansion and encounter part of the story, more can be said about the encounters already covered (China, Japan, Russia, the Ottoman Empire, indigenous peoples) and much more about those not covered much or at all (e.g., Egypt, India, Iran). Certainly more needs to be said about the colonized parts of the world, which tend to drop out of the story until decolonization brings everyone inside international society after 1945. In line with this, there is also a need to recover the story of the non-Western international societies that the Europeans overran. Acharya (2008) makes the good point that some of these contain interesting expansion stories of their own – for example, the peaceful expansion of Indian world society into East Asia. The Hellenistic, Islamic and Chinese expansion stories are also possible comparators, having, like Europe's, but unlike India's, a strong military element supporting the cultural one.

For both the expansion and post-1945 parts of the story, Halliday (1999: 1–23) argues that, despite its conspicuous place in Wight's three traditions and Bull's work, too much of the subsequent English School writing leaves out or downplays the role of revolutions in the history and evolution of international society. Armstrong's (1977, 1993) work belies Halliday's assessment, though it remains true that revolution does not figure broadly in the English School literature. Revolutions often specifically challenge aspects of international society (sovereignty, diplomacy) or are specific projects aimed at building societies different from the West, and the existence of a dominant international society is thus itself a permanent spur to such revolutions. This has long been the case. There is now an emerging recognition, for example, that the revolution that brought about the United States posed a significant challenge to the dynastic international society that prevailed at that time in Europe and that the United States went on to play a key role in the transformation of some of the defining institutions of the European international society.[5]

The story of the expansion of international society is one of the centre-pieces of the English School and is crucial to what differentiates its offering from realist, liberal, Marxist and constructivist understandings of international relations. Like all good grand narratives, the expansion story is not just an attempt to create a hegemonic discourse but also a site of contention, where many people contribute both to developing it and debating over its content and interpretation. The perspective it gives ties history and current affairs together into a coherent and meaningful whole that is unique both in its depth and mode of historical analysis and in its ability to frame many current policy dilemmas in a sophisticated way. The expansion/evolution story about international society explains what the international order is, how it came to be, and why resistance to and defence of it take the forms and have the intensities that they do. Many criticisms have been made about whether the English School has told this story accurately enough, what it has left out or exaggerated, and whether its approach is the optimal one for the job. But these criticisms are not for the most part aimed at suggesting that this story should not be told; rather they indicate an energetic and spirited debate whose desire is to get it right. That desire is in turn driven by an appreciation of how important it is to do so in order to understand how we got to where we are, what our options are, and what our priorities should be, from here going forward.

CONCLUSIONS TO PART II: THEORIZING INTERNATIONAL SOCIETY AS SOCIAL STRUCTURE

Both the comparative and the expansion/evolution historical approaches discussed in the previous two chapters make extensive use of the idea of primary institutions (introduced in chapter 2). They do this sometimes explicitly and sometimes implicitly. Such institutions also feature strongly in the pluralist/solidarist debate, and I will explore this in much more detail in chapters 6 to 9. Recall that primary institutions are differentiated from secondary ones (purposefully designed regimes and IGOs) by being deeper and more evolved, and by having a much longer history. Primary institutions range from diplomacy and trade, through balance of power, war, international law and great power management, to nationalism and the market. These and other primary institutions provide a way of describing and differentiating international societies and tracking their evolution. This was Wight's approach to thinking about the international societies of the ancient and classical world, and it remains the basis of English School theory.

Primary institutions offer a way of seeing international society, and possibly also world society, as a form of social structure. In other words, any given international society can be defined in terms of the set of primary institutions that compose it. Building on both the structural hints in earlier English School work and the approaches of Waltz and Wendt noted above, Buzan (2004) has made a strong call for an explicitly structural approach to be developed along these lines.[1] He wants to differentiate a purely structural approach from the normative one and make this a core element of English School theory alongside normative approaches. He sets out in some detail how this might be done and argues that, *inter alia*, it will provide sharper concepts than the existing undifferentiated approach has done. Buzan (2004: 14–15) notes that a structural approach does not have any necessary normative content in the sense of promoting preferred values (though that is not excluded). Norms and ideas play their role here as different forms of social structure: not normative theory, but theory about norms. It is about finding sets of analytical constructs with which to describe and theorise about what goes on in the world, and in that sense it is a positivist approach, though not a materialist one. . . . I hope to expose the dynamics and driving forces underlying international society more clearly, and to break out of the somewhat stultifying opposition between a self-paralysed set of pluralists, and a self-confined set of solidarists. Will this still be English School theory? Definitely, for it remains linked to the classic texts, the focus on international social structure, and the methodological pluralism. But it will not be English School theory as we have known it so far.

Buzan (2004: 228–49) and Holsti (2004) show how the rise, evolution and sometimes obsolescence of primary institutions can be used to frame a historical account of how international societies evolve. This approach can usefully be applied to the expansion story, showing how and why expansion and evolution played into each other, and I develop this in some detail in chapters 7 and 9. Buzan (2004: 207–12; see also Buzan and Gonzalez-Pelaez 2009; Buzan and Zhang 2014) uses this approach to differentiate regional international societies both from each other and from the global level. Tapping into the pluralist–solidarist spectrum, he sets out a typology of international societies based on the thickness and type of their primary institutions (Buzan 2004: 190–5). He argues that such a social structural approach dissolves the necessity for a concept of international system by folding all into types of international societies. His types are as follows.

- *Power political* represents here much the same as Hobbesian does for Wendt (1999) and the traditional English School's 'international system' pillar – namely, an international society based largely on enmity and the possibility of war, but where there is also some diplomacy, alliance making and trade. Survival is the main motive for the states, and no values are necessarily shared. Institutions will be minimal, confined mostly to rules of war, recognition and diplomacy. This is a pluralist society of offensive realism.
- *Coexistence* occupies some of the zone taken by Wendt's (1999: 279–97) uncomfortably broad Lockean category, focusing on the exemplar of modern Europe and meaning by it the kind of Westphalian system in which the core institutions of interstate society are the balance of power, sovereignty, territoriality, diplomacy, great power management, war and international law. In the English School literature this

form is labelled pluralist and incorporates the realist side of Grotianism. The guiding principle of coexistence defines a pluralist society of defensive realism.

- *Cooperative* requires solidarist developments that go significantly beyond coexistence, but short of extensive domestic convergence. It incorporates the more solidarist side of what the English School calls Grotian but might come in many guises, depending on what type of values are shared and how/why they are shared. Examples of interstate cooperative projects might include the creation of a shared market economy, the pursuit of human rights, the joint pursuit of big science, and collective environmental management. Such cooperation probably downgrades war as an institution, and other institutions might arise to reflect the solidarist joint project(s). This form incorporates liberal international society.

- *Convergence* means the development of a substantial enough range of shared values within a set of states to make them adopt similar political, legal and economic forms. The range of shared values has to be wide enough and substantial enough to generate similar forms of government (liberal democracies, Islamic theocracies, communist totalitarianisms, etc.) and legal systems based on similar values in respect of such basic issues as property rights, human rights, and the relationship between government and citizens. Convergence is deep solidarism, and one would expect quite radical changes in the pattern of both primary and secondary institutions of international society. In a society of states the Kantian form of solidarism around liberal values identified by the English School and Wendt is one option, but not the only one.

This kind of social structural approach to international society through primary institutions raises two sets of theoretical questions:

1 How are primary institutions to be theorized? Are they just empirically observed, or is there some principle of differentiation, whether functional or something else, that can be used to put bookends around the possible set?

2 Is it possible to create comprehensive taxonomies of types of international society? If it is, do we need the concept of international system that has been an important part of the English School's classical triad, or does the system element reduce to a mere rump of interaction capacity?

Before considering these questions further, it helps to have a more detailed understanding of primary institutions and how they have evolved. This is provided in Part III, and I pick up these theoretical questions in chapter 10.

PART III NORMATIVE ORIENTATIONS: PLURALISM AND SOLIDARISM

INTRODUCTION

This part focuses on the normative structure of the English School's 'great conversation', which was manifested throughout the first three chapters as the concern about order and justice formalized in the pluralist/solidarist debate. Its normative structure is a key feature distinguishing the English School from realism and much constructivism. The pluralist/solidarist debate is about how international, or more specifically interstate, society relates, and should relate, to world society – or, in other words, how states relate, and should relate, to people. The key issue has been human rights and the seeming tension between the states' claim to sovereignty, on the one hand, and the idea that universal rights are vested in people, on the other. The order/justice, states/people issue can be looked at in two ways. It can be seen in terms of the rights of states versus the rights of people. Or it can be seen more in terms of the nature and potentiality of interstate society, and particularly the actual and potential extent and type of shared norms, rules, practices and institutions within interstate societies. In this view there is no necessary contradiction between the rights of states and those of peoples if states deploy their sovereign right (and, in the solidarist view, also responsibility) to recognize and implement human rights. Important to this debate are questions about international law as the foundation of international society, and especially about whether the international law in question should be (or include) natural law (as it was for Grotius) or positive law (as it was for Bull).

The main empirical issue at stake in this debate has been human rights, and particularly the question of humanitarian intervention. As Rengger (2011: 1160) points out: 'the language of human rights is for many the lingua franca of ethical discussion of international politics.' Reus-Smit

(2011b: 1217) underpins this with the point that 'what makes individual/ human rights particularly compelling moral principles is their universaliz- ability: the fact that they cannot coherently be claimed by one but denied to another.' And as Wheeler (2000: 11) notes: 'humanitarian intervention exposes the conflict between order and justice at its starkest.' Also in play was the responsibility of the West towards the Third World.[1] It can, however, be argued that solidarism ranges much more widely than human rights and world society, also covering issues such as the global economy and environmental stewardship and reflecting state-centric logics of coop- eration and convergence (Buzan 2004: 139–60). More on this below.

It is crucial to understand that the pluralist and solidarist positions are not just 'objective' descriptive categories framing how things are, or might be, or have to be. Nor are they simply opposed positions. In some ways they are opposed, but the key is to see them as constituting the normative framing principles for a debate within the English School about the limits and possibilities of international society. And this is not just an abstract debate. As de Almeida (2006: 68) argues powerfully, 'world order is and always has been both pluralist and solidarist', which means that the practi- cal debate is not about either/or but about how to blend and mix the two qualities. Order/justice and pluralism/solidarism have yin/yang qualities in which each is a necessary presence in the other.

Both positions express preferences about how things should be: they are practice-guiding theories. This normative quality is obvious in relation to solidarism/justice, which is expected to be about the 'ought' side of things. It is perhaps less immediately obvious in relation to pluralism, which is more easily thought of as being about the 'is' side. Yet, as Bull (1972: 270; see also Mason and Wheeler 1996) makes very clear about pluralism, interstate order is purposive, represents preferred values, and has to be defended in terms of its contribution to world society. Jackson (2000: 1–10), who comes close to pure pluralism, likewise makes very clear the latter's essentially normative quality. The debate, like that in much of political and legal theory, is mostly about how best to blend the demands and needs for both order and justice. Its distinctive focus is in applying those arguments to international relations, and how best to rec- oncile the desires and needs of both people and states. This debate goes on both within and between the individuals participating in the great con- versation of the English School.

Should further evidence of the normativity of this debate be needed, even a superficial reading of the English School literature, both classical and contemporary, quickly reveals a deep grounding in the normative clas- sics of political theory and international law. It is no accident that the three traditions are named after Hobbes/Machiavelli, Grotius and Kant. Also to be found are Arendt, Berlin, Burke, Cobden, Elias, Gentili, Hart, Heeren, Hume, Locke, Marx, Mill, Oakeshott, Oppenheim, Popper, Pufendorf, Rawls, Rousseau, Schwarzenberger, Vattel, Vitoria, Weber, and many others.[2] Hurrell (2001: 493) rightly observes that 'within English School writing the emphasis on the history of thought about international relations occupied a particularly important place', and more than a few English School writers have made their own contributions to the history of ideas literature.[3]

These pluralist and solidarist dispositions form the mechanism that connects the core English School debates about rationalism/international society to the other two sections of the triad: realism/international system and revolutionism/world society. The links can be expressed in various tempting dyads:[4]

- pluralism as the normative character of international society and solidarism as the normative character of world society (Williams 2010a);
- pluralism as situational ethics and solidarism as cosmopolitan ethics (Reus-Smit 2002: 501–2; Jackson 2000);
- pluralism as identified with positive law and solidarism with natural law;
- pluralism, following Nardin's (1983) distinction, as a 'practical association' (in which actors pursuing different purposes seek some rules about coexistence) and solidarism as a 'purposive association' (in which actors seek to pursue collective goals);
- pluralism following the realist injunction to focus on the empirical study of what is and solidarism following the normative path of campaigning for what should be;
- pluralism as about order and solidarism as about justice.

But, as the four chapters in this part will show, these are oversimplifications. As Williams (2005; see also Bull 1977: 276–81) argues, the inherent diversity of humankind means that world society is in many ways also pluralist even in its cosmopolitan framing. It is also the case, as argued by liberal democratic peace theory, that interstate society can be solidarist along cooperative and convergence lines. Pluralism's logic of coexistence is not just about 'is' but contains room for 'ought', as in arms control and environmental management as responses to shared existential threats. Conversely, solidarism's logics of cooperation and convergence contains room for 'is', as in the study of existing regimes or purposive cooperation. The pluralist and solidarist strands of English School thinking are thus complex and closely interwoven. As Weinert (2011) argues, there is a need to rescue the pluralist/solidarist debate from the excessive polarization into which it has fallen and to recover the sense from the classical three traditions of the English School that both are always in play. Yin and yang never stand alone.

The English School not only brings together international system, international society and world society but also keeps the normative and the structural approaches to these in continuous play. Because it does this, the English School is better able than narrower theoretical approaches to develop a holistic perspective on international relations. Thus, although pluralism and solidarism might at first sight look simply like restatements of liberalism and realism, this is not the case. Rather than being separate, zero-sum positions, they are two sides of an ongoing, and permanent, tension in the subject matter of International Relations around which the normative and structural debates of the English School are organized. This is what enables the English School to incorporate, and up to a point integrate, what most other approaches to IR separate, compartmentalize and put into zero-sum competition.[5]

Much of the debate around pluralism and solidarism is about how to find ways of reducing the tension between the needs and imperatives of states and the needs and imperatives of humankind, both singly and collectively – what Cochran (2009) calls 'middle-ground ethics'. Most English School writers operate within this debate, taking the tension between the imperatives of order and justice as the core problem to be addressed. The tension is visible even within the work of individual writers – most famously in Bull's work between order (1977) and justice (1984a) – and the debate about it (Dunne and Wheeler 1996; Wheeler and Dunne 1998). A similar case in point is within Vincent's (1974, 1986) work. That tension is what makes sense of the debates about human rights, international order, great power responsibilities, (non)intervention, the institutions of international society, and the rest of the English School's agenda. If, as Wheeler (1996) argues, international society requires some degree of moral community among state leaders, then it is legitimate to ask how much that creates, or can create, a sense of moral responsibility towards citizens. That is how international society links to world society. The English School is about finding a working balance between how power and interest, as well as standards of justice and responsibility, operate in international society, how the ideal and the real meet up, and how the normative and the empirical are intertwined.

Several recent English School works make this search for a synthesis between the demands of order and justice abundantly clear.[6] The four chapters in this part look at pluralism and solidarism in both theoretical and historical perspective. The aim is to distil the essence of each position by looking at the literature advocating it, and then to survey the primary institutions that represent them in the historical development of international society. Readers should keep in mind that this is not a setting out of opposites like the standard chapters in IR texts covering realism and liberalism. These chapters are about the yin and yang of justice/order, solidarism/pluralism and states/people. Readers should also keep in mind that the historical accounts in chapters 7 and 9 of how primary institutions have evolved are intended as much to unfold the story of the developing structure of international society as they are to illustrate the practical interweaving of pluralism and solidarism.

6 CLASSICAL PLURALISM AND ITS SUCCESSORS

Introduction

This chapter explores the more conservative side of English School thinking whose intellectual leanings take it closest to realism. The main concern of pluralism is international order, and its vision of international society is state-centric and limited largely to norms of coexistence. Pluralism presupposes that states are *de facto* the dominant unit of human society and that state sovereignty means giving political primacy to both positive international law (Hurrell 2007b: 49ff.) and nonintervention. More discreetly, pluralism, like realism, is about the preservation and/or cultivation of the political and cultural difference and distinctness that are the legacy of human history (Jackson 2000: 23). The assumption of major differences among states and peoples in the system is amplified by the English School's preference for thinking of international society on a global scale. If international society must cover the whole system, then the historical evidence is overwhelming that states are culturally and ideologically unlike. During the Cold War, when this position was first crystallized within the English School, the evidence for the depth of cultural and ideological differences among states was all too palpable (Bull 1977: 257–60).

Pluralism defines international societies with a relatively low, or narrow, degree of shared norms, rules and institutions among the states, where the focus of international society is on creating a framework for orderly coexistence and competition, or possibly also the management of collective problems of common fate that concern the 'existence' part of coexistence (e.g., arms control, environment). At the pluralist end of the spectrum, where international society is thin, collective enforcement of rules will be difficult and rare. Like Bull, Hurrell (2007b: 29) sees the limits of pluralist thinking not so much in a denial of common interests, but more in consciousness of the difficulty of agreeing action in the face of differences in power and values. On a more negative note, pluralism can be defined as 'little more than a name given to the voice of scepticism that regards the scope for international agreement as falling well short of encompassing questions pertaining to the enforcement of international law' (Bain 2007a: 560). Pluralists give political, though not necessarily moral, primacy to states over people. They are more sovereigntist and nationalist than internationalist.

Among the pluralists, James (1984, 1986) is particularly strong on the defence of sovereignty as the prime organizing principle and states as the only entities with full capacity to act as international persons. He stages sovereignty as 'the constitutive principle of inter-state relations' (James 1999: 468). Pluralism's focus on sovereignty sets up the solidarist promotion of cosmopolitan human rights as a danger to the stability of international society, because, if human rights are given independent of the state, then the principle of sovereignty and the right of nonintervention are necessarily challenged in a fundamental way.

The pluralist framing in terms of coexistence restricts international society to fairly minimal rules. Pluralist international society lacks much potential for development beyond institutions centred on shared concerns about the desired degree of international order under anarchy. It is thus confined largely to agreements about mutual recognitions of sovereignty, rules for diplomacy, and promotion of the nonintervention principle. As Mayall (2000a: 14) puts it, pluralism is:

> the view that states, like individuals, can and do have differing interests and values, and consequently that international society is limited to the creation of a framework that will allow them to coexist in relative harmony . . . For pluralists, one of the features that distinguishes international society from any other form of social organization is its procedural and hence non-developmental character.

Pluralism thus shares with realism the view that states are separate and different, but does not follow it into an assumption of a permanent crisis of survival and the primacy of conflict. Unlike realism, it moderates that view with the idea that, despite their separateness and difference, states might nevertheless desire, and be able to construct, relations that display a degree of order and up to a point peace. Whereas the basic principle of realism is *survival*, that of pluralism is *coexistence*.

Despite its state-centrism, there is also some place in pluralism for the great society of humankind. Like realism, pluralism is not devoid of ethical concerns. Its ethical orientation is grounded not in one specific vision of the good, but rather in acceptance, and normative defence, of the ethical diversity of human communities. The normative stance of pluralism is thus grounded in a conception of the responsible management and maintenance of a diverse international society (Jackson 1990b). This commitment to ethical diversity, whether as a normative preference or as acceptance of a profound, historically generated reality, means that the ethics of pluralism are much concerned with avoiding conflict promoted by the intolerant pursuit of universalist ideologies. This is the root of pluralist concern about the liberal pursuit of universal human rights. Pluralism is not only a conservative disposition. It is a practical ethics in which justice is framed as a concern with order under conditions of cultural and political diversity (Cochran 2008). That it is a normative choice to work to sustain international society, as pluralists want to do, is made clear by Jackson (2000: 366; see also Williams 2011), who uses situational ethics to argue that pluralism 'is a greater international good than democracy'. Pluralism stresses the instrumental side of international society as a functional counterweight to the threat of excessive disorder. Such disorder can come either from the absence of states (a Hobbesian anarchy) or from excesses of conflict between states, whether driven by simple concerns about power and survival (as in the warring states period in China or in early modern Europe – see Hui 2005) or by rival universalist ideological visions (as during the Cold War). In empirical terms, pluralism therefore defines international societies in which the ethical diversity of the members dictates a relatively low degree of shared norms, rules and institutions among the states, and where the focus of society is on creating a framework for orderly coexistence and competition, and possibly also the management of collective problems of common fate. Both Wight (1991: 134) and Bull (1991: xi) are aware that the minimalist, state-centric position of pluralism tends to support the status quo: in Wight's terms, it 'makes a presumption in favour of existing international society'.

The setting up of the pluralist/solidarist debate started in the early years of the British Committee and unfolded in both its internal discussions and the wider debate they inspired (Dunne 1998: 100–3; Vigezzi 2005). Foundational to this debate was the prior differentiation of international society from international system. Only when the idea of international society is the guiding concept do the essentially social and normative issues of pluralism/solidarism come into play. This explains why the pluralist/solidarist debate is distinctive to the English School and largely absent in the systems-based theories dominant in American IR.

Bull's pluralism

The originating work was a paper first written by Bull in 1962 (Bull 1966b; see also Bull 1990). Bull set out the terms for solidarism and pluralism by exploring the positions represented respectively by Hugo Grotius and Lassa Oppenheim. The core of the argument is about whether the international law on which international society rests is to be understood as natural law (Grotius, solidarist) or positive law (Oppenheim, pluralist). According to Bull (1966b: 64), it was Grotius's view, deriving from natural law, that 'individual human beings are subjects of international law and members of international society in their own right.' Because Grotian solidarism comes out of natural law, it is inherently universalist in the sense of having to be applied to all humankind. While Bull accepted the universalism, he rejected natural law as a basis for international society, and particularly dismissed the idea that individuals have standing as subjects of international law and members of international society in their own right. He argued (ibid.: 68) that Grotius's attachment of solidarism to natural law was rooted in the needs of his own times 'to fill the vacuum left by the declining force of divine or ecclesiastical law and the rudimentary character of existing voluntary or positive law', and that (ibid.: 66) 'Grotius stands at the birth of international society and is rightly regarded as one if its midwives.' Seeing the Grotian position as relevant to a long-past set of historical conditions, and fearing that Grotius's blending of individual rights and state sovereignty was a recipe for conflict, Bull (ibid.: 73) opted for Oppenheim's view: 'it may still be held that the method he [Oppenheim] employed, of gauging the role of law in international society in relation to the actual area of agreement between states, is superior to one which sets up the law over and against the facts.' This view seemed to strengthen over time: 'there are no rules that are valid independent of human will, that are part of "nature". Natural law cannot accommodate the fact of moral disagreement, so prominent in the domain of international relations' (Bull 1979: 181). For Bull, international society is, and should be, based on positive law.

The rather stark package of arguments that Bull deployed in this article did much to set the tone and content of pluralism. He restricted the idea of international society to states (see also James 1989), and in that sense he helped to draw a clear boundary between international society (states) and world society (individuals, peoples, humankind). Bull (1966b: 51–2) argued that states are 'capable of agreeing only for certain minimum purposes which fall short of that of enforcement of the law', and that this made Grotian solidarism defined in terms of enforcement of law unrealistic. He also argued (ibid.: 53–7) that, while pluralists see war as a right of the state, solidarists see it as an instrument of international society. Adopting the positive law position reinforced all this by putting international law wholly into the hands of states. It identified pluralism with positive international law (ibid.: 64–8) and excluded individuals as subjects of international law.

In another paper at the same time Bull (1966c) set out the pluralist case for international society more broadly as a third option between chaotic anarchy and empire. Wight (1966b: 95–7) is clearly thinking along parallel lines, characterizing international society as a middle position between the atomization of realism and the unification of cosmopolitanism, resting on a sense of common humanity combined with a recognition of states as similar types of unit. Bull (1977: 46–51; see also Suganami 1989) rejects the Hobbesian analogy of international with domestic politics, like Wight (1966a: 23), seeing greater prospects for order in international than in domestic anarchy.

Yet, despite their state-centric, positive law leanings, neither man abandons the world society element entirely, and both remain highly conscious of the tension between order and justice (Bull 1984a; Wight 1966b: 104–5). Bull (1977: 77–98) initially seems to take the harder line, arguing that order is a necessary condition for justice, but that justice is only a desirable condition for order. Surprisingly, he also remains open to natural law as a way of thinking about moral questions free from cultural relativism (Bull 1979). Wight (1966b: 106–11) likewise starts with order as a precondition for justice, but he goes on to argue that decolonization suggests a case where justice is a precondition for order. Later on in the same book, Bull (1977: 318–20) also begins to think of international society as a way station towards world society, which provides the moral basis for it and the standard by which it should be judged. This seems to lean towards his description of Grotius's vision of international society as informed by natural law, and therefore blending states and people: 'International society for Grotius is not just the society of states, it is the great society of all mankind' (Bull 1990: 83). Again, Wight (1991: 36) takes a parallel view that 'in the last analysis international society is a society of the whole human race.' Despite favouring a pluralist, state-centric understanding of international society, both men see the need to retain a moral anchor in world society, and it is this that set up pluralism/solidarism as a debate rather than a taking of mutually exclusive positions.

Although realism and pluralism start from different ontologies (system versus society), they share a similar vulnerability to pessimism. Starting from mechanical assumptions about survival imperative and a self-reproducing balance of power, realism excludes hope of any major change in the condition of insecurity and is pessimistic by definition. Starting from an assumption that a coexistence international society is possible though not inevitable, pluralism is already less pessimistic to begin with. But, since pluralism does not allow much if any scope for development of international society beyond mere coexistence, it too can easily breed, or reflect, pessimism.

This effect is easily visible in Bull. Vigezzi (2005: 291) notes Bull's growing pessimism about the future of international society, given both the superpower ideological polarization of the Cold War and the rising dissatisfaction of the Third World with Western values and institutions. In the logic of the three traditions, the relative strengths of international system, international society and world society are in continuous flux. Pluralism contains no teleological assumption that international society will necessarily grow stronger, and a real possibility that it might decline. Writing in the depths of the Cold War, and not too long after the main round of decolonization following the Second World War, Bull clearly thought that international society was going downhill. The two superpowers he characterized as 'the great irresponsibles' (Bull 1980). Visible throughout his work is concern about the dilution of international society by decolonization, which brought in both weak states and non-Western cultures, so reducing the political efficiency and the shared cultural foundation of Western international society (Bull 1977; Bull and Watson 1984c; Bull 1984a). He concludes his best-known work (1977: 319) with the evaluation that 'International society today is in decline, but such prospects as there may be for order in world politics lie in attempts to arrest this decline rather than to hasten it.'

Successors

Bull's pessimism seems to have been mainly empirical: that, even though he wanted a better world, the facts of international politics seemed to stand firmly in the way of achieving it. The principal legatee of this reluctant pluralism is James Mayall (2000a). His position, like Bull's, is pragmatic, taking the view that the world is pluralist whether we like it or not and that the risks of ignoring this fact are likely to outweigh any gains. In earlier writing Mayall (1984) excluded the development of the market as a solidarist institution of contemporary international society by seeing it as having become subordinated to economic nationalism as a consequence of the broadening of security. More recently (Mayall 2000a), his review and critique of the shortcomings and pitfalls of solidarism leave him nowhere else to go. He sees the state, sovereignty and territoriality remaining strong and indispensable even though war has declined as an institution of international society. Popular sovereignty and nationalism open the way to solidarist pursuit of human rights and democracy, but human rights is hugely problematic in practice, as is self-determination. Both reopen reasons for war, while democracy is simply unavailable in many places because the conditions for it are lacking (ibid.: 92–8). Mayall therefore sees mainly continuity in practice, with solidarist rhetoric often being hypocritical or dangerous, and he prefers an honest realistic pluralism stressing prudence and responsibility over unrealistic solidarist projects.

Although making many of the same arguments, Robert Jackson (2000) manages to shrug off the mantle of pessimism. He presents the glass as half full rather than half empty, focusing more on what pluralist international society and good professional statecraft have accomplished in the provision of order than on what they have not done or cannot do. In a strident defence of pluralism, Jackson mounts a polemic in favour of a pluralism of prudence, tolerance and nonintervention against what he sees as the destabilizing and utopian solidarist promotion of humanitarian intervention and democracy. He argues that responsibility between states is low and that cosmopolitanism is imperialist and dangerous, and he joins those who see the pursuit of human rights as a new 'standard of civilization' (ibid.: 287–93). But, as Bain (2007a: 562) argues, 'Jackson's global covenant can be little other than a pluralist society of states that in effect extinguishes the solidarist voice of human community.'

Jackson and Mayall both share Bull's fear that attempts to promote solidarism based on cosmopolitan values (especially human rights and democracy) will not only undermine sovereignty as the basis of international order but also increase disorder, because of the lack of any plausible agency other than the state to provide order on a global scale. Both are keen to point out in detail why democracy and human rights are not values universally shared within pluralist international society, as well as the risks of conflict that arise if it is assumed that they are or should be. Both authors are firmly against postmodern approaches to IR. Both defend the importance of prudence and responsibility in the practice of statecraft. Both are impressed by the stability of pluralist interstate values, while at the same time conscious that substantial changes not only in some of the core institutions (war, sovereignty, colonialism) of international society but also in the nature of states also reveal considerable flexibility and adaptiveness. Both have deep reservations about the pursuit of human rights on the basis of cosmopolitan principles. Both (Mayall 2000a: 21; Jackson 2000: 105) oppose the solidarist project of transforming international society from a practical into a purposive or 'enterprise' association. And both oppose the practice of the strong trying to impose any 'standard of civilization' on the weak.

Coming from the next generation of English School writers, and also from a rather different perspective, Morris (2004) reinforces the pluralist story and picks up the pessimistic tone of earlier writers noted above. He sees the European great powers as having been the leading norm entrepreneurs pre-1945, driven by a sense of exceptionalism in relation to the rest of the world. But the Cold War and decolonization wrecked this position and reduced international society to little more than 'unlimited pluralism'. The possible post-Cold War reopening for a progressive agenda has been sullied by US unilateralism and coercion.

Classical pluralism accepted the ideological and cultural diversity of humankind and sought to embed this diversity in a logic of coexistence. Because pluralists are looking to enhance order in world politics, they fear that any attempt to impose ideological or cultural homogeneity, such as the promotion of universal human rights, will provoke conflict and undermine the sovereignty-based international order. Pluralist order is based on the *raison de système* of cultivating a shared interest in a degree of stability in international relations. It rejects the hope that ideological or cultural convergence will bring peace.

Building on this legacy, John Williams (2002, 2005, 2006, 2011) has started to reclaim the normative foundations of pluralism and to challenge the solidarists' claim to the moral high ground. He starts from the proposition that pluralism is 'the defining feature of human life and possibly the universal feature we all share as humans – that we are different' (Williams 2011: 1251). He sees the state system as a possible solution to this condition, noting that territoriality has a normative side as an 'important aspect of community-based accounts of the nature of the good life for humans', and that tolerance is a key normative value for pluralists (Williams 2002; 2011: 1252). He mounts a probing attack on the assumption that solidarism must be associated with world society and pluralism with the society of states, showing how world society is inherently pluralist and the society of states at least potentially solidarist (Williams 2005). He questions the universalism of solidarism and argues that globalization is challenging the Westphalian model by changing the balance between international society and world society more towards the latter (ibid.). Because this shift is a major restructuring of world politics, understanding that world society is in fact intensely pluralist rather than inherently solidarist matters a lot.

With these arguments and inclinations in mind, we can now look at the historical record in terms of primary institutions. How does the English School's discussion of these institutions, and their emergence and evolution, line up or not with the theoretical pluralist assumptions and expectations sketched above? Is the structure of international society in fact pluralist?

7 PLURALISM IN HISTORICAL PERSPECTIVE

Introduction

Pluralism, like much of IR theory, is rooted in European history mainly from around 1500 until 1945.[1] More particularly, it rests on the emergence of the modern international system of sovereign territorial states out of the religious wars of the seventeenth century, a process usually bench-marked in IR by 1648 and the Treaties of Westphalia. There is a lot of argument in IR about the appropriateness (or not) of Westphalia as a benchmark for the emergence of the sovereign state (see Carvalho et al. 2011; Buzan and Lawson 2012), but this need not detain us here. 1648 is a reasonable tipping point to signify the emergence of the absolutist sovereign, territorial state, a process stretching from the late fifteenth century, through the Glorious Revolution in England in 1688, to the Treaty of Utrecht in 1713. This system generated the sovereignty-based form of 'Westphalian' international society that went on to impose itself on the rest of the world through the process of colonization and decolonization. It symbolizes a deep and widely agreed change in both the organizing principle and the nature of the dominant unit in (European) international relations.

Bull's foundational account of Westphalian international society drew on the debates within the British Committee and focused on five primary institutions as characterizing this pluralist society: the balance of power, diplomacy, great power management, international law and war. Given the discussion above, sovereignty is a surprising absence from this list, but one that is easily explained. Bull (1977: 65–76) frames his account within a functional conception of society in which human societies of whatever sort must be founded on understandings about three issues: security against violence, observance of agreements and rules about property rights.

Within society he argues that there are three levels of rules.

1 *Constitutional normative principles* are the foundation, setting out the basic ordering principle (e.g., society of states, universal empire, state of nature, cosmopolitan community, etc.). In Bull's view, what is essential for order is that one of these principles dominates. Because the principles are usually zero-sum, contestation equals disorder. Contestation at this level is what defines Wight's revolutionists.[2] For a Westphalian international society, the key principle is sovereignty.

2 *Rules of coexistence* are those which set out the minimum behavioural conditions for society, and therefore hinge on the basic elements of society: limits to violence, establishment of property rights and sanctity of agreements.[3]

3 *Rules to regulate cooperation in politics, strategy, society and economy* About these Bull (1977: 70) says: 'Rules of this kind prescribe behaviour that is appropriate not to the elementary or primary goals of international life, but rather to those more advanced or secondary goals that are a feature of an international society in which a consensus has been reached about a wider range of objectives than mere coexistence.' Here one would find everything from the UN system, through arms control treaties, to the regimes and institutions for managing trade, finance, environment, and a host of technical issues from postage to allocation of orbital slots and broadcast frequencies.

Given this starting point, several things become clear about Bull's formulation of pluralist international society. First, the absence of sovereignty from his list of primary institutions is explained by his prior choice of 'society of states' as the constitutional normative principle. In this formulation, states, and therefore sovereignty, are already given before we get to primary institutions. More subtly, but just as surely, so also is territoriality, which is a deep institutional choice about how to package sovereignty. If one sees primary institutions as constitutive of international society, then sovereignty, and its corollary nonintervention, plus territoriality are the keys to constituting the new type of state that emerged in Europe during the centuries around 1648. We can therefore add these two primary institutions to Bull's original five. Since 'cosmopolitan community' is given as an alternative to society of states under constitutional normative principles, that also tends to stage solidarism as a competing, revolutionist form of basic order, and therefore a potentially major source of disorder.

Second, once the choice is made for a society of states, Bull locks in the pluralist form of international society by defining his second level of rules as being about coexistence. His five primary institutions plus the two implicit ones are nicely linked to the three elements in his functional view of society: limits to violence (war, the balance of power, great power management), establishment of property rights (sovereignty, territoriality) and sanctity of agreements (diplomacy, international law).

Third, his regulatory rules seem to point mainly to secondary institutions and to be the location where state-centric solidarism might develop in the form of 'consensus . . . about a wider range of objectives than mere coexistence'. The formulation of such rules as being 'more advanced' but 'secondary' is curious. It seems to suggest that solidarist rules are both more advanced than those of coexistence and secondary to them, and to deny them status as primary institutions.

It is of course unfair to pick apart a formulation of Bull's that was written so long ago. But his ideas remain influential, and in trying to get to grips with the pluralist/solidarist debate it is helpful to expose its foundations. Bull's scheme limits primary institutions to pluralism, but a clearer understanding of what is at stake emerges if human rights and other solidarist values are also classed as possible primary institutions. To embark down that road one needs to unpack the classical set of primary institutions further, and also look at the framework of legitimacy that both supports them and marks important points of transformation in their historical development.

The emergence of pluralist primary institutions

Talking about the classical package of seven primary institutions risks not just setting up a kind of model for pluralist international society but also sliding into the assumption that this package came into being all of a piece, thereafter existing as a relatively stable and static social structure. This risk is enhanced both by the iconic status in IR of 1648 as representing the transformation from mediaeval to modern and by the relative disinterest in the details of history among a majority of those in the field. Yet, when viewed in the perspective of English School writing about them, nothing could be further from the truth. Rather than a big bang, there was a slow and quite differentiated emergence. And rather than stasis, the internal social structure of pluralism has been surprisingly fluid and evolutionary. Sketching out this dynamic process tells us a lot not just about the nature of pluralism but also about the linkage between pluralism and solidarism. I start this process here and carry it on in chapter 9.

There is also a problem about the use of the term 'modern'. In IR, this is often attached to the mediaeval to 'modern' transition benchmarked by Westphalia. The mainstream, state-centric approaches in IR tend to think of the emergence of the 'modern' sovereign territorial state as happening during the sixteenth and seventeenth centuries, and carrying on from there. This view is at odds with the opinions of most sociologists and world historians, who associate modernity with the package of industrial, social, political and economic revolutions that transformed the world from the late eighteenth through the nineteenth centuries. The English School, in line with most of IR, underplays this 'great transformation' of the nineteenth century (Buzan and Lawson 2013), yet it is a crucial factor in understanding the evolution of pluralist international society.

Bull (1990: 75) shows some awareness of all this but does not take it far. He argues that Westphalia marks the beginning of modern international society in Europe but not the beginning of the modern state, which he rightly places in the late eighteenth and nineteenth centuries. He fails to identify this gap as problematic. Using his distinction between system and society, he sees the emergence of a European international *system* of states as happening in the late fifteenth century. Several other writers agree that Westphalia marks the coming into being of a self-conscious international society of states in Europe that was a deep transformation from the mediaeval arrangements.[4] But this international society was still far from being 'modern' in the sociological sense. It was not the absolutist states of 1648 that Europeans went on to spread around the world, but the modern ones that emerged from the French, American and industrial revolutions.

In a powerful argument building on the assumption of territoriality and sovereignty, Reus-Smit (1999: 87ff.) makes the case that the moral purpose of the state set up by Westphalia was fundamentally still premodern. It was to preserve the divinely ordained hierarchical social order of aristocratic dynasticism, while at the same time undercutting the political authority of the papacy. This generated the absolutist territorial state, dynastic diplomacy, reliance on natural law, and a status hierarchy of states based on dynastic standing rather than sovereign equality. The shift to true modernity, as Bull and Wight hint, took place during the nineteenth century, when the moral purpose of the state shifted to the liberal aim of 'the augmentation of individuals' purposes and potentialities' (ibid.: 122–9) or, in Wight's (1977: 153–73) terms, from dynastic to popular sovereignty. This generated popular sovereignty, positive international (contractual) law, multilateral diplomacy, and a greater degree of sovereign equality. It also changed the norms and principles by which states accorded each other recognition (Fabry 2010).

The idea of society raises the question of what principles of legitimacy underlie it, an idea prominent in Watson's (1992: 130–2) main work, and one which will play importantly throughout the rest of this part of the book. Hurrell (2007b: 77–91) provides a thoughtful discussion of the complexity of legitimacy, in the end associating it with belief as opposed to coercion or calculation (a framing parallel to that used by Wendt [1999] and also picked up by Buzan [2004]). James (1978) sets out a similar case to Bull's for thinking of states as forming a society, focusing on international law as defining rightful (i.e., legitimate) behaviour, sovereignty as defining rightful membership, and diplomacy as formal communication. This approach is developed by Clark (2005, 2007), who defines legitimacy in terms of rightful membership and rightful conduct. Wight (1977: 153–73) likewise defined legitimacy in terms of rightful membership and the determination of rightful sovereignty. But he also noted that the principles on which these are determined can change, as in the transition from dynasticism to popular sovereignty (see also Watson 1992; Reus-Smit 1999; Navari 2007). This point echoes Bull's awareness that the modern state did not emerge for a couple of centuries after Westphalia. Yet it is pretty clear that by 1500 the transformation from the constitutional normative principles of feudalism to an order based on centralized, sovereign territorial states was well under way (Wight 1977: 129–52; Watson 1992: 135–81).

If the international society that emerged around 1648 was undergoing substantial changes in the nature of its members and what was considered rightful conduct among them, then it is necessary to chart the evolution of these changes, and this can be done in terms of primary institutions. Within the frame of European history, the early story of primary institutions is almost entirely pluralist in character, and in what follows I briefly sketch the emergence of eleven such institutions, mainly as seen through the English School literature: territoriality, sovereignty/nonintervention, diplomacy, international law, the balance of power, great power management, war, imperialism/colonialism, human inequality, dynasticism and nationalism.

Territoriality

As Ruggie (1986: 141–8; 1993: 161–4) argues, territoriality and property rights emerged strongly during the transition from the many cross-cutting rights of the mediaeval order to the state-centric Westphalian one (Watson 1992: 138–97). Territoriality became an underpinning principle of the new anarchic international order, reinforced in Europe by its development as a colonial practice to deal with the 'empty' spaces of the Americas (Branch

2012). The ever more precise demarcation of borders steadily tightened up over the succeeding centuries, becoming a constitutive element of international society (Holsti 2004: 75–88).

Sovereignty/nonintervention

In tandem with territoriality, sovereignty/nonintervention also unfolded from the sixteenth century onwards (Brewin 1982; Sørensen 1999; Holsti 2004: 118–28). Together, these two primary institutions laid the foundations for, and indeed constituted, the Westphalian order of a states-system. As noted in chapter 6, James (1984: 12–13, 17; 1986; 1999: 468) takes a strong view of sovereignty as the defining institution of modern international society, linking it to territoriality and stressing the difference between fully sovereign states, 'which are independent in their constitutional arrangements', versus those lacking full international capacity to act. And, as Mayall (2000a: 11) points out, the removal by Westphalia of religion as a legitimate reason for war was the 'ancestor of the modern practice of non-intervention'.[5]

Diplomacy

Ruggie (1993: 164–5) notes that sovereignty created the necessity to invent a particular form of diplomacy with extraterritorial rights (see also Holsti 2004: 178–98). There is a good deal of discussion in the English School about diplomacy as one of the key practices of states-systems generally, but also the particular modern form of it that emerged in Europe from the fifteenth century onwards.[6] One particularly interesting argument about the evolution of this primary institution is Reus-Smit's (1999: 87–121) about the nineteenth-century shift from a diplomacy based on dynastic interests and concerns to a modern form of multilateralism reflecting the interests and concerns of the rational, bureaucratic state, where sovereignty was vested in the people rather than the prince.

International law

Sovereignty also generated a new international law, starting with Spanish debates during the sixteenth century, but often benchmarked to the classical texts of Hugo Grotius in the first part of the seventeenth century. As noted above, Grotius was a key reference point for the first generation of English School writers (Bull et al. 1990; Keene 2002). The English School has retained a stronger connection to international law than most other approaches to IR.[7] Indeed, several writers accord international law pride of place among the primary institutions:

> 'The most essential evidence for the existence of an international society is the existence of international law.' (Wight 1979: 107)
>   International law is 'the bedrock institution on which the idea of international society stands or falls'. (Mayall 2000a: 94)
>   In the legal positivist view, 'international society is not merely regulated by international law but *constituted* by it.' (Nardin 1998: 21)

Despite this focus, and despite the importance of it in Bull's foundational work (discussed in chapter 6), the English School has not had much to say about the shift from natural to positive law as the dominant form that took place during the transformation to modernity during the nineteenth century (Reus-Smit 1999: 94–134).

The balance of power

The balance of power was slower to emerge, though Watson (1992: 181) argues that it was preceded in Europe by the idea of anti-hegemonism, especially against the Habsburgs. Somewhat later, after the Treaty of Utrecht (1713), the balance of power began conspicuously to challenge dynastic principles as a key institution for regulating relations among states.[8] In this usage, the balance of power is an agreed social convention among the powers, not just a mechanical quality of the system (Bull 1977: 104–6; Little 2007a), and it was this understanding that emerged after Utrecht (Bull 1977: 101–6). The balance of power principle was then enshrined in the Treaty of Vienna (1815) (Reus-Smit 1999: 134–40; Simpson 2004: 96–7).

Great power management

Great power management is in a sense implicit in all of the big war-settling congresses from 1648 onwards, and Bull (1977: 200–29) provides a statement of its mechanics. Like the balance of power, the logic and legitimacy of great power interests grew as the dynastic principle weakened. Holsti (1991: 114–37; see also Wight 1977: 42, 136–41) argues that this practice becomes much more evident and formalized from the Treaty of Vienna (1815) and the Congress of Europe, a transformation that Simpson (2004) defines as a shift from the relatively pure and undifferentiated practice of sovereign equality set up at Westphalia to a quite strong form of 'legalized hegemony' in which great powers saw themselves as having, and were recognized by others to have, managerial responsibility for international order (see also Watson 1992: 138–262). That practice continued through the League of Nations after 1919 and the UN Security Council after 1945, both of which embodied a hybrid structure with sovereign equality recognized in the general assembly of all members and the legalized hegemony of the great powers in the smaller council.

War

War, like diplomacy, is a perennial practice found in most international societies throughout history. Bowden (2009: loc. 1933) cites the sixteenth-century international lawyer Vitoria as saying: 'it is a universal rule of the law of nations that whatever is captured in war becomes the property of the conqueror.' What is particular about war as a primary institution of 'modern' European international society is what kind of restraints are put both on the ways in which it is fought and on the reasons that are considered legitimate to justify resort to it (Williams 2010b; see also Howard 1966, 1976; Bull 1977: 184–99). In this sense, Westphalia opens the way for war to become an institution of international society, largely by taking religion off the list of legitimate reasons for war *within* the realm of Christendom – relations with the Islamic sphere were another matter (Holsti 1991: 38)! Holsti (2004: 131–4, 277–83) also notes the formalization and legalization of war during the eighteenth century and the erosion of the right of conquest after 1815.

So far, this account of the classical seven primary institutions exposes two types of dynamism in the evolution of 'modern' pluralist international society. The first dynamism concerns the seven primary institutions themselves, which do not arrive as a coherent set but unfold in an extended, interwoven sequence. Sovereignty, territoriality and diplomacy (or at least the latter's distinctive form in relation to absolutist sovereign states) emerge from the sixteenth century. International law emerges during the sixteenth and seventeenth centuries. War (in the sense of restraints on war) emerges from the seventeenth century. The balance of power as a political principle emerges from the eighteenth century. And great power management, although detectable earlier, emerges strongly from the nineteenth century.

The second dynamism concerns major changes of practice *within* several of these institutions which reflect changes in the underlying principles legitimating them. A number of writers note that sovereignty did not initially come with equality, and that the emergence of sovereign equality was contingent on the decline of dynastic hierarchy from the late eighteenth century onwards (Wight 1977: 136; James 1992; Reus-Smit 1999: 87ff.). At the same time the basis of sovereignty shifts from dynastic to popular, and the basis of diplomacy shifts from dynastic to multilateral (Reus-Smit 1999: 87ff.). International law starts out mainly as natural law but, particularly from the nineteenth century onwards, becomes dominated by positive law (Holsti 2004: 146–50). Thus, although the general framing of these classical primary institutions remains stable, the core practices within some of them change very dramatically indeed.

This quite pervasive and deep dynamism is at odds with the conservative and rather static image often attached to pluralism. This dynamism is easy to miss even though defenders of pluralism, such as Jackson (2000: 419–26), stage it as demonstrating the flexibility, adaptability and therefore desirability of the decentralized pluralist approach to international order. One explanation for the static image of pluralism is that, by seeing the development of international society as being confined by the dictates of sovereignty and difference, pluralism mainly limits its view of international society to being a practical association going no further than a logic of coexistence. That limitation in turn generates a rather restricted view of the range of primary institutions that international society can have.

Even with the internal changes noted above, a striking feature of this classical set of seven pluralist primary institutions is how neatly they fit together. They define clearly the criteria for membership of international society in terms of sovereign territorial states, which settles the issue of property rights. They provide for means of formal communication among these entities via diplomacy. And they provide for a degree of order in terms of the balance of power, war (and agreed limits on its use), international law and great power management. It is theoretically and practically possible for all of these elements to work together in mutually complementary harmony around a logic of coexistence. Nothing determines that they *have* to work in that way, and pluralists regularly remind us of the contingent and fragile character of international society: it can easily fall apart if some powers defect from the rules of the game of coexistence. But the classical seven institutions can work together in a relatively smooth and coherent fashion if the powers want them to, and as they did for a time during the nineteenth century.

Yet the story of pluralist primary institutions does not end here. There are extensions to it – imperialism/colonialism, human inequality and nationalism – that have unsettling implications for the harmony of the classical seven. Imperialism/colonialism is the ghost at the table (or skeleton in the closet), hidden away, or at least marginalized, and yet continuously present to haunt all other proceedings, not least because of the ethical implications of its association with human inequality. Imperialism conveys the general legitimacy of a culture of domination, while colonialism is more about the formalities of foreign rule and occupation.[9] Nationalism picks up the relentlessly evolutionary thread of the story and suggests that this dynamism is an unceasing characteristic of modern international society. If fluidity and evolution are ongoing features of modern international society, then pluralism is at risk of becoming just the opening phase of modernity. The continuous rise, evolution and sometimes decline and obsolescence of the primary institutions of international society (Holsti 2004) put the package of the classical seven increasingly at risk of destabilization.

Imperialism/colonialism

So the eighth pluralist primary institution is imperialism/colonialism, which, supported by the prevailing interpretations of war and international law, created a two-tier international society based on divided sovereignty. Colonialism began to soften after the First World War with the development of the mandate system and became rapidly obsolete after the Second World War. The mind-set of imperialism as a legitimate culture of domination was slower to fade and arguably still remains influential in some international practice. Only a handful of authors have addressed imperialism/colonialism in an English School framing. As noted in chapter 5, Keene (2002) and Holsti (2004: 239–74) both point out the failure of the classical story to identify that imperialism/colonialism was a core institution of classical European international society. It is not that the classical story was unaware of imperialism/colonialism, but it failed to construct it as a core institution of European international society and therefore obscured the key reality of divided sovereignty in its operation.

Keene (2002) makes a quite different interpretation of Grotius from that of Bull and Wight, seeing Grotius's ideas as underlying the divided sovereignty and the very particular view of property rights that underpinned European imperialism/colonialism. Keene highlights colonialism and imperialism pre-1945 as emblematic of divided sovereignty in which the core develops a Westphalian principle of sovereign equality and tolerance within itself, but practices divided sovereignty and the 'standard of civilization' against the periphery. He argues that 'we need to appreciate the importance of the idea of civilization not merely as a standard for regulating the entry of new states in international society, but also for validating an entirely different set of legal rules and political institutions in its own right' (Keene 2002: 117). Phillips (2012) also picks up the importance of 'civilization' as a concept, noting how it could be, and was, used both to justify and to oppose imperialism.

This idea of a two-tier imperial/colonial international society has been taken forward by Suzuki (2005, 2009) in the context of Japan's and China's encounters with Western international society. Although colonialism is formally dead, its imperial legacies remain to haunt much of contemporary international politics between the (Western) core and the periphery, despite the notional uniformity of sovereign equality. Keene, like many other English School writers, considers the logic of human rights as the successor to the standard of civilization, albeit now *within* a universal international society rather than being about the relations between insiders and outsiders.[10]

While Keene sees imperialism/colonialism as going right back to the beginning of the European states-system, Holsti (2004: 239–74) focuses on colonialism, arguing that this gets formalized as state practice only during the late nineteenth century. Before that it was practised, but mainly informally and led by private actors. Holsti notes the enduring parallels between colonial discourses about bringing the natives up to the 'standard of civilization' and contemporary ones about development (ibid.: 250).

Reflecting on imperialism/colonialism as a primary institution of European international society raises the thought that, during the four and a half centuries of its imperial period (late fifteenth century to 1945), two more primary institutions also existed: the ninth being human inequality and the tenth, closely associated, being dynasticism as the legitimate form of government.

Human inequality

An assumption that humans were not equal underpinned many practices of this historical period (and earlier ones), most notably slavery, racism, gender inequality, dynasticism and empire. As Hobsbawm (1975: 312) notes, the aristocracy's ideas about good breeding and their class superiority as rulers were not far removed in essence from racist thinking and eugenics. Perhaps the most extreme manifestation of this was the 'scientific' racism that blossomed throughout the West during the nineteenth century (Hannaford 1996: 155–84; Smaje 2000: 1–8; Keal 2003: 56–83). Its 'scientific' standing was strengthened by the evolutionary ideas of Darwin. These translated easily into the view that different races represented different steps on the ladder of evolution, and this view in turn was easily reinforced by the huge power superiority of the white race during the latter half of the nineteenth century (Taylor 1840; Ferguson 2004: 196–203, 262–4). Hobsbawm (1990: 107–8) refers to racism as a 'central concept of nineteenth century social science'.[11] An interesting and important twist in Japan's encounter with Western international society was the rejection in 1919 of its claim for recognition of racial equality (Clark 2007: 83–106). As noted, Vincent (1982, 1984b) is one of the few English School writers to pick up on racism in the context of international society. Yet, while human inequality was certainly, in the sense defined in chapter 2, a primary institution during this historical period when pluralist international society was the dominant form, it is not intrinsic to the logic of pluralism, and arguably contradicts it. Although human inequality buttressed imperialism/colonialism, its essential idea goes against both the pluralist logic of coexistence and the pluralist acknowledgment of the great society of humankind.

Dynasticism

In addition to Wight's (1977: 110–73) focused discussion of the shift of legitimacy from dynasticism to popular sovereignty and Watson's (1992) more diffuse accounting of it in Europe and elsewhere, Reus-Smit (1999: 87–134) is one of the few writers associated with the English School to give much specific attention to dynasticism. Like Wight, his focus is on the shift from absolutism to popular sovereignty as the basis of the state during the nineteenth century. Another is Navari (2007), who shows how three different types of state in Europe – absolutist (seventeenth and eighteenth centuries), constitutional (nineteenth century) and democratic (twentieth century) – generated different practices and therefore different forms of international society. As the dominant form of legitimate government in Europe (and many other places), dynasticism shaped not only, in Reus-Smit's term, 'the moral purpose of the state' but also the rightful membership of international society. Diplomacy was orientated towards dynastic concerns, and wars were fought for dynastic interests. In this way, dynasticism had a major impact on the nature of international society, an influence perhaps best illustrated by the Holy Alliance after 1815, which was concerned to defend a dynastic status quo against any resurgence of the republicanism unleashed by the French and American revolutions. To the extent that dynasticism backed empire and sustained a hierarchical international society, it too is not a good fit with pluralism's emphasis on sovereign equality. Some tension remains to be resolved between the view of Simpson (2004), that Westphalia ushered in a strong period of sovereign equality, and that of Reus-Smit (1999), that the intervening effect of hierarchy linked to dynasticsm meant that sovereign equality did not really emerge until popular sovereignty replaced dynasticism during the nineteenth century.

In this sense, imperialism/colonialism, human inequality and dynasticism destabilize the classical seven primary institutions of pluralism even though they coexisted with them historically. While there might have been a pluralist international society among the Western states up until the First World War, there was certainly not one on a global scale. As Keene and Suzuki argue, what Europe experienced as pluralist international society along coexistence lines, Africa, Asia and the Middle East experienced as the inequality, intolerance and humiliation of imperialism/colonialism and racism. And, while imperialism/colonialism, human inequality and dynasticism have all been obsolete as institutions of international society since 1945, their legacies linger on.

Nationalism

The eleventh pluralist primary institution is nationalism, which burst onto the European scene with the French revolution in the late eighteenth century and was consolidated alongside the other pluralist primary institutions during the nineteenth. As Hurrell (2007b: 121–2) notes, 'political nationalism has been the most persistent and pervasive ideology of the modern state system', and national self-determination provided 'the political power and the moral meaning to the idea of an international society'. Nationalism can be explained multiply as a product of romantic thinking, as a political tool for peoples seeking to free themselves from empires (primarily Ottoman and Austro-Hungarian), and as a response by state elites both to military pressures (the use of the *levée en masse* by revolutionary France) and to the class tensions identified by Marx as arising from the practices of industrial capitalism. As Hobsbawm (1962: 116–17) says of its impact: 'It was now known that social revolution was possible; that nations existed as something independent of states, peoples as something independent of their rulers.' Nationalism transformed people from being subjects of their ruler to being citizens of their state, in the process relocating sovereignty from the ruler (*l'état c'est moi*) to the people (popular sovereignty).

The English School *locus classicus* for this story is Mayall (1990; see also Porter 1982; Watson 1992: 228–51). In one sense, the rise of nationalism to the status of primary institution can be seen as an extension of the successive rise of pluralist institutions. After all, nationalism reinforces in a deep way the basic ideas of difference, historical legacy and political separateness that underlie pluralism and justify its prioritizing of coexistence. Yet, in another way, the rise of nationalism was profoundly disturbing to the pluralist package. As Mayall charts in detail, nationalism changed the meaning and practices of key elements of the classical seven, in the process upsetting the harmony of the pluralist package in profound ways. Indeed, along the lines suggested above by Reus-Smit's transformation in the moral purpose of the state, it changed the meaning of the state itself, generating the true modern state. Mayall (2000b) goes so far as to argue that this impact, along with that of liberalism (on which more in the next chapter), is sufficiently profound to create a disjuncture with the classical pluralist story about the rise and expansion of international society. This disturbance effect is precisely what pluralists fear about human rights and democracy, which places the rise of nationalism as an interesting bridge between pluralism and solidarism. As Gellner (1992: 289) notes, national-ism had the paradoxical quality of being deeply rooted in modernity, on the one hand, while appealing to premodern understandings of community and identity, on the other. This Janus face was perhaps what made it so successful in bridging the transition from traditional to modern society.

The transformative effect of nationalism on the state came through its key idea that the nation should be the basis of the state. The core idea seems simple: 'nations', being self-identifying groups sharing some com-bination of culture, language, ethnicity and history, should have the right of political self-determination to claim their own state. Ideally, all states should be nation-states, with the state therefore becoming the container and protector of its particular national identity. Indeed, despite the rela-tively late arrival of nationalism to the pantheon of primary institutions, this nation-state model underpins pluralism much more that does the abso-lutist one, in which cultural and ethnic identity counted for much less. Nationalism delegitimized dynastic absolutism as the dominant form of the state (Mayall 1990: 35) and, because of that, and despite its military advantages, was widely resisted in Europe as a revolutionary threat to the post-1815 order (Kadorcan 2012). It increased the social cohesion of the state by the cultivation of commonly understood national languages and high cultures. As nationalism took root, people who would not formerly have thought of themselves primarily, or even at all, as French, Italian, Spanish, British or German increasingly did so, helped along by the state in the form of a national language, a national education system and national military service. This consolidating and centralizing of the state worked both where a unified state already existed but needed to be consolidated (France, Spain, Britain) and where a new state had to be created out of previously disparate parts (Germany, Italy). It also worked in some settler colonies where diverse immigrant populations needed to be forged into nation-states (Americas, Australia), though this was not without problems in differentiating colonial 'nations' from their metropolitan origins.

Since dynastic rule was closely correlated with empire, in principle undermining one undermined the other, but in practice the nineteenth-century picture was mixed. Dynastic rule was a powerful device for constructing conglomerate empires containing many nations – or at least many peoples with different languages, cultures, ethnicities and histories. By adding to the power of the leading states in Europe, nationalism initially helped to consolidate their overseas empires. Only in the twentieth century did the spread of nationalism (and liberal political ideas about human rights and equality), along with the upheaval of the First World War, corrode first the Austro-Hungarian and Ottoman empires, and, after the further upheaval of the Second World War, the overseas colonial empires of Britain, France, the US and other Western states (Mayall 1990: 38–49; 2000a: 39–66). This, in turn, as Mayall (1990: 45–63, 111–44) argues, sowed the seeds of the contemporary economic and political problems of the successor Third World states which struggle to cope with institutions and practices designed by and for the core states. Nationalism in the Third World had to be created, often in unpromising conditions, and it as easily fragmented and weakened the postcolonial state as unified and legitimized it. Nevertheless, despite all of the problems, as Mayall (ibid.: 152) notes: 'nationalism has become structurally embedded, in all parts of the world, as the basis of the modern state.'

In interplay with its transforming of the state, nationalism changed both the meaning of and the practices associated with several of the pre-existing institutions of pluralist international society. Most obviously, nationalism changed sovereignty by shifting the foundations of political legitimacy from the dynastic claims of ruling aristocracies to the popular sovereignty of the people constituted as a nation (Mayall 1990: 26–8). At the same time, by giving special standing to nation-states, it strengthened the move towards sovereign equality already noted as a feature of the nineteenth century. Nationalism also transformed the other foundation of the state – territoriality. When the absolutist state became the nation-state, territory became sacralized by its relationship to the people in a way that was not present in the politics of dynastic territoriality (Mayall 2000a: 84; Holsti 2004: 83–8). By tightening the link between states, populations and particular territories, nationalism raised the prominence of territoriality in relations between states and generated new problems of irredentism and secessionism (Mayall 1990: 57–63). The seizure of Alsace-Lorraine by Germany from France in their 1870 war is perhaps the exemplar of this effect, poisoning relations between the two and playing its part in the making of the First and Second world wars. The states of East Asia are replaying this game of sacralized territory in their ongoing disputes over a variety of small islands in the East and South China seas.

By changing territoriality in this way, nationalism also provided new reasons for war. In its extreme social Darwinist form, nationalism gave a justification for the expropriation of the weak by the strong. More generally it set up a tension between the status quo of fewer than two hundred territorial states and the potential existence of several thousand cultural nations demanding their own state (Mayall 1990 63–9). It also changed the method of war. The 'nation in arms' and the '*levée en masse*' enabled the mobilization of huge numbers of troops and imbued them with the motivation to fight heroically.

We can see, therefore, that the pluralist model did not emerge all of a piece at Westphalia but evolved over several centuries, with some of its key elements not coming into play until the nineteenth century. During this process of emergence, the ostensibly 'modern' pluralist international society remained imbued with a number of much older institutions, not all of which were a comfortable fit with the pluralist model. The early, pre-modern European international society was mainly pluralist but was highly dynamic, evolving new practices and new institutions on a regular basis. By the nineteenth century, a truly modern international society was taking shape. But then the comfortable coherence of the classical set of seven primary institutions was being both reinforced and placed under stress by the new and very powerful institution of nationalism. Mayall (1990: 2) notes that nationalism was also one of the strands leading to the development of human rights in the West. This observation, along with the theme of the disruptive dynamism of international society generally, suggests that it is time to move to the solidarist side of the English School's normative story.

8 CLASSICAL SOLIDARISM AND ITS SUCCESSORS

Introduction

This chapter covers the debate from the solidarist side, exploring the progressive, mainly liberal, wing of the English School. Here the main concern has been with the justice side of the order/justice dilemma, particularly with human rights and the question of intervention. This wing gives much more attention to the role and significance of an emergent world society, though generally combining this with interstate society. It views the state not as a sovereign actor in its own right but as an agent representing its population (Hurrell 2007b: 65–7). Solidarism as seen by pluralists was discussed in chapter 6, where it was staged partly as the threatening cosmopolitan 'other' to pluralism's culturally diverse, state-centric, sovereigntist order and partly as the necessary moral foundation against which state-based orders should be judged. This chapter focuses on solidarists through their own voices, and the following one continues the historical developmental perspective on primary institutions. With this structure I hope to capture, on the one hand, that there is a necessarily endless normative debate about current affairs and what should be done and, on the other hand, that there is some real evolution of international society towards more solidarist practices and institutions. The core theme remains that pluralism and solidarism are not zero-sum positions but interlinked sides in an ongoing debate about the moral construction of international order.

Solidarist conceptions lean towards the Kantian side of rationalism. As Mayall (2000a: 14) notes, solidarists root their thinking in cosmopolitan values: 'the view that humanity is one, and that the task of diplomacy is to translate this latent or immanent solidarity of interests and values into reality.' It is probably fair to say that most solidarists believe that some cosmopolitanism, and concern for the rights of individuals, is necessary if international society is to be stable. In other words, order cannot work without some underpinning of justice in which interstate society takes account of the needs and rights of its citizens. On this most pluralists and solidarists agree, even though they draw different conclusions about what then should follow. Solidarists presuppose that the potential scope for international society is much wider than the 'non-developmental character' that limits the pluralist vision. Their vision embraces the possibility of shared norms, rules and institutions about functional cooperation over such things as limitations on the use of force and acceptable 'standards of civilization' with regard to the relationship between states and citizens (i.e., human rights). In this view, sovereignty can in principle embrace many more degrees of political convergence than are conceivable under pluralism (as it does, for example, within the EU). Solidarism focuses on the possibility of shared moral norms underpinning a more expansive, and almost inevitably more interventionist, understanding of international order.

State-centric and cosmopolitan solidarism

Because the pluralist position is mainly state-based, it easily appears relatively straightforward and coherent. Because the solidarist position ties together state and non-state actors and draws on cosmopolitan notions of individual rights and a community of humankind, it is more complex and potentially problematic. Given the present reality of a state-centric world order, it cannot help but blur across the boundary between international and world society. Solidarism is partly, perhaps mainly, about the creation of consensual beliefs across international and world society. For solidarists, ethical issues transcend state boundaries, and, as Hurrell (2007b: 63–5) argues, at least for some, solidarism can also be about the exercise of power to enforce beliefs that are held to be universal but are not in fact universally held.[1] This coercive approach to solidarism is at the heart of disputes about human rights and has a long record in the economic sector, as in the mid-nineteenth-century 'opening up' of Japan and China by Western gunboats to the 'universal' principle of free trade. As Hurrell (2001: 490) also notes, the Kantian label is unfortunate because it 'has consistently involved claims and arguments that are essentially concerned not with transcending the state system but rather with reforming the character of the international legal order.'

In the previous chapter I hinted at a distinction between state-centric solidarism (states sharing norms and institutions that take them beyond a logic of coexistence) and cosmopolitan solidarism (based on the idea that there are universal rights vested in people) (see Williams 2010a). This distinction is implicit throughout the English School literature, but in practice the two are usually discussed together in an intertwined way. Making this distinction explicit provides a helpful way of untangling many elements of the pluralist/solidarist debate. It exposes which tensions are real and which merely rhetorical, so, at the risk of going against the orthodoxy of the English School, I feature it here. Clarifying the distinction between the two solidarisms is, perhaps, a practical reply to de Almeida's (2006: 68) and Bain's (2007a) appeals that we should abandon the habit of thinking about pluralist and solidarist orders as representing opposed ideas.

One way of understanding the issue is to locate it across a spectrum of internationalism (Navari 2000: 361). In this perspective, pluralism becomes at best a very weak form of internationalism limited to a thin logic of coexistence by its commitment to difference at the level of state and nation. State-centric and cosmopolitan solidarism are strong forms of internationalism, but based on different ontologies (states, people). Ontologically, pluralism and state-centric solidarism are more alike, both being based on states. But, politically and morally, state-centric solidarism is closer to cosmopolitan solidarism because it is open to moving beyond a logic of coexistence into logics of cooperation and convergence. In one important sense the question is about the location of solidarism: is it rooted in the great society of humankind, or is it rooted in the society of states, or must it somehow be present in both?

This line of reasoning might suggest that state-centric solidarism is the middle ground, and therefore a *via media* between the two extremes. There is something in that argument inasmuch as state-centric solidarism provides an exit for pluralists who want to stick with the state-centric ontology but abandon the constraints of coexistence. In my view, however, that is not the main point. The two forms of solidarism are much closer to each other than either is to pluralism, and that is why they are so interwoven in the literature. Partly this entanglement arises because, under existing conditions, states necessarily play a key role in implementing and defending cosmopolitan principles. As many have pointed out, the great society of humankind may have force as a moral referent, but for the most part it lacks the agency to implement and defend universal rights. Only states, or secondary institutions largely under the control of states, can do that, even though states of course can also be the main violators and opponents of cosmopolitan principles.

The other link is that state-centric solidarism may well be driven, or motivated by, cosmopolitan principles, either because such principles are part of its identity (as most obviously in the US) or because of political pressure from below. This is not necessarily the case. In pure logical terms, state-centric solidarism might have nothing to do with cosmopolitan principles and be driven by other kinds of instrumental logics (for example, capitalism). Even in that case, however, the two types of solidarism are similar, both aiming to achieve higher order commonalities, making peoples and states more alike in their common rights and obligations and pursing more than merely a logic of coexistence. Solidarists of both persuasions think that international society can develop quite wide-ranging norms, rules and institutions, covering both coexistence issues and cooperation in pursuit of shared interests, including some scope for collective enforcement.

The entanglement of state-centric and cosmopolitan solidarism in the literature of the English School is thus perfectly understandable, and to some extent justified. But the logics of the two solidarisms are distinct, and the overall picture of the pluralist–solidarist, order–justice, states–people debate within the English School becomes considerably clearer if the two solidarist logics are kept separate from each other as well as from pluralism. As I will show in this chapter and the next, the pluralists' rhetorical tendency to construct solidarism in largely cosmopolitan terms is misleading to the point of being simply wrong. In practice, while cosmopolitan logic is the main moral impetus for the solidarist camp, state-centric solidarism is the dominant practical theme.

State-centric solidarism

State-centric solidarism is about the possibility that states can collectively reach beyond a logic of coexistence to construct international societies with a relatively high degree of shared norms, rules and institutions among them. In state-centric solidarism the focus is not only on ordering coexistence and competition but also on cooperation over a wider range of issues, whether in pursuit of joint gains (e.g., trade) or realization of shared values (e.g., human rights, environmental stewardship, pursuit of knowledge). In its stronger forms, state-centric solidarism can also include convergence, where, as in the EU, states not only seek cooperation but also redesign themselves to become more alike in their domestic rules and structures (Buzan 2004: 45–62, 139–60).[2]

State-centric solidarism rests on a juridical view of sovereignty, in which the right to self-government derives from international society. Sovereignty is a social contract rather than an essentialist condition, and the terms in which it is understood are always open to renegotiation. A view of sovereignty along these lines poses no contradiction to solidarist developments among states. Manning (1962: 167–8) was crystal clear on this point: 'What is essentially a system of law *for* sovereigns, being premised on their very sovereignty, does not, by the fact of being strengthened, put in jeopardy the sovereignties which are the dogmatic basis for its very existence. Not, at any rate, in logic.' In this view, so long as one does not insist that individuals have rights apart from, and above, the state, there is no contradiction between development of human rights and sovereignty. Solidarist laws, even about issues such as human rights, can be cast in terms of individuals as the objects of international law rather than as independent subjects carrying their own rights. So, if they wish, states can agree among themselves on extensive guarantees for human rights, and doing so is an exercise of their sovereignty, not a questioning of it. They can even agree that in doing this they are recognizing some deeper universal right, though this is not a necessary condition. This logic extends even towards a degree of collective enforcement in some areas, as has happened already for aspects of trade and human rights, and somewhat less clearly in relation to arms control.

Arguably, state-centric solidarism harks back to Bull's (1966b: 52) original formulation stressing the collective enforcement of international law by states. Yet, even though his rules about cooperation seem to make room for it, Bull's vision of state-centric solidarism is very much at odds with the one just outlined, which rests on cooperation and convergence. Bull paints a picture based not on cooperation and convergence but on the awkward combination of a pluralist's strong toleration of ideological diversity alongside a solidarist's effective collective security system (Bull 1977: 238–40). By the device of discussing it only in relation to 'high politics' issues such as collective security and human rights, his enforcement criterion is made to seem more demanding than it often is. In this perspective, solidarism opposes alliances as sectional and favours collective security on a universal basis. Pluralists argue for the centrality of sovereignty and nonintervention as the key principles of international society, 'and the only purposes for which they could be overridden were that of self-preservation and that of the maintenance of the balance of power' (Bull 1966b: 63). It is this very demanding concept of solidarism within pluralism, attached to collective security, that goes forward into *The Anarchical Society* (Bull 1977: 238–40).

One can see how Bull's view related to the history within which he lived, and we cannot know what he would have made of the ideological convergence towards varieties of capitalism that followed the Cold War. Because it largely excludes the possibility that states might share values and goals beyond coexistence, Bull's vision sets up state-centric solidarism as an unlikely development. It also reflects the blindness of the classical English School to developments in the world economy and at the regional (i.e., EU) or subglobal (i.e., Western) level. In fact, much of the solidarist literature is precisely about how to get states to take shared values on board, and thereby become more alike. It is about building, or recognizing, convergence among states on values that extend beyond coexistence. Such a logic is broadly visible in both debates and practices around democratic peace theory, economic liberalism, human rights and environmental stewardship.

Cosmopolitan solidarism

Cosmopolitan solidarism means a disposition to give moral primacy to 'the great society of humankind', and to hold universal, natural law, moral values as equal to or higher than the positive international law made by states. The impetus for cosmopolitan solidarism comes mainly from the desire to establish foundations for a moral critique of the state and the logic of an interstate society. This is accomplished by taking the community of humankind as a whole as a moral referent against which to judge the behaviour and purpose of states. This is a philosophical move, well rooted in the texts of political theory that play a large part in fuelling the pluralist/ solidarist debate. Humankind does not actually have to exist as an actual empirical community in order to be used as a moral referent in this way. It is important to keep distinct the moral and the empirical aspects of the community of humankind because the moral argument can be made even when the empirical one cannot. The absence of a real, existing community of humankind does not invalidate its use as a moral referent (Williams 2010a), and the empirical reality of world society is very much one of extensive and complex fragmentations (Bull 1977: 276–81; Williams 2005). The existence of this distinct moral use of the community of human-kind goes a long way towards explaining why solidarists have put so much focus on human rights, and pluralists so much on the potentially disruptive effects of solidarism.

Within the pluralist/solidarist debate, cosmopolitan solidarism has a somewhat strange dual role. On the one hand, it is the key source of the moral energy and engagement with normative issues that is a noted feature of the English School. On the other hand, it is very much present on the pluralist side of the debate as the bogeyman that threatens international order by undermining the sovereignty that underpins the society of states. In both of these roles, cosmopolitan solidarism functions mainly as a source of moral principles rather than as a practical political programme for international order. Few if any solidarists are looking towards a world without states as either a theoretical or a practical option. Rather, they regard cosmopolitan values as a way of leveraging the society of states towards more progressive, just and stable positions.

Pluralists have two views about cosmopolitan solidarism. First, there are those, such as Bull and Mayall, who have sympathy for the idea that international society should in some profound way reflect the moral demands of the great society of humankind. But they cannot see how this can be done given the pluralist realities of both the historical and contemporary society of states. Although they can see the force of the argument for grounding international society in some form of respect for world society, they see even more the dangers of opening up a moral agenda for interventionism that would threaten the foundations of sovereign order. Their acknowledgment of cosmopolitan solidarism makes them reluctant pluralists. Others, such as Jackson, take a more straightforward view of the dangers by focusing on the essential contradiction between interstate and world society. This is achieved by staging cosmopolitan solidarism as a fundamentally different form of order necessarily opposed to an order based on sovereign states. Authority for this view can also be taken from Bull. Recall from the chapter 6 that Bull (1977: 67–8) sets out three levels of rules about society. Within his deepest level of rules (constitutional normative principles) he identifies a 'cosmopolitan community of individual human beings' as an *alternative ordering principle* to a society of states. It is not posed as a matter of having or not having some kinds of solidarist institutions, but as a completely different (and under contemporary conditions unrealistic) mode of order. Jackson (2000: 175) picks up this angle, taking the view that world society is the domain 'in which responsibility is defined by one's membership in the human race', contrasting this with responsibilities to the state, to international society and to the global commons. He then goes on at great length to unfold a pluralist defence of nonintervention against human rights on the grounds of the threat that pursuit of them poses to international order (ibid.: 210–93). Jackson is a militant, enthusiastic pluralist, not much troubled by the morality of states and, even though acknowledging an element of humanitarian responsibility, mainly happy to argue against cosmopolitan solidarism.

The view that pluralism and solidarism are mutually exclusive rests on an argument over whether primacy of right is to be allocated to individuals or to states. If one takes the reductionist view that individual human beings are the prime referent for rights, and that they must be subjects of international law, carrying rights of their own, then this necessarily falls into conflict with the view that the claim of states to sovereignty (the right to self-government) trumps all other claims to rights. Either individual human beings possess rights of their own (subjects of international law) or they can claim and exercise rights only through the state (objects of international law). If pluralism is essentially underpinned by realist views of state primacy, and solidarism is essentially a cosmopolitan position, then they do look mutually exclusive. This rift can be reinforced by different views of sovereignty. If sovereignty is given an essentialist interpretation, seeing it mostly in what Jackson (1990a) calls 'empirical' terms (in which sovereignty derives from the power of states to assert the claim to exclusive right to self-government), then states cannot surrender very much to shared norms, rules and institutions without endangering the very quality that defines them as states.

Because of these two different ways in which it can be understood and used, solidarism is a tricky concept. The literature is not always clear about this, and it matters hugely to the whole order/justice, pluralist/solidarist debate which meanings are in play. Both of these meanings have validity, but some of them pose order/justice and pluralism/solidarism as irreconcilable and mutually exclusive and others more as ends of a spectrum that can be blended and mixed in different ways. Because the existential threat to sovereignty is especially acute in relation to questions about human rights, it is in some ways unfortunate that this issue has featured so much in English School debates. Humanitarian intervention, as Wheeler (1992: 486) observes, opens up fundamental issues about the relationship between states and their citizens and 'poses the conflict between order and justice in its starkest form for the society of states'. There have been advantages in pursing the 'starkest form' hard case, but one cost has been to steer the pluralist–solidarist debate towards an excessive polarization in which non-intervention and human rights become seen by some as mutually exclusive positions. This threatens at times to reproduce within the English School the zero-sum style of division between liberals and realists. Putting universal cosmopolitan principles to the fore highlights an apparent contradiction with sovereignty, reducing states to mere implementers of such principles rather than being capable of solidarism in their own right. This overemphasis on cosmopolitan principles is amplified by the English School's disposition to sideline both economic questions and subglobal developments, where state-centric solidarism is more obviously on display. This distortion is ironic. While it has given moral energy and legitimacy to both pluralists and solidarists, it has made the tension between them worse than it needs to be. It has given ammunition to some pluralists, and obscured the fact demonstrated below that much of what the solidarist wing has to say is in fact about how to promote state-centric solidarism.

Bull's solidarism

The solidarist position is driven both normatively (what states should do, and what norms should be part of international society) and empirically (what states do do, and what norms are becoming part of international society). Since it was Bull who did the most to set up the pluralist/solidarist debate within the English School, it seems fair to start with him, even though he has already had a considerable airing above as a pluralist. As Reus-Smit (2011b: 1205) astutely notes, Bull provided 'a language and set of arguments that subsequent writers have used to great effect and struggled to escape'. That case is reinforced by the unfolding theme in this part of how closely intertwined the pluralist and solidarist positions are, and in a sense must be, given that they are about the balance between order and justice. Further justification, if any is needed, can be given by the fact that two leading solidarists (Dunne and Wheeler 1996; Wheeler and Dunne 1998) make the case that, despite his distaste for both natural law and foundationalist universalisms, Bull's thinking contains significant openings for pragmatic elements of what I understand as state-centric solidarism. They find in Bull a weakening belief in the willingness of the great powers to underpin a pluralist order under Cold War conditions. And they find acknowledgement of both the possibility of some enforcement of international law and some responsibility for human rights.

As Alderson and Hurrell (2000: 9–10) note, there is a well-formed conception of solidarism in play throughout Bull's work. Bull saw solidarism as putting the interests of the social whole above those of independent states and as reflecting normative goals beyond mere coexistence, such as strong restrictions on the use of force, pursuit of human rights, or management of common problems in the economy or environment. Actors other than states would be active and legitimate players in the development of these normative goals, and international society would have effective measures in place to implement and if necessary enforce its rules. Particularly in his later works, Bull (1984a, 1984b) seems to display solidarist sentiments when he sympathetically, and with full awareness of the many hypocrisies in play, takes up the justice claims of the Third World against the West. He makes plain that the sovereign rights derive from international society and are limited by its rules and that, in terms of justice, the rights of states are derivative from those of humankind (Bull 1984b: 11–13).

Yet there can be no doubting the strength of Bull's rejection of cosmopolitan solidarism. He continued to identify solidarism with Grotius's natural law position, and this led him to the view that:

> Carried to its logical extreme, the doctrine of human rights and duties under international law is subversive of the whole principle that mankind should be organised as a society of sovereign states. For, if the rights of each man can be asserted on the world political stage over and against the claims of his state, and his duties proclaimed irrespective of his position as a servant or a citizen of that state, then the position of the state as a body sovereign over its citizens, and entitled to command their obedience, has been subject to challenge, and the structure of the society of sovereign states has been placed in jeopardy. (Bull 1977: 152)

This position did not change much in his later, seemingly more solidarist, work. Despite enjoining states to take a wider morality than their own immediate self-interest into account, Bull (1984b: 13) still argues that 'The promotion of human rights on a world scale, in a context in which there is no consensus as to their meaning and the priorities among them, carries the danger that it will be subversive of coexistence among states, on which the whole fabric of world order in our times depends . . .'

The fierceness of Bull's defence of pluralism is understandable when seen as a response to a normatively driven cosmopolitan solidarism, based in natural law, pitting a universalist principle of individual rights against the state, and so compromising the principle of sovereignty. But it does not make sense against the logic of Bull's own positive law position, in which like-minded states are perfectly at liberty to agree human rights regimes among themselves without compromising the principle of sovereignty. Since Bull rejected natural law and cosmopolitanism and focused on the state as the only available agent to provide order, and indeed justice (Wheeler and Dunne 1998: 53–5), positive law provides the only pathway out of his thinking towards solidarism. Remembering Bull's third tier of rules to regulate cooperation, it seems clear that adherence to positive law does nothing to prevent states from developing such an extensive range of shared values, including in the area of human rights, that their relationship would have to be called solidarist in the state-centric sense. As Cutler (1991: 46–9) notes, this move undercuts the assumption of cosmopolitan universalism that is the basis of Bull's critique of solidarism. Within a positive law framework, states can by definition do what they like, including forming solidarist regional or subsystemic international societies. Acceptance of positive law draws a connecting line between the pluralist and state-centric solidarist positions and eliminates the logic of their being necessarily opposed, as they must be if solidarism is understood only in its cosmopolitan sense. Pluralism simply becomes a lower degree of shared norms rules and institutions (or a thinner body of positive law), solidarism a higher one (or a thicker body of positive law).

Yet, despite this obvious opening, Bull (1977: 245) rejects the idea that an ideologically homogeneous state system equates with solidarism. He does so partly on the weak ground that it is unlikely to happen, and the process of arriving at it would be highly conflictual (because of inability to agree on universal values), and partly on the basis of a distinction between genuinely harmonious Kantian world societies (an idea he rejects as utopian) and international societies that have learned to regulate conflict and competition but have not eliminated it. In effect, Bull tries to eliminate the idea of a Kantian model of ideologically harmonious states altogether, so closing the door in his own work to state-centric solidarism. But the door nonetheless remained, and others have walked through it.

Successors

The first to lead the way was John Vincent. Dunne (1998: 161–80) presents Vincent as a progressive pluralist who chafed against the support for the status quo that was implicit in pluralism regardless of whether the status quo embodied justice or not.[3] Vincent (1974, 1986: 113–18) started from Bull's concerns about the dangers posed by cosmopolitan universalisms to sovereignty and nonintervention, and therefore to international order. And, like Bull, he accepted the importance of the great society of humankind as the necessary moral foundation for the society of states (Vincent 1978: 27–9). He agreed with Bull's view that the great society of humankind, no matter what its moral force, had no agency and therefore that practical progress towards solidarism had to be made through the society of states. On this basis, Welsh (2011) counts Vincent as more pluralist than solidarist, and from a perspective of cosmopolitan solidarism that might be a correct judgment. Reus-Smit (2011b: 1206) labels him a 'qualified solidarist'. Linklater (2011a: 1182) puts him squarely in the middle ground between pluralism and solidarism. Vincent was clearly a man with a foot in both camps. But, unlike Bull, he found a way around the pluralist impasse between sovereignty and human rights by developing the view that sovereignty was a right granted by international society and might therefore be made conditional on states observing some minimum standards of basic rights towards their citizens. In practical terms, Vincent became a state-centric solidarist looking to change the normative structure of interstate society to take more account of human rights (Dunne 1998: 169). Dunne (1995b: 143–5) rightly characterizes his approach as practical ethics.

Vincent's primary concern was with human rights, and within the English School this focused his work precisely on the tensions between the individual and the state. For Vincent (1978: 40) it was the standing of individuals in Western thought that gave them the right to make claims against the state and international society, and, in the twentieth century, this way of thinking was embodied in the human rights discourse. His angle of attack hangs on the degree to which the rights of states derive from their being manifestations of the right of self-determination of peoples (Vincent 1986: 113–18). This right, in his view, requires that states have some minimum degree of civil relationship with their citizens. If a state is 'utterly delinquent in this regard (by laying waste its own citizens, or by bringing on secessionist movements)' (ibid.: 115), and 'by its conduct outrages the conscience of mankind' (ibid.: 125), then its entitlement to the protection of the principle of nonintervention should be suspended. He qualifies such suspensions by saying that the circumstances triggering a right of humanitarian intervention must be extraordinary ones, not routine (ibid.: 126). He was fully aware that he was making a normative argument, and that in practice international society was only weakly developed on this point. He was also very aware of both the need for prudence and the dangers of opening up a licence for intervention.

In this way, Vincent offers a minimalist, state-centric solidarist solution to the tension between a pluralist international society (focused on sovereignty and nonintervention) and the cosmopolitan, or even revolutionist, world society implicit in a doctrine of universal human rights. He wanted to put a basic rights floor under the societies of the world. His idea is the development of a more solidarist interstate society, in which states become more alike internally, and therefore more likely to find common ground in agreeing about when the right of humanitarian intervention overrides the principle of nonintervention (Vincent 1986: 104, 150–2). The trick here is for states to translate human rights into citizens' rights (ibid.: 151). This issue of homogeneity in the domestic structures of states was perhaps Vincent's key point of departure from Bull. That Vincent is mainly a state-centric solidarist is clear from his choice of basic rights as a ground floor from which to build a more solidarist interstate society (Gonzalez-Pelaez and Buzan 2003; Gonzalez-Pelaez 2005). In the right to food he is looking for a lowest common denominator of human rights on which most states might agree, and from there perhaps to work up to the more contentious elements of the human rights agenda such as freedom from arbitrary violence. He was absolutely not looking to start from the moral high ground of universal human rights as a way of challenging the interstate order. His strategy was to get a foot on the first step of the ladder of human rights and hope to climb further once that was established. He wanted to avoid starting with the more difficult issues of human rights for fear of gaining the moral high ground at the expense of any possibility of practical advances towards solidarism.

For Vincent (1986: 104, 150–2) a solidarist international society would be one in which all units would be alike in their domestic laws and values on humanitarian intervention, or at least would recognize their common duty in relation to it. In this context, Vincent notes (ibid.: 151) that 'the spread of a global culture makes international society work more smoothly', and he takes hope in the historical record by which the state has made deals with civil society 'coopting the ideology of individualism by translating human rights into citizens rights'. With this line of thinking, Vincent begins to blend together a state-based international society with an underlying world society. Thus: 'international society might admit institutions other than states as bearers of rights and duties in it, recognizing to that extent their equality and welcoming them into what would then have become a world society' (Vincent 1978: 37). Vincent's preferred future is one in which a Westphalian type interstate society, defining itself as an exclusive club of states, gives way to a world society that is defined by an inclusive, somewhat neomediaeval, mixture of states, groups, transnational entities and individuals, all sharing some key values and having legal standing in relation to each other (Vincent 1986: 92–104). Yet even in his late work, and despite his desire to bring other actors into international society and so push towards a more inclusive type of world society, it is clear that Vincent still puts the state at the centre of his solidarist world order (Vincent 1992: 261–2).

After Vincent's untimely death in 1990, his breakout from Bull's impasse was taken up by two of his followers, Tim Dunne and Nicholas Wheeler. As already noted, in their joint writings (Dunne and Wheeler 1996; Wheeler and Dunne 1998) they try to reinterpret Bull as a kind of proto-solidarist, opening wider the door that he left behind and Vincent discovered. They draw attention, rightly, to the later Bull's concerns for justice as a component of order and to his awareness of the limits of pluralism exposed by the Cold War ideological polarization of the great powers. They even (1996: 92) want to pull out of Bull 'three paradigms of world politics: realism, pluralism and solidarism . . . centred upon the themes of, respectively, power, order and justice'. In Vincent's tradition, they see solidarism as intimately bound up in the transition from international to world society, extending the Grotian line that solidarism crosses the boundary between international and world society. They follow Wight in locating on normative ground the entire theoretical foundation of the English School triad. Their later work (Dunne and Wheeler 2004) pushes strongly the line that order without justice is unsustainable, and uses this to critique realist, pluralist and neoliberal positions.

In his solo works Dunne (1998: xi–xv, 5–12, 187ff.) is keen to distance the English School from attempts to classify it as a soft branch of realism, seeking to emphasize the fundamentally normative grounding of its central concept of international order, and seeing it as in some ways more akin to critical theory. Like Vincent, but pushing the vision of state-centric solidarism a bit further, Dunne (2001b: 7) also built on the idea of conditional sovereignty, arguing that modern states should 'only exist to promote the welfare and security of their citizens'. He too envisages an international society combining states and other actors:

> Bull is arguably mistaken in interpreting international society as a 'society *of states*' since many of the rules and institutions of international society predated the emergence of the modern state. It is time that the English School jettisoned the ontological primacy it attaches to the state. . . . International society existed before sovereign states and it will outlive sovereign states. (Dunne 2001a: 227)

Dunne goes further (2001b: 37–8) to argue that world society should be folded back into international society.

Wheeler (1992) follows Vincent in unpicking Bull's dilemma between order and justice, and between human rights and nonintervention, and finding the path to greater solidarism in making the right of nonintervention conditional on some minimal observance of human rights. He sees an improving prospect for human rights in the post-Cold War period, albeit slow and modest in extent. Wheeler departs from Vincent in focusing particularly on humanitarian intervention as the hardest case for solidarism. Like Vincent, he is fully conscious of the many risks that humanitarian intervention can pose to international order, both practical and philosophical (Wheeler and Morris 1996; Wheeler 2000: 11–13, 29–33). And he frames solidarism on this issue in state-centric terms, arguing that, if all states observed human rights internally, then no contradiction between human rights and sovereignty/nonintervention would arise (Wheeler and Morris 1996: 135). Wheeler (2000: 27–9, 41) does not want to undo the principle of nonintervention, which he recognizes as the core of international society, or to bring human rights into conflict with international law. From his perspective, solidarists see human rights as universal, but, until such time as civilization is developed enough to support this, states have the right, and possibly the obligation, to act in support of human rights beyond their borders, especially so when violations are on a large scale (ibid.: 11–13). There is more than a whiff of cosmopolitan solidarism underlying Wheeler's view. Yet, in the spirit of Vincent's practical ethics, he constructs an essentially state-centric solidarist position. He pushes it further than Vincent's basic rights by building a case from just war theory and customary international law that international society already recognizes and accepts some elements of humanitarian intervention, especially where legitimized by the UN Security Council (ibid.: 33–51). Although it is fair to say that Wheeler draws his normative force from cosmopolitan solidarism, both his empirical analysis and his policy prescriptions are firmly rooted in state-centric solidarism. He wants states to take more responsibility for 'saving strangers'.

By contrast, Linklater takes a more robustly cosmopolitan solidarist position where people are more clearly in the foreground. His strategy, like Vincent's, is to demolish the logic by which sovereignty and nonintervention are held to be necessarily contradictory to a cosmopolitan view of human rights. Echoing Bull's thinking, but not his conclusions, Linklater (1998: 24) starts from the proposition that 'An elementary universalism underpins the society of states and contributes to the survival of international order' and notes the already achieved contributions of this in the delegitimation of racism and colonialism. Linklater (1981) is concerned about the way in which the system of states separates people into different citizenships, in the process posing citizenship against the moral community of humankind in terms of how people weigh their moral obligations. He seeks to address this opposition by constructing a moral obligation both to fellow citizens and to the rest of humankind. He argues against the realist and pluralist view that the anarchic structure of the states-system forces citizens into rival or oppositional stances in relation to the citizens of other states (ibid.: 31–5). He views humankind as a developing species, and considers the constitutional character of states as also playing a significant role in how they relate to other states and peoples. On that basis he sees room to strengthen the sense of cosmopolitan obligation without undermining the duties of citizenship. Linklater's (ibid.: 34–5) vision is initially one of state-centric solidarism akin to liberal democratic peace, with states and their citizens internalizing 'the idea of humanity' as part of what would now be referred to as their 'logic of appropriateness'.

In later work, Linklater (1996b) casts this argument within a more explicitly English School framing. He advocates a wider sense of citizenship extending above and below the state as a necessary response to the opening up of the states-system by globalization. There are strong elements of cosmopolitan solidarism underlying this, but also strong elements of state-centric solidarism in play, with states 'mediating between the different loyalties and identities present within modern societies' (ibid.: 78). In *The Transformation of Political Community* (1998) Linklater continues his assault on the moral and intellectual tyranny of excessive state-centrism and the trumping of cosmopolitan by communitarian logics. He argues that the assumption that the sense of community resides almost exclusively within the state is wrong, as many religious, class and national solidarities across state borders demonstrate (ibid.: 3). He also argues (ibid.: 213) that the most successful types of state are those with relatively open stances between their citizens and the rest of the world.[4] The essence of Linklater's argument is that the recovery of a greater sense of 'humanity as a whole' is most likely to be achieved by making the meaning of citizenship itself more cosmopolitan.

Linklater (Linklater and Suganami 2006: 117ff.) continues to unfold this line of argument in favour of a progressive development of international society towards a more solidarist position on humankind, along the way rejecting on empirical and social theory grounds the anti-progressivist assumptions within realism and pluralism. He sees scope for social learning by states and citizens, and nicely points out how even an ideological pluralist such as Jackson (ibid.: 223–34) makes room for moral obligations beyond the state and for 'good international citizenship'. He later adds into this critical theory mix Norbert Elias's idea of a 'civilizing process', seeking to make new connections between the English School and process sociology by showing how the analysis of international society can contribute to the study of civilizing processes and vice versa. He sees this process as now moving beyond the state to the international sphere, carrying with it a growing, if still minimal, consciousness of wider obligations to humankind (Linklater 2010; 2011a: 1190). He perceives empirical validation for this in the simultaneous occurrence of 'attachment to survival units' and 'transnational solidarism' as exemplified in the contemporary human rights movement (Linklater 2010: 160, 164).

Linklater makes a nice critique of the English School's misuse of Kant to represent revolutionism, arguing that Kant is in fact a radical rationalist who is far from wanting to transcend the state system, and whose cosmopolitanism is aimed mainly at changing states internally as a way of changing their relationships with each other (Linklater and Suganami 2006: 155–69). He clearly sees himself as a Kantian in this sense. Evoking the harm principle (the imperative to do no avoidable harm, and the right of people to have a say in things that might harm them), he unfolds a vision of a merged international and world society not dissimilar to Vincent's, in which states, people and non-state actors all have rights in relation to each other (ibid.: 155–88; Linklater 2011b; see also Clark 2013). It might be argued that there is a parallel between Linklater and Vincent inasmuch as both are searching for a normative lowest common denominator (respectively the harm principle and the right to food) on which to build a more solidarist society of states. Like Vincent and Dunne and Wheeler, Linklater is thus primarily a state-centric solidarist in terms of means, albeit with a stronger and more obvious cosmopolitan solidarism just under its surface. Linklater is seeking to open up and humanize the state and citizenship, not to overthrow them (Linklater and Suganami 2006: 199–221, 246–55).

William Bain (2003: 1–26) picks up the problem of the obligation of states and their citizens to outsiders in the specific case of trusteeship: the idea that dominion over others is justified only if it is used to protect and improve those whose right of self-rule is suspended. He notes the troubled background to this in the unequal, often racist, doctrines of nineteenth-century empire that put an obligation on more advanced races to bring those lagging behind up to the 'standard of civilization'. On this basis the Europeans considered the Turks unfit to be imperial rulers (ibid.: 95). Bain (ibid.: 92, 78–107) argues that, after the First World War and the breakup of empires, trusteeship became an institution of Western international society. This institution was, however, short-lived. Along with colonialism, within which it might be seen as an evolution of practice, it was largely swept away by the tide of decolonization after the Second World War, in which formal inequality among peoples was delegitimized, and the right to self-determination trumped all considerations of capacity for self-government under modern conditions (ibid.: 134–9). Bain sees a substantial ghost of trusteeship haunting contemporary international society both in its attempts to deal with failed and failing states and in its deployment of conditionality, human rights and good governance as entry criteria into various international clubs (ibid.: 155–63). He ends with an argument that seems to push Linklater's attempt to narrow the gap between citizens and humankind even further. He sees the world of states and the world of people as having merged, so that 'it makes little sense to speak of insiders and outsiders' (ibid.: 188–9). Bain elaborates this theme in later work: 'We are not moving towards a solidarist world, we began there and we are still there' (2007a: 573).

Bain's solidarism harks back to natural law. He makes the telling point that 'human beings have always appealed to some sort of higher law in protest against the intolerable' (Bain 2007a: 573). Knudsen (2009) is also committed to the natural law approach, and he uses a Grotian position on human rights and international society to argue that human rights can be (and in his view already are) an institution of international society. He brings individuals into international society through natural law but still holds solidarism to be an empirical feature of state-based international society. One could read Bain and Knudsen as, *inter alia*, an extension of Linklater's argument that there is indeed a civilizing process going on in recent history in which obligation to others plays an increasing, if in many ways still modest, role in international society. There may still be a long way to go towards almost any version of universal human rights. But general acceptance since 1945 of the ideas that all humans are equal and that all peoples have the right of self-government nevertheless marks very significant progress from the formal inequalities of slavery, racism, gender and empire.

Despite de Almeida's (2006: 63–9) classification of him as a solidarist along with Dunne, Linklater and Wheeler, Buzan (1993; 2004: 45–62, 139–60) is not a solidarist in the sense of pursuing a normative agenda. Nor is he a pluralist who sees solidarism as necessarily threatening to the interstate order. Buzan's solidarism is based mainly on the pragmatic line of argument from Bull and Manning that states can agree to whatever arrangements they like. On this basis, he understands solidarism as being about anything that moves international society beyond the logic of coexistence into the realms of cooperation and convergence. The scope for solidarism so defined is much wider than human rights, including as well cooperation on the global economy, the environment and big science. For Buzan, the EU is a living example of a thick solidarist society that has done precisely that. Arguably such potential diversity puts it beyond the reach of a normative approach (Williams 2011).

While sharing neither the background in normative political theory nor the promotionalism of the mainstream solidarists, Buzan is on side with their arguments in two ways. First, he (1993: 336–40) argues that, beyond some very basic point, international and world society can only develop in tandem with each providing necessary elements of support to the other. Second, his more encompassing definition of solidarism allows him to support quite strongly the argument that international society in fact already contains very substantial elements of solidarism woven through its pluralist framing. In contemporary international society there is a lot more than just a logic of coexistence in play, most obviously in relation to the construction and maintenance of a global economy. Buzan's particular focus on primary institutions as a way of looking at international society, along with Holsti's (2004) way of tracking their rise, evolution and decline, provides a quite fine-grained way of following the growth of solidarist content in international society. More on this in the next chapter.

Andrew Hurrell is perhaps best positioned, like Vincent, as standing between the pluralist and solidarist positions, acknowledging the virtues and flaws of both, and focusing on how to understand the complex interplay between them. Hurrell's work, like Buzan's, supports the solidarist view that international society has already moved beyond the pluralist model. Hurrell (2002b: 137–41) is generally committed to the idea of the English School as the best site within IR theory to address the normative aspects of the subject, both empirically and in terms of a progressive agenda. But he is also committed to exploring the empirical reality of a durable pluralist international society that, under the pressure of globalization, has irreversibly taken on a variety of solidarist elements, needing to do so, and to continue doing so, in order to support its own legitimacy. Globalization and global governance are driving international society from the minimalist pluralism of the Westphalian model towards a much more solidarist model (Hurrell and Fawcett 1995: 309–10).

Hurrell (2007b) picks up this earlier argument, aiming to set out a comprehensive view of contemporary international society in its full complexity. He sees it in terms of the mix of actors and institutions, the blending of pluralist and solidarist elements, and the interplay of the state, the market and civil society that feature in the solidarist literature. Hurrell blends the expansion story into an evolving, deepening one, so carrying forward the classical historical discussions into the complexities of contemporary globalization and global governance. Yet he is always conscious of how power and inequality play through this blend, and not only as a consequence of differences in state strength and power. Echoing Clark (2007), Hurrell (2007b: 111–14; see also Armstrong 1998) notes how the non-state actors increasingly populating global civil society, being mainly Western, serve to enhance Western dominance by projecting Western values.

Hurrell (2007b: 63–5, 71, 35–6) reflects on 'coercive solidarism' and US extraterritorialism, brings in the role of the market much more than most other English School writers, and echoes the earlier arguments of Watson and others that the juxtaposition of equalities (sovereignty, racial, human) and inequalities (elements of hierarchy) in international society is problematic. Although he is conscious of the clashes caused in a multicultural world by Western-driven solidarist deepening, in terms of both the global market and human rights, he concludes that pluralism cannot work in today's complex world (ibid.: 287–98). In one sense, his book can be read as a critique and updating of the classical expansion story, but in the process it moves the focus from widening to evolution and deepening. The deepening perspective highlights the inequalities and differences between the West and the rest that are the unresolved legacy of the original monocentric expansion. This view pushes Hurrell, like others, to question the image of a relatively homogeneous 'global level international society' resting on sovereign equality, and to hint at a West-plus-regions view of overlapping and in some ways competing international societies.

Conclusions

What is striking about this survey of mainstream solidarist literature is how little of it fits with the classical pluralist bogeyman image of radical cosmopolitanism. The main thrust of solidarism in the English School debates is much more about how to make solidarism work within the society of states than, as Bull would have it, necessarily being revolutionist in the sense of setting out to replace the society of states. Even in its normative thrust, this solidarist literature is mainly moderate, and pragmatic to a fault – almost, in a word, classically English. While it may be motivated by an underlying cosmopolitanism, in practice it is almost all about state-centric solidarism. In its historical understanding it shows convincingly how what was initially a mainly pluralist society of states has become increasingly solidarist in its practices and institutions, including even on the tough issue of human rights, albeit still being very far away from any sort of solidarist utopia. Both Barkin (1998) and Reus-Smit (2001) underline this inherent unity of the pluralist–solidarist debate by showing how sovereignty is not a rigid social construction necessarily opposed to human rights, as Bull and Jackson contend, but a rather open construction whose meaning and practice has been continuously renegotiated, not least in relation to human rights. In a similar vein, Hill (1996) argues that 'world opinion' comprises both the voices of states and the voices of global civil society, which together shape 'the empire of circumstance' within which world politics takes place. More broadly, Brown (1995b: 105–6) argues that the society of states serves as a useful *via media* between the narrow particularity of communitarianism and the universalist pretensions of cosmopolitanism.

While Bull rejected the idea that states might become more alike, convergence plays a key role in much of the argument reviewed above. Although states with steep ideological differences might form a pluralist international society, it is quite difficult to imagine them progressing much beyond the principle of coexistence. But, when states and societies become more alike, then more possibilities for solidarist developments open up. This is particularly so if they converge along liberal democratic lines, in which case there is convergence of outward-looking values and practices between not only states but also their societies. Armstrong (1999) follows up changes in the nature and interests of the leading states as they have become more democratic and interdependent. He talks in terms of world society, seeing a shift from international law for a society of states to 'world law' for a world society of people. In this sense, as Hurrell (2007b) makes plain, history is more on the side of the solidarists than of the pluralists. Compared with the Cold War, and even more so the period between the First and Second world wars, states are more alike internally. In a loose sense, we are all capitalists now, and the great ideological divides of the twentieth century have lost much of their traction (Buzan and Lawson 2014).

And it is not just history that is on the side of solidarists. There is a fair amount of theoretical backing for homogenization as a feature of international relations. Waltz (1979) argues that the structural logic of anarchy produces like units through a logic of socialization and competition. Similarly, Tilly (1990) shows how, between 990 and 1990, war made the sovereign territorial state the dominant type of unit. Halliday (1992) focuses on the issue of homogenization of domestic structures among states as one of the keys to international (and by implication world) society. He notes the normative case for homogenization (Burke and democratic peace), the Marxian idea of capitalism as the great homogenizing force, and the Kantian/Fukuyama idea of science and technology and democracy as homogenizing forces. The members of the Stanford School (Meyer et al. 1997: 144–8) also take the striking isomorphism of the 'like units' of the international system as their key phenomenon for explanation. The large literature from the last quarter century backing the idea of a liberal democratic peace rests on the assumption that increasing likeness of units along these lines opens the way to more peaceful and cooperative relations within the group of like units (if also still competitive – this is capitalist society after all).

This convergence logic, is, however, discussed largely in universalist terms. The bias of much English School literature towards the system level continues, with the danger that the English School will continue to neglect the potential for regional differentiation. Logics of convergence can, after all, work just as powerfully to differentiate parts within a whole as they can to unify it, arguably more so. A logic that brings democracies (or Islamic states, or Confucian ones) together will generate different forms of solidarism that might strengthen regions in relation to the whole. As the relative power of the West weakens, so too does the case for assuming system-level homogenizing logics.

With all of this in mind, we can now return to the story of how the primary institutions of international society have continued to unfold and use this story to check empirically both how the balance between pluralism and solidarism and the social structure of international society in terms of primary institutions are evolving.

9 SOLIDARISM IN HISTORICAL PERSPECTIVE

Introduction

When we left this story at the end of chapter 7 (and the end of the nineteenth century), nationalism was dramatically reconfiguring both the foundations for legitimacy (rightful membership and rightful behaviour) and the meaning and practice of several key primary institutions of international society (territoriality, sovereignty, war, dynasticism). It was both reinforcing and beginning to break down the age-old institution of human inequality: reinforcing via racism and social Darwinism; breaking down by establishing principles of political legitimacy that were corrosive of both dynasticism and imperialism/colonialism. Under the impact of modernity, other primary institutions were undergoing internal revolutions of practice, most obviously international law and diplomacy. We saw that in historical perspective the abstract pluralist package of institutions contained other elements (imperialism/colonialism, human inequality, dynasticism) much more obvious in historical view than in the theoretical construction of the pluralist canon. And we saw that this supposedly stable minimalist package was in fact dynamic and becoming more so in destabilizing ways.

In the review of solidarist thinking above, there was a strong thread of argument not only that international society should pay more attention to world society and the solidarist agenda but that up to a point it was already doing so, even in the contentious area of human rights. As we pick up this story from the late nineteenth century, the question is to what extent, if any, do we see a trend towards solidarism in the way the primary institutions of international society have arisen, evolved and declined? The general backdrop to this question is the extraordinary global transformation to modernity, with its package of multiple revolutions both material and social, that dominated the nineteenth century. This transformation took off in Northwest Europe, North America and Japan during the nineteenth century. It quickly imposed itself on the rest of the world and continued to spread, evolve and diversify during the twentieth century and up to the present day. Given both the centrality of the idea of progress to modernity and the massive impact of its multiple revolutions on the human condition everywhere, it would be astonishing if the primary institutions of international society had not undergone profound changes during that time. And given that liberalism, with its emphasis on individual rights and free markets, was a leading part of the modernist package, it would be equally astonishing if some, or indeed most, of these changes were not in a solidarist direction. Nationalism was but the harbinger of further modernist assaults on the classical seven pluralist primary institutions and their three darker companions, imperialism/colonialism, human inequality and dynasticism. The global transformation to modernity needs to become an explicit part of how the English School tells its story about the evolution of international society and the changes in primary institutions that defined it (Buzan and Lawson forthcoming).

The emergence of solidarist primary institutions

In what follows I look first at the market, which arose alongside nationalism during the nineteenth century and, like nationalism, had major impacts on other primary institutions. I turn then to the classical seven, followed by the additional four (imperialism/colonialism, nationalism, dynasticism and human inequality), and finally to some new ones (democracy, environmental stewardship). Throughout this review I will be looking not just for the changes that mark the evolution of the social structure of international society but also for changes that can be understood as moving towards (or away from) solidarist values. For this purpose I understand solidarist values to mean both bringing world society more into play in relation to interstate society and moving interstate society beyond a logic of coexistence into one of cooperation and convergence. The move beyond coexistence might happen for either pragmatic calculation or convergence in values, or both.

The market

The English School literature is rich in allusions to the need to take account of the economic sector in thinking about international society, but poor in instances of anyone actually doing so (Gonzalez-Pelaez and Buzan 2003: 336–7). Vincent (1986; see Gonzalez-Pelaez 2005) came close with his solidarist argument for a right to food. That he understood the political side of the international economy is clear from his statement that, 'in regard to the failure to provide subsistence rights, it is not this or that government whose legitimacy is in question, but the whole international system in which we are all implicated' (Vincent 1986: 127, 145). But his work was not aimed at seeing the market as an institution of international society. Mayall (1982, 1984, 1989, 1990) gets closest to seeing the market (economic liberalism) in this way, at one point (Mayall 1982) even arguing for the existence of a sense of community in the economic sphere despite differences between North and South. But he seemed to lose faith in his earlier interpretation (Mayall 1984). His more recent works (1990, 2000a) focus on nationalism, and see economic nationalism returning on the back of national security concerns in such a way as to undermine economic solidarism. Nevertheless, Mayall (1990: 70, 150ff.) considers nationalism and liberalism not as simple opposites, though they are often staged as such, but also as complementary in many ways.

The development of thinking about economics within the English School is indeed so poor that there is no consensus, and hardly any discussion, about how to characterize primary institutions in this sector. Mayall (1990) talks about economic liberalism and economic nationalism, while Holsti (2004) focuses on trade. It might be argued that capitalism should be a master institution. I choose to talk about the market both because the term is relatively neutral and because it encompasses trade and other things. I am conscious of the critique that the market needs to be differentiated in terms of derivative institutions (Beeson and Breslin 2014), but doing that work is beyond the scope of this book.

The rise of the market as a distinctive institution of international society began, like nationalism, in the late eighteenth century. But, whereas the rise of nationalism followed a relatively smooth trajectory, becoming almost universal by the late nineteenth century, the rise of the market was a much more contested and very up-and-down process. While nationalism quite easily reinforced (while also changing) the classical pluralist institutions, the market was much more directly disturbing to them. It was one of the core features of the liberal modernist project to separate politics from economics, both intellectually and practically, and to give the market a considerable degree of autonomy from the state (Ruggie 1982: 385; Rosenberg 1994). This was a radical departure from the previous practice of mercantilism, which tied the economy closely to the state. Indeed Holsti (2004: 211–18) very much takes that view, arguing that mercantilism was simply a competition to establish monopolies. Mercantilism could nevertheless be seen as an institution of Westphalian international society inasmuch as it was a shared practice constituting legitimate behaviour. It fitted nicely with the classical seven, simply folding economy into sovereignty, territoriality and war, and also with colonialism (imperial preference) and nationalism (economic nationalism, protectionism). Even if it was largely a shadow institution, not really separable from the state, it is still useful to have a sense of it if only to occupy the space that the market later comes to fill.

Ruggie (1982: 386; see also Holsti 2004: 211–38) charts a shift in the social purpose of the state, away from the embedding of the economy within its political and social structures and towards using the state to 'institute and safeguard the self-regulatory market'. During the nineteenth century, Britain, then the first and pre-eminent industrial power, led the beginnings of a long struggle to institute and safeguard the market (free trade) as an institution of Western-global international society. The story of this struggle is too long and complicated to recount in detail here. Some – most obviously totalitarians of all stripes – opposed it because they preferred to keep their economies under political control. Others opposed it because they saw themselves in a weak position, being late industrializers needing, at least for a time, to protect infant industries against competition from more efficient established producers – most obviously Germany and the US during the nineteenth century. Yet others opposed it because they reacted against the consequences of the market in generating inequality and crass materialist cultures. And then there was the issue of periodic instability, sometimes on a heroic scale and with devastating consequences for millions of people, as after the downturn of 1873 and the crashes of 1929 and 2008. Yet, despite all these problems, the market seemed to be a necessary accompaniment of industrial capitalism and to offer greater prospects for economic growth and development, and therefore power, in the long run (the short run was sometimes a quite different matter). The price of living with a global market was the need to engage in a continuous learning process about how to adapt to, and stabilize, the ever unfolding challenges that it generated.

Although the idea of liberating the market from the state had been influential since Adam Smith's *Wealth of Nations* (1776), it did not begin to gather pace as an international practice until the middle of the nineteenth century, when Britain dropped its agricultural tariffs. Thereafter followed a general expansion of rules governing the legitimate practice of trade and finance, albeit with some backsliding during the recession of the 1870s and 1880s (Holsti 2004: 218–21). The last quarter of the nineteenth century saw the creation of permanent secondary institutions such as the International Bureau of Weights and Measures (1875), the Universal Postal Union (1874) and the International Telecommunications Union (1865). These were set up in response to growing trade and communication and the rapid shrinking of the world by railways, steamships and the telegraph. The First World War, compounded by the great depression of the 1930s, triggered a major setback for the global market. The war itself was a huge disruption to trade and finance, and it pushed Russia into a totalitarian revolution deeply hostile to the global market. The great depression pushed all the major powers of whatever ideology, even Britain, into an economic nationalism that lasted until after the Second World War.

Partly in reaction against the association of economic nationalism with war and totalitarianism, the market was revived as a key institution of American-led Western international society, with a host of new secondary institutions governing international trade and finance. Yet the Soviet Union remained largely outside and opposed to the global market, and so too did communist China after 1949 and some major postcolonial states such as India. The Cold War was thus another round in the struggle for dominance between the market and the communist/socialist version of mercantilism. The market was a powerful and defining primary institution of Western-global international society. Within the West, and particularly so within the developing EU, sovereignty, territoriality and borders were adapted to meet the conditions created by a more extensive embracing of the market.

But not until the end of the Cold War did it achieve for the first time something like fully global status as an institution of international society. China changed sides in the late 1970s, Russia, more arguably, after the collapse of the Soviet Union, and India during the 1990s. Thus, over a period of some two centuries, the market has moved from being an elite idea held by few to being a mainstream institution of international society (Bowden and Seabrooke 2006). Many support it on normative grounds of being good in itself. But many go along with it either on instrumental grounds that it has proved to be the most efficient way to generate power and wealth or because they are coerced into it by stronger powers. It remains contested, and the dialectic between economic nationalism and economic liberalism is far from finished. Very few states are completely open to the global market, and many cultivate forms of state capitalism in which economic nationalism is still prominent. But now the main game is about how to relate to the global market, and how to make it work best. The twentieth-century struggle over whether to have it or not is over. And since the building and maintaining of a global market goes far beyond the remit of mere coexistence, this is a major solidarist development in the structure of international society even though it has no necessary roots in cosmopolitan values or human rights.[1]

Sovereignty and nonintervention

Sovereignty, with its corollary nonintervention, has remained central to constituting the state and is one of the core primary institutions of international society. These two institutions together continue to define the form not only of world politics but also of international law and diplomacy. So, in a deep sense, there is tremendous continuity in the centrality of this most distinctively pluralist institution within the structure of international society. Yet at the same time, and without changing the basic idea of independent self-governing collectivities, there have also been profound changes in the nature of sovereignty and the practices associated with it. Nationalism redefined the basis of legitimacy for sovereignty by shifting its foundations from dynasticism, where the sovereign virtually was the state, to popular sovereignty, where the state was in a sense owned by its people. This move weakened the hierarchy of sovereignty among princes, kings and emperors (Reus-Smit 1999: 101–2) and facilitated the move towards a norm of sovereign equality that picked up speed during the nineteenth century (Hjorth 2011: 2588–95). Just as sovereignty under dynasticism was unequal because princes, kings and emperors had unequal status, so there was a matching link between the idea of the equality of people and the sovereign equality of their states (Bain 2003: 173–92; Hjorth 2011: 2590). This kicked in with particular force after 1945 and the beginning of large-scale decolonization, prompting James (1992: 391) to argue that it had 'taken on a new vitality' by extending 'the concept of equality to encompass the formal renunciation of many of the pressures which might be thought to be natural in a society without a government, and in which there are huge imbalances of power between its members'.

While nationalism had a big impact on sovereignty, it is harder to make the case that the market did so. This is notwithstanding the widespread argument that the market undermines sovereignty because it reduces the autonomy of states in a large and vital sector of activity. The key point here is once again Manning's argument that such decisions do not affect the basic principle of sovereignty if states consent to them. As Holsti (2004: 135–42) maintains, the basic constitutive functions of sovereignty that underpin the state, international law and international society have remained robust despite changes in the relative autonomy or autarchy of

states. Sovereignty would not be compromised unless, by allowing themselves to be penetrated in this way, states eliminated themselves as the
dominant political unit. So far this has not happened, and it does not look
like happening any time soon. The effect of the market is more on the
institution of territoriality than on sovereignty, as will be shown below.

A more difficult question is the classical English School chestnut about
the impact of human rights on sovereignty, and particularly on nonintervention. How one views this depends on how much weight is given to a
juridical interpretation of sovereignty. If sovereignty is understood mainly
as juridical, then it is largely given by international society in the form of
diplomatic recognition and acceptance as a rightful member. In that case,
sovereignty is in its essence conditional. Thus, to the extent that international society embraces human rights as a form of state-centric solidarism,
there can be legitimate erosion of the right of nonintervention on those
grounds, without such erosion affecting the institution of sovereignty itself.
As I will argue below, human rights is an emergent but still hotly contested
institution, which means that there are sharp differences of opinion within
international society at the global level as to whether intervention on
human rights grounds is legitimate or not. Ralph (2005), for example, uses
the case of US opposition to the International Criminal Court to explore
the ongoing tension between sovereignty in the context of international
society and individual rights rooted more in world society.

The other big change in the practices of sovereignty comes not from
other primary institutions but from the expansion of international society.
Holsti (2004: 128–30) charts the shift in criteria for recognition (what
Jackson 1990a terms 'juridical sovereignty') from the strict rules of the
'standard of civilization' during the nineteenth century through to the
almost anything goes attitude during the post-1945 decolonization. Colonial international society during the nineteenth century was very much a
two-tier affair, with the Western core moving towards sovereign equality
for interstate relations within it but outsiders being subject to the entry
criteria of the Western-defined 'standard of civilization'. This involved
conditionality on such issues as law, property rights, human rights and
good governance. Colonized peoples were notionally under tutelage on
such things. Non-colonized peoples, such as in China, Japan and the
Ottoman Empire, were not given full recognition until they could meet the
standard. Their unequal status was inscribed in the humiliating extraterritorial rights demanded by Westerners in treaties with them.

Although a handful of non-Western countries made it into international
society, this system of divided sovereignty stayed largely in place until the
breakdown of imperialism/colonialism as an institution of international
society after the Second World War. As Bain (2003: 92) argues, this was

a system in which a 'superior' West decided on the readiness for self-government of less developed peoples: 'self-determination implied granting powers of self-government and autonomy in proportion to the capacity of a people to make good use of them.' The Second World War, with its catalogue of barbaric behaviour by Westerners to each other, delegitimized rule by 'superior' over 'inferior' on grounds of the 'standard of civilization'. It opened the way to mass decolonization on the basis of a transcendental right of self-determination that trumped all arguments about unreadiness for self-government in the modern world (ibid.: 134–5). This in turn set up the problem of failed states and humanitarian intervention which after 1989 brought the return of a modicum of conditionality to recognition of sovereignty, and more so to rights of entry into various international clubs. As Holsti (2004: 131–4) points out, decolonization also removed the right of conquest as a legitimate ground for claiming sovereignty. He traces this back to 1815, but it became robust only after the Second World War, when it was reinforced by the political dynamics of decolonization and anti-colonialism.

In two very significant ways, then, the quintessentially pluralist primary institution of sovereignty has taken on board profoundly solidarist characteristics: its legitimacy now rests on peoples rather than on dynastic leaders, and its practice has been extended to all on the basis of a link between the principle of human equality and that of sovereign equality.

Territoriality

Along with sovereignty, territoriality has retained its strong role as one of the two definers of the state, and therefore as a key principle for how humankind organizes and legitimizes its political life. Holsti (2004: 73–111) shows how borders have become firmer and more precisely defined over time, both as a result of improved survey techniques and because administrative, political and military needs demanded it. Jackson (2000: 317–35) notes the centrality of boundaries to international relations and their relative neglect in IR theory. I have already noted how nationalism transformed the dynastic meaning of territoriality by sacralizing boundaries linked to the nation. As Zacher (2001: 246) argues, this move consolidated a new norm of territorial integrity in which 'mutually recognized and respected boundaries are not what separate peoples but what binds them together'. This cumulative firming up of territoriality has progressively delegitimized transfers of territory by force, as Saddam Hussein discovered when he invaded Kuwait in 1990. Transfers of territory are now legitimate only by consent and, after the major round of decolonization following the end of the Second World War, the political map of the world has taken on an increasingly fixed character. It is notable how even major state disintegrations, such as that of the Soviet Union and Yugoslavia, have happened along the lines of internal administrative boundaries. Williams (2002) makes the case for territoriality as an institution of modern international society whose ethical justification is that it supports a desirable social pluralism that to some extent defends people against oppression.

Nationalism has both reinforced and challenged territoriality. It has reinforced it by linking territory to people in an emotional way and transforming the idea of the state to that of the nation-state. So effective has this been that the term 'nation' has become a synonym for 'state', and we talk without thinking about it of 'international relations' and 'international society' rather than using the term 'interstate'. But nationalism has also challenged territoriality because of the large disparity between the number of ethnic nations and the number of states. This causes major problems of secessionism and irredentism if nationalism is interpreted in an ethnic way, and it was instrumental in breaking up empires during the twentieth century. Civic nationalism addresses this problem by creating overarching 'national' identities, such as British, American, Nigerian and Indian, to allow a variety of ethnicities to coexist as a nation within a given territory. Both types of nationalism reinforce territoriality but may do so in conflicting ways, as when Kosovars do not want to be part of Serbia, or Kurds part of Iraq, Syria or Turkey. The ongoing strength of territoriality plays to pluralism by reinforcing the dividedness and difference of states. Yet, at the same time, this consolidation of a firmer territoriality seems to play a major role in the decline of war – another of the key pluralist institutions – by delegitimizing territorial transfers by conquest (Holsti 2004: 103–11).

The market, reinforced by huge improvements in the technologies of transportation and communication, has, on the other hand, made major modifications to the practice of territoriality that unambiguously strengthen state-centric solidarism and the logics of cooperation and convergence. The rise of the market has in one sense been a struggle about territoriality. Economic nationalists have wanted to impose territoriality onto the economic sector, while economic liberals have wanted to open borders to flows of goods, ideas, capital and, up to a point, labour (i.e., people). This struggle hinges on the liberal trick, central to modernity, of conceptually separating the economic and political sectors. Most types of economic nationalist reject this separation and think that opening up to the world economy necessarily involves major impacts on domestic politics. Economic liberals think that the autonomy of the national political sphere can be preserved even when borders are opened to economic flows. Without taking a position on this complex dispute, one can still say that the rise of the global market has in many ways, and in most places, shot territorial borders full of what look like rather large and permanent holes. Here the argument links to sovereignty, because much of this opening up of borders has been done by the consent of the states concerned, whether consensually out of belief or under coercion from liberal powers. The rise of the market as a primary institution has thus radically changed the practice of territoriality, or, from another perspective, compromised its core principle in relation to the economic sector. The contemporary form of this debate is about globalization, and whether the deterritorializing tendencies of the global economy are challenging the state as the core political player in international society. If they are, then the global market perhaps poses a more serious threat of cosmopolitan revolutionism to pluralist international society than human rights has so far managed to do.

The balance of power

The balance of power is another key pluralist institution. Recall that this is not about the purely mechanistic understanding of realism, where rival powers compete for dominance or survival. It is about the essentially constructivist idea that the great powers in particular agree to a principle of balance as a way of maintaining international order. Little (2007a: 66–7) labels these *adversarial* and *associational* balancing. While theoretically distinct, these two understandings of the balance of power are not mutually exclusive in practice, and observation of the mechanistic tendency may have played a role in the development of balancing as a social convention. Both depend on the idea from Vattel that no one power should be in a position to lay down the law to the others (Bull 1977: 101). It is not uncommon in the English School to infer from this definition that a balance of power is a necessary condition for international society and, in some sense, the foundation on which other institutions rest (ibid.: 106–7; Hurrell 2007b: 32, 51; Clark 2009a: 203–5, 220–3). In the absence of a balance, either one power would indeed be laying down the law to the rest, which does not constitute an international society, or there would be insufficient interaction to require a society. Both types of balancing are essentially motivated by anti-hegemonism: the imperative to stop any one power from dominating the international system.

Associational balancing emerged after 1713 and was consolidated after 1815. The Concert of Europe during the nineteenth century provides the model for the balance of power as a conscious institution of international society. As Little (2006: 113–15) observes, by the nineteenth century, colonial acquisitions were feeding back into the European balance of power. The great power Concert broke down in the run up to the First

World War, had a flawed and feeble revival during the 1920s under the League of Nations (with the US refusing to join in), and broke down again catastrophically during the 1930s. Hope for reconstruction of an associational balance after the Second World War was quickly dashed by the onset of the Cold War and another adversarial balance, this time between the two superpowers. Anti-hegemonism remained the driving motive throughout. The rise of nationalism made little impact on the balance of power. Neither did the rise of the market except in an inverse way, when the return of economic nationalism during the 1930s was associated with intense adversarial balancing. Likewise the market did not much affect balancing between the US and the Soviet Union because their economies were largely separate.

The appearance of nuclear weapons after 1945 made a substantial difference to the operation of the balance of power (Bull 1977: 117–26). In a strictly classical sense, the balance of power assumes that power (meaning mainly military power, the capacity to destroy) is a scarce resource. Balancing is therefore about ensuring that no one power accumulates a preponderance of this resource. But nuclear weapons quickly created a surplus capacity of destructive power such that more than one country could acquire sufficient of it to lay waste the entire planet. This technical change did not eliminate balancing behaviour between the US and the Soviet Union, but it added deterrence logic into the equation. The huge destructive capacity of nuclear weapons changed equations by making it possible for states with fairly small nuclear arsenals to deter much larger adversaries. Nuclear weapons also added to the balance of power an imperative to prevent nuclear wars if humankind was to survive. During the later Cold War this survival imperative led to some reassertion of associational balancing in the form of superpower arms control negotiations and agreements.

The big question about this institution comes with the ending of the Cold War in 1989. The implosion of the Soviet Union abruptly ended the adversarial balancing game between the US and the Soviet Union and left the US as the sole superpower. The frenzy of balancing that realists assumed should be triggered by this structure did not take place. China decided to rise peacefully and integrate itself into the Western-global economy. Russia remained prickly, but too weak to mount more than nuisance tactics. Europe and Japan retained their Cold War ties to the US. At best there was some 'soft' balancing. This generated a variety of explanations as to why there was no balancing. These included geography (the distance of the US from Eurasia), politics (the liberal, non-threatening character of the US and the democratic peace), economics (the impact of the market in reducing the importance of territorial control to the pursuit of power and wealth) and power gap (the idea that the US lead, especially military, was too daunting for anyone to challenge). While the US was clearly the biggest power, it was not really in a position to lay down the law to the others, although it did claim exceptional rights for itself.

So, probably for a mix of reasons, after 1989, balancing and anti-hegemonism weakened markedly. Adversarial balancing remained in the background with a possible revival in a US–China rivalry. Associational balancing was loosely present both in ongoing nuclear deterrence among most of the major powers and in the unwillingness of any of the other major powers to pose a serious challenge to US primacy. But even associational balancing was hardly a major theme of international order. There was a quite widespread willingness among the powers both to open their economies and accept the risks of interdependence and to collaborate in various big science projects. Asking whether the balance of power as a master institution was in decay was at least not an unreasonable question. Nau (2001: 585), for example, argues that 'when national identities converge, as they have recently among the democratic great powers, they may temper and even eliminate the struggle for power.' Such democratic peace and liberal market effects might have been operating within the West during the Cold War, but this effect is difficult to separate from that of their joint alliance against the Soviet Union. After the Cold War at least the market effects, less so the democratic ones, became more global.

To the extent that this weakening of a key pluralist institution can be linked to the global market and a degree of ideological convergence among the great powers around economic liberalism/capitalism, then aspects of state-centric solidarism can be seen as changing the normative composition of international society.

Great power management

As Hjorth (2011: 2591–8) argues, the privileged status of great powers is a practical derogation from the principle of sovereign equality. Great power management strongly implies collective hegemony, which in turn raises questions about sovereign equality. This poses a theoretical challenge to the English School. Existing English School scholarship has focused mainly on international societies close to the anarchic end of Watson's (1992: 13–18) spectrum. It could be argued that the concept of international society is relevant only for the anarchic side of the spectrum because hierarchy removes the multi-actor condition required for a society. The institution of great power management is closely tied to an associational balance of power (Little 2006), with the strength of adversarial balancing and great power management being inversely correlated. Thus the ups and downs of this institution follow much the same trajectory as that of associational balancing, with major breakdowns around the First and Second world wars. Bull's (1980) castigation of the two superpowers during the Cold War as 'great irresponsibles' is about the failure of the US and the Soviet Union to take adequate responsibility for managing international society.

This parallel breaks down after 1989, when the unchallenged rise of the US as the sole superpower raises doubts about the basic principle of balance of power but causes much less disturbance to that of great power management. Post-Cold War, the US was perfectly willing to see itself as the leader and to claim privileges for itself on that basis. Up to a point, the US retained followers, though after 2001 under the Bush administration it did not seem to care much whether anyone followed its lead or not, and its legitimacy as leader consequently declined (Hurrell 2002a: 202; 2007b: 262–83; Buzan 2008). Hurrell (2002c: xxii) rightly posed the question: 'How stable and how legitimate can a liberal order be when it depends heavily on the hegemony of the single superpower whose history is so exceptionalist and whose attitude to international law and institutions has been so ambivalent?' Morris (2005) argues that the US sullied its normative opportunity by its unilateral and coercive approach to promoting its liberal agenda. Dunne (2003) even questions whether, after 9/11, US policy amounted to suzerainty, moving it outside of international society.

This concrete situation of a sole superpower made manifest in acute form a broader question that had been under discussion within the English School for many years. The legitimacy of contemporary international society is based on the principles of the sovereign equality of states and, up to a point, post-decolonization, on the equality of people(s) and nations. Yet it is still riddled with the hegemonic/hierarchical practices and inequalities of status left over from its founding process and largely favouring great powers in particular and the West in general.[2] Simpson's (2004) work has a lot to say about this tension over the last two centuries, providing a useful link between English School concerns and international law. Clark (2009a, 2009b, 2011) has tackled this problem with an argument that hegemony can be a primary institution of international society. This in turn picks up the dissatisfaction of Wight and Watson, noted in chapter 4, about wanting the British Committee to explore hegemonic international societies. Clark (2011: 1) notes the contradiction in English School thinking between a strong commitment to anti-hegemonism as a condition of international society and its simultaneous acceptance of great power management as an institution, with the inequality of status that that implies. The key to both great power management and hegemony as institutions of international society is that the powers concerned attract legitimacy to support their unequal status as leaders. They do this both by displaying good manners and by efficiently providing public goods (Clark 2009a: 207–20). Clark, however, is arguing mainly in theoretical terms that hegemony as a variant of great power management is possible. He is not arguing that the US has successfully achieved hegemony in this sense, seeing it as at best a limited and partial hegemon.

Great power management, like the balance of power, is a classical pluralist institution. It is also one that places pluralism close to realism in the sense of accepting and legitimizing an uneven distribution of power in the face of a broader commitment to sovereign equality. In historical perspective, this institution also looks to be weakened for two reasons. First, because for most of the twentieth century the great powers pursued adversarial balancing and, second, because anti-hegemonism has been a continuing and robust feature of post-decolonization international society more broadly. There is of course no doubt that the larger powers remain disproportionately influential, and Clark (2011: 235–44) makes much of the veto power of the US in world politics. Yet whether their right to manage can be legitimized is open to question. Although it is beyond the scope of this book, this line of argument points towards the literatures on secondary institutions and global governance, and the idea that the management of international society is diffusing downwards and outwards from the great powers. It is notable how both minor powers (most notably in ASEAN) and non-state actors (e.g., in the Land Mine Treaty) take leadership roles in specific aspects of the management of international society. This might be thought to support solidarism, but whether or not it does so depends on the nature of the actors in play. Even great powers or hegemons might promote state-centric solidarism (as in the promotion of the market), whereas world society actors and/or lesser powers might work against solidarist goals (e.g., religious extremists) as well as for them (most human rights international non-governmental organizations [INGOs]).

International law

Unlike the balance of power, the primary institution of international law is not intrinsically pluralist. Bull (1977: 106–9) emphasizes its pluralism by arguing that 'international law depends on its very existence as an operating system of rules on the balance of power.' Mayall (2000a: 84–95) likewise presents international law as mainly a pluralist institution. As shown above, Bull rejected Grotius's natural law precisely because it gave too much scope to human beings and world society; he preferred positive law for the clarity of its state-centrism. Natural law is therefore attractive to cosmopolitan solidarists, and positive law to pluralists. On that basis, the trajectory of international law might at first glance seem to favour pluralism. As with sovereignty, while the basic principle of international law has remained stable, the sources of legitimacy, content and practices within it have changed quite radically. The distinctive type of international law that emerged during the sixteenth and seventeenth centuries as a response to the rise of sovereignty was initially dominated by natural law. Positive law developed alongside this, and during the nineteenth century positive law became dominant while natural law was pushed increasingly to the margins (Holsti 2004: 146–50). This development was driven, among other things, by the rising global market and the general increase in interaction flows of all kinds across international society consequent on the nineteenth-century revolutions of modernity. There was a major expansion in functional regimes of all sorts starting in the late nineteenth century to regulate and coordinate the new global infrastructures of rail, steamship, post, telegraph and radio, as well as the expanding activities of international trade, investment and finance and the rights of European citizens abroad (Armstrong 2006: 129–33).

It was this rapidly growing body of positive international law with its universalist pretentions that the newly empowered West projected outwards during the nineteenth century, overriding pre-existing Chinese and Islamic systems that also saw themselves as representing universal systems of law (Onuma 2000). The process of an ever expanding and more elaborate body of positive international law along functional lines has continued, and international law has also adapted to changes in other institutions, such as the demise of imperialism/colonialism and the growth of restraints on war. The triumph of positive law suggests that the evolution of this primary institution favours the pluralist position. Yet, as Holsti (2004: 156–61) observes, there has also been growth in human rights law despite the difficulties posed by potential clashes with the principle of nonintervention. Bull (1977: 127–61) remained opposed both to erosion of positive law by infringement of the principle that states had the right to consent and to extension to non-state actors and individuals of status as subjects of international law. Yet, although international law has remained overwhelmingly positive, it has also been extended in various ways to take in non-state actors and individuals. Armstrong (1999) reviews the case for and against seeing international law as still predominantly state-based or moving towards being a world law for a world society of people. He arrives at a conclusion in line with what I have called state-centric solidarism. International law is still state-based rather than cosmopolitan, but its content has been driven into a more solidarist direction by the changing nature of the leading powers and their commercial and moral interests. Elements of human rights and environmental and commercial law transcend mere coexistence and open out into cooperation.

One interesting point to watch is whether the weakening of the balance of power since 1989 has implications for international law. If the balance of power underpinned international law, as Bull and others thought, then there could be substantial implications. Yet so far, other than some awkward and inconsistent behaviour on the part of the US (Armstrong 2006: 125–9), international law seems to be going from strength to strength. That would make sense if, as some think, the mechanisms of global governance are beginning to displace the balance of power.

Diplomacy

Diplomacy certainly starts as a core pluralist institution concerning communication in state-to-state relations. In historical perspective, it is another story of continuity in the basic principles but substantial changes in practice. Like international law, it emerged in modern form to meet the needs of sovereignty, albeit initially in dynastic form, becoming professionalized only during the nineteenth century (Holsti 2004: 179–98), during the shift from dynastic to multilateral diplomacy (Reus-Smit 1999: 101–10). Multilateralism takes root during the nineteenth century, symbolized by the advent of permanent IGOs, but really this takes off under US leadership after the Second World War, when the US promoted multilateralism as the main way of doing diplomatic business. After the First World War there was considerable public reaction against the secret diplomacy seen as one of the causes of the war, but the institution weathered this storm.

Great pressure on the institution has come from the impact of communications technology, the huge increase in both the number and type of actors and the volume of interactions throughout the international system, and the pressures of ideological competition and propaganda (Hall 2006a). Vastly improved communications have not just centralized diplomacy but also bypassed it. State leaders can talk directly to each other, and so can representatives of lower tiers of government from different states. This kind of development has gone furthest within the EU, where diplomacy in its traditional sense no longer really describes the process of governance within the grouping, and embassies and ambassadors are of decreasing relevance (Holsti 2004: 206–10). Generally, the huge proliferation of functional IGOs and international conferences has created not only new actors and new nodes of communication but also a structure of global governance that has taken on a life of its own alongside interstate diplomacy (Hurrell 2007b: 96–9). Decolonization has centralized much diplomacy into IGOs for new states unable to afford diplomatic representation in two hundred countries (Buzan and Little 2000: 316–18). Given the massive increase in trade, investment and financial flows, firms have increasingly become players in diplomacy (Stopford and Strange 1991). And, given the increasing strength of civil society, so too have INGOs, both as advocacy groups and as participants in diplomatic conferences (Holsti 2004: 198–205; Clark 1995: 508–9; Clark 2007; Hurrell 2007b: 99–104). At the same time as all of this, what Der Derian (1992) labels 'antidiplomacy', the propagandist, coercive and self-promoting behaviours designed to '*dis*order international society' (Hall 2006a:160) have grown in strength. Some violent non-state actors have acquired elements of diplomatic standing, as have elite conclaves such as Davos. From the late 1990s multilateralism itself came under hard questioning, as Washington adopted more unilateralist attitudes and practices and turned against many of the secondary institutions it had been the prime mover in creating.

Watson (1982) notes how diplomacy has changed and adapted to new circumstances, but it will remain central so long as states continue to be the principal players in world politics. Holsti (2004: 206–10) sees greater complexity in diplomacy but no fundamental change of principle, and Jackson's (2000) defence of pluralism gives 'statecraft' a central role in preserving order. But Hall (2006a: 160–1) is perhaps closest to the truth when he sees diplomacy as a weakening institution: 'The erosion of "diplomatic culture" might thus be welcomed, at least by cosmopolitans, for it may signify the end of [pluralist] international society.' For better or worse, diplomacy looks to be another pluralist institution evolving in such a way as to make some room for non-state actors and solidarist issues.

War

The last of the seven classical pluralist primary institutions is war. Holsti (2004: 277–83) outlines the institutionalization of war during the eighteenth century, making it more professional, putting limits on conduct, legalizing its status, and confining it to states as legitimate practitioners. Pejcinovic (2013) tracks the history of war as an institution of European/ Western international society, looking particularly at the changing rationales for war and the difference between the use of war among insiders, and between insiders and outsiders (see also Buzan 1996). Making war an institution of international society is about limiting who may resort to it, how it is conducted, and the purposes for which it can legitimately be used. This poses something of a paradox about how to understand the strength/ weakness of war as an institution of international society. Is it strong when war is legitimate for a wide range of purposes or strong when war is heavily constrained? Would an agreement to abolish war completely be an instance of a strong institution of war?

Up until the end of the First World War states were pretty free to go to war for a wide variety of legitimate purposes, from extending their home territory and preventing a rival from rising, to empire building abroad and the pursuit of economic gain. The two Hague conferences before the First World War sought mainly to begin imposing some limits on the *means* by which wars could be fought. Mayall (2000a: 17–19) argues that, after the First World War, war was discredited as an institution and became seen more as 'the breakdown of international society'. The League of Nations attempted to restrict the right of war, but this quickly broke down. Except for the conspicuous non-use of chemical weapons arsenals, the Second World War was a pretty unrestrained affair in terms of both motives and means. Thereafter there was a more serious attempt to limit the use of war to self-defence and purposes ordained by the UN Security Council, although, as Pejcinovic (2013: ch. 6) argues, for a time the shift to decolonization after 1945 legitimized wars for independence against colonial powers such as France and Portugal.

Pressure to narrow the legitimacy of war even among states has arisen from a variety of sources. Navari (2007) remakes the Kantian argument that the propensity for states to resort to war has declined as the state has evolved from absolutist through constitutional to democratic forms. Looking at the internal political dynamics of these three types, she sees a progression from war as a normal and regular activity of absolutist states through to war as a last resort among democracies. A host of more particular explanations for the increasing restraint on war can also be found. As discussed above, the rise of nationalism made the claiming of legitimate sovereignty over territories seized by force more difficult than in earlier times. Holsti (2004: 131–4) claims that removal of conquest as a legitimate ground for claiming sovereignty can be observed from 1815 onwards. The major round of decolonization begun after the Second World War, and the parallel demise of imperialism/colonialism as an institution (more on this below), consolidated this norm. The rise of the market downgraded or removed economic motives for war by delinking wealth and the possession of territory (Bull 1977: 195), but this effect did not really kick in until after the Second World War, and even more so after the end of the Cold War. The incentives to resort to war, especially among the great powers, were being reduced by the impact of technology in raising its costs and scale of destruction (ibid.: 189–99), though, as Pejcinovic (2013) argues, the use of the threat of war was still very much in play in Cold War policies of nuclear deterrence. These impacts also increased incentives to restrict the use of war. This dynamic became plainly visible after the First World War, with its unprecedented costs and casualties, its undoing of empires, and the fear that technologically driven powers of destruction threatened to wreck European civilization. Fear of war began to rival fear of defeat in the minds of the great powers (Buzan 2007 [1991]: 217–33). The Second World War happened anyway, of course, but its climax in the use of nuclear weapons against Japan signalled clearly that all-out war among great powers would soon be an irrational act of mutual suicide. The means of destruction had outgrown both the states that deployed them and the institution of war that justified them.

Up until 2001, the combined effect of these pressures served mainly to narrow the utility and legitimacy of war, restricting it to the right of self-defence and for purposes mandated by the Security Council. With the terrorist attacks of 9/11, this steady squeeze on the legitimacy of war came to an end. The US reacted to this attack by declaring open season on terrorists and their supporters and claiming a much wider right to resort to war in its self-defence against the new type of threat (Holsti 2004: 146–50; Jones 2006; Ralph 2010). At the time of writing, the full impact of these US moves on the institution of war is not clear. They have received some support from other states which share US fears of terrorism (or simply like the idea of opening up the legitimacy of war again), but the legitimacy of the US as a hegemon is sufficiently under question that these moves do not automatically change the accepted practices within the institution, though they certainly do challenge them.

The picture is now very mixed (Holsti 2004: 283–99; see also Hurrell 2007b: 165–93). War is pretty much obsolete within the West, and more arguably among the great powers as a whole, though Pejcinovic (2013) argues that it is still an important institution of international society. By contrast, in many other parts of the world it is suffering de-institutionalization and a return to pre-eighteenth-century practices and norms, whereby any sense of professionalism, restraint on violence or limits to use have eroded away. Between the West and the rest is a murky zone of actual (Iraq, former Yugoslavia, Afghanistan, Libya) and potential (North Korea, Iran) interventions and more or less noninterventions (Rwanda, Somalia, Syria). Here the debates hinge around legality versus legitimacy in moral terms, and motives range from the solidarist (humanitarian intervention) to the pluralist (preventing nuclear proliferation, removing regimes seen as threatening to international order). As Mayall (2000a: 95–6, 102–4; 2000b: 70; see also Hurrell 2007b: 63–5) notes, the rise of human rights as an institution extends the right of war beyond self-defence, and he is highly critical of sanctions as a surrogate for war. These cases fall between the institutionalized and non-institutionalized extremes. There is much dispute about the legitimacy of these uses and non-uses of war in relation to the right of nonintervention that is a corollary of sovereignty and the obligation to protect against acts of genocide. Holsti (2004: 294–7) offers an intriguing speculation that the development of high-precision weapons might offer a possible route in these cases for restoring some limits to both the use of force and political objectives. The intensive use of drones by the US and others in the war against terrorism is perhaps a move in this direction.

It is very difficult to draw any conclusions about this in relation to a historical perspective on pluralism and solidarism. War has been, and mainly still is, a pluralist institution. But it is also one that can and does sometimes serve solidarist ends, and, arguably, much of the narrowing of war's legitimacy since 1945 and the increasing role of IGOs in providing legitimacy pushed war in a solidarist direction. The trend towards de-institutionalization in some parts of the world serves neither pluralism nor solidarism, undermining both and constituting a curious turn in the structure of international society.

Imperialism/colonialism/development

If one were looking for a date to mark the beginning of the end of imperialism/colonialism, Japan's defeat of Russia in 1904–5 would be a good choice. Although it was the precursor to yet more empire-building by Japan, it was also the major opening move in breaking the myth of white power. For the first time in the modern era, a non-Western, non-white people had won not just a battle (there were several examples of that) but a whole war against a major European great power. This gave hope to non-whites everywhere who were under the heel of white domination, thus fuelling the revolt against the West. Imperialism/colonialism as an institution did not begin visibly to weaken until after the First World War, when the mandate system questioned its legitimacy (Mayall 2000a: 17–25). At the same time, several empires broke up, and there was a major consolidation of national self-determination, popular sovereignty and, to a lesser extent, democracy within European international society (Wilsonianism). These corrosive ideas began to seep into the colonies.

The widespread de-legitimation and collapse of imperialism/colonialism as an institution happened quite rapidly after the Second World War. There were many reasons for this (Holsti 2004: 262–74). There was, of course, anti-colonial resistance within the colonies, but this was just one of several factors. There was also public opposition to empire within the metropolitan states and a growing contradiction between democratic politics at home and imperial ones abroad (Mayall 2000b: 64–5). There was a shift in the general framing ideas that supported imperialism/colonialism, especially against racism and towards human equality and the right of self-determination (Bain 2003: 134–9). The two superpowers that dominated post-1945 world politics, although fiercely opposed to each other ideologically, both understood themselves to be anti-colonial and did not want to see the continuation of European overseas empires. And the European metropolitan powers (and Japan) were weakened materially and discredited as 'superior' cultures by the war. In terms of interplay with other primary institutions, nationalism and liberalism – both economic (market) and political (human equality and human rights) – were corrosive of imperialism/colonialism. In some contrast to Keene (2002), Holsti (2004: 274) rightly perceives the obsolescence of colonialism as one of the most important developments in twentieth-century international relations. Seen in longer perspective, it is arguably more important than the onset of the Cold War that happened at the same time and still dominates the IR landscape for that period.

The great wave of decolonization after 1945 hugely expanded international society. Rather than being a formal, two-tier colonial society with divided sovereignty, it became formally a global-scale society based on sovereign equality. But many of the new states were poor and lacking in modernization. The colonial construction of non-Europeans as being at a lower stage of development within a single model of development carried over into trusteeship and the postcolonial discourse of development (Bain 2003: 13–21). Although the 'standard of civilization' as a criterion for entry was gone, it left as its legacy to the postcolonial world the discourse of aid and development (Holsti 2004: 250; Bowden 2009: locs. 1000–84, 2173–220). The colonial obligation of the metropolitan powers to bring the indigenous peoples up to a European 'standard of civilization' morphed into an obligation on the part of the rich world to assist in the development of the 'Third World' or 'less developed countries'. Indeed, it is an interesting thought that development, understood as the right to acquire modernity, might well have become the successor primary institution to imperialism/colonialism. It appears as a goal in countless diplomatic documents and IGO constitutions and charters. It draws legitimacy from a sense both of obligation by the former colonial powers (aka 'developed states') and of entitlement by the postcolonial states. It also draws legitimacy from its synergies with the welfare and basic needs end of the human rights and human security discourses, with their emphasis on rights to adequate nutrition, clean water, shelter, education and suchlike, all of which are associated with better developed societies (Clark 2013). Whether this right to development is about resources transfers from rich to poor, or about the necessity for the 'underdeveloped' to undergo their own revolutions of modernity, is of course hotly contested.

As discussed in chapter 5, for the English School, the great postcolonial expansion in the membership of international society, with its ending of divided sovereignty, raised the problem of whether or not the cultural cohesion of international society had been seriously undermined. For solidarists, the problem of multiculturalism, and the embedded inequality that went along with it, was more complex than it was for pluralists. Pluralists had lower expectations of what international society could be or do, and so could set their sights lower and hope that a modicum of cultural cohesion via Westernized elites would somehow offset the otherwise depressing prospects for a multicultural international society that would lack any shared moral foundations. Solidarists had higher hopes for international society and were more challenged by the need, on the one hand, to accept multiculturalism on liberal grounds,while, on the other, wanting to promote universal values such as human rights and equality. As Donnelly (1998: 1–11) argues, contemporary international society can be seen as open (because, although European in origin, others can join if they meet specific terms and conditions) or as imperial (seeming to offer pluralism while in fact requiring extensive Westernization). O'Hagan (2005) takes a similar view, noting the complacency of pluralists such as Jackson (2000), who think that the global covenant on coexistence among states largely takes care of this by providing a Western framework for dialogue across cultures. She contrasts this with critics such as Keal (2003) and Keene (2002), who focus on the coerced unequal character of international society in which non-Western cultures were devalued and forced into Western moulds. From this perspective, pluralism is not so much about respect for multiculturalism as *de facto* assimilation. Fidler (2000), Gong (2002) and Bowden (2009: loc. 2398–448) see the ongoing inequality in the world economy as perpetuating the 'standard of civilization' logic, or, as Fidler puts it, 'the standard of liberal, globalized civilization'. These tensions echo many of the concerns in the pluralist story and suggest that contemporary international society is less stable, egalitarian and consensual than it might at first appear to be.

Linklater and Suganami (2006: 147–53) pick up this problem of expansion, having created a multicultural underpinning for international society and having caused inequality, exclusion, and the 'revolt against the West' noted in the classical expansion story. They are interested in both international order and moral progress and suggest a kind of pluralist, coexistence approach to interstate society, in which progress is measured not by the adoption of a common hegemonic culture but by the working out of a set of cross-cultural values 'which reveal that very different societies can agree on forms of human solidarity in the context of radical cultural and religious differences'. In this process, they think, lies the possibility of 'progress towards a universal community'. Cronin (1999) emphasizes the possibility for identity change on the grounds that political community is constructable, and therefore international and world society remain open to transformation. This view, however, leaves open the question as to whether what is constructed is a new consensus or a hegemonic imposition.

Assessing imperialism/colonialism and its demise in terms of the pluralist/solidarist debate produces a surprisingly mixed picture. Imperialism/colonialism was not part of the classical construction of pluralism, and it could be construed as both compatible with it (if empire is acceptable) and opposed to it (if pluralism values sovereign equality as a universal value). Solidarist attitudes towards colonialism are even more mixed. While liberal-minded solidarists would be unanimously opposed to imperialism/colonialism on many grounds, they are vulnerable to some forms of trusteeship, state-building and international administration that have strong imperialism/colonial overtones. Despite these mixed feelings, imperialism/colonialism served both pluralist and solidarist goals in highly significant ways. The main service of imperialism/colonialism to pluralism was in transplanting the European system of states to the whole of humankind, along with the classical seven primary institutions plus nationalism. It also transferred human equality, though not before it had also implanted racism and colonialism into many cultures. Imperialism/colonialism remade the political world in Western, pluralist form. The price of independence was to take on the trappings of a sovereign, territorial state participating in diplomacy and accepting international law.

The main service of imperialism/colonialism to solidarism was in moving humankind some way along the path towards an interconnected human community, or at least a world society based on some common knowledge, ideas and mutual awareness. The idea of human equality served both pluralist and solidarist ends. Imperialism/colonialism transplanted lingua francas, nationalism, sovereignty, human equality, and some elements of modernity to the four corners of the world (Ferguson 2004). For better or worse (usually both of these together), it enmeshed everyone in a single global economy. This was often a cruel and coercive process, with many casualties and huge amounts of pain and disruption to both individuals and cultures. But it cannot, and should not, be denied that, in addition to being only an abstract moral referent, it created the conditions for 'world society' and 'the community of humankind' to begin to take practical form. Humankind now knew about itself on a global scale for the first time. Imperialism/colonialism provided some of the basic tools to make that happen. The end of imperialism/colonialism left a historically unprecedented solidarist legacy in the form of the principle that all people(s) are equal.

Nationalism

In one sense there is not too much more to be said about nationalism. By the late nineteenth century it was well consolidated in Europe, underpinning the formation of new states in Germany and Italy and undoing old empires such as Austria-Hungary (whose name already gives away its fate) and the Ottoman Empire. Imperialism/colonialism transmitted it beyond Europe, where it began to eat away at the legitimacy of overseas empires. Within Europe (and Japan), nationalism began to take on extreme forms. It fused first, and quite widely, with Social Darwinism and the ideas of natural selection and survival of the fittest. Then, and more selectively, it fused with 'scientific' racism to form fascism. In that guise during the Second World War it reached a violent and exterminist peak so ghastly as to speed the delegitimation of racism, human inequality and empire once the fascist powers had been defeated. Fascism delegitimized itself, but it did not weaken the overall position of nationalism as one of the key institutions of international society. Decolonization indeed strengthened nationalism, albeit with a difficult and dangerous ongoing legacy of tension between its ethno and civic interpretations (Mayall 2000a: 39–66).

Nationalism was always primarily a pluralist institution, the main counterpoint to cosmopolitanism and therefore having little to offer to solidarists other than the idea that all peoples are equal. That remains the case. The ongoing strength of nationalism rests on its being an institution not just of interstate society but also of world society in the sense that, as demonstrated in many types of sport, it is widely internalized and embedded as a legitimate idea in most of the populations of the world. Even as the state comes under question because of globalization, nationalism still reinforces the pluralist vision of the human condition.

Dynasticism

I have already traced the demise of dynasticism in some detail, and there is not much to add here. Dynasticism as the legitimate form of rule gave way over a long period to the balance of power, nationalism and popular sovereignty, sovereign equality, and the equality of peoples. Dynastic rule was closely associated with empire, and in some ways these two institutions declined together. Dynasticism did not, like colonialism, become illegitimate. Instead, it faded away into the background, being seen as increasingly incompatible with modernity. It hung on in residual form in a few places as constitutional monarchy and in more substantive, if archaic, form mainly in some Arab countries. Political (as opposed to aristocratic) dynasties can still be found in some democracies (the US, India) and some dictatorships (North Korea, Syria). But these are now more quirks of particular domestic societies, and they do not constitute an institution of international society in the same way that aristocratic rule once did in Europe and many other parts of the world. As with imperialism/colonialism, and for many of the same reasons, the demise of dynasticism supported both pluralist and solidarist ends: pluralism because it cleared the way for an international society of sovereign equals, and solidarism because it cleared the way towards human equality.

Human equality and human rights

I argued in chapter 7 that human inequality was a primary institution up until the Second World War, that this was closely linked to dynasticism and imperialism/colonialism as supporting institutions, and that in the century up to 1945 inequality was also buttressed by 'scientific' racism and gender inequality. The norm of human inequality prevailed despite some counter-moves such as the successful campaign against slavery during the nineteenth century (Clark 2007: 37–60; Keene 2007) and moves towards human rights in the Covenant of the League of Nations. It peaked during the Second World War and collapsed afterwards, along with imperialism/colonialism. It was replaced by a norm of human equality embedded in the Charter of the United Nations and most visibly expressed in the 1948 Universal Declaration of Human Rights (UDHR). The UDHR made individual human beings 'right holders on their own behalf' (Mayall 2000a: 33). On the face of it, this by itself is an enormous advance for solidarism. Human equality is a necessary, or at least a strongly supporting, condition for human rights because without it the universality of the human rights principle cannot apply (Reus-Smit 2011a, 2011b). As also argued above, even though the shift from natural to positive law might be seen as mainly pluralist and as weakening the solidarist position, it also opened the door to the development of state-centric solidarism in this area. Under positive law, human rights are legal rather than natural, which is a weaker (because reversible) position, but in a practical sense there might not be much to choose between them.

This is not the place to enter into detailed accounts of either the complex history of human rights or the many disputes about the interpretation and implementation of them. Suffice it to say that human rights are now embodied not only in the Charter of the UN (Clark 2007: 131–51), but also in many UN conventions and committees and in many regional bodies. The UN has a Human Rights Council, and there is a body of international humanitarian law. Serious questions can be raised as to how much of this is merely rhetorical posturing and about the often feeble or ineffective or cynical responses to human rights crises (Gonzalez-Pelaez 2005). Yet it is clear that there has been some advance of state-centric solidarism on human rights and that, for all the contestation about it, human rights has acquired legitimacy as a basis for public policy and appeal for international action. Welsh (2011) sees progress since the 1990s in attaching responsibility for human rights to sovereign states (e.g., the responsibility to protect – R2P) but still also great hesitation on the part of international society to intervene on humanitarian grounds. Wheeler (2000: 40–8, 283–8) argues that since the end of the Cold War a new norm of humanitarian intervention is emerging, linked to legitimation by the UN Security Council. Mayall (2000b: 64) and Donnelly (1998: 20–3) both see human rights as having becoming influential in international society, albeit far from universally.

It is probably fair to say that human rights is at best still only emergent as an institution of international society, though it does have a wide standing as a legitimating principle. It is much more strongly held in some parts of international society, mainly the West, than in others, and elements of it are strongly opposed by states that fear erosion of their right to nonintervention, most prominently Russia and China. Indeed, as noted above, there is a quite widespread view within the English School that human rights has in some ways become the new 'standard of civilization' wielded by the West against the rest. The Vincentian idea that sovereignty is a function of recognition by international society, and therefore comes with conditions about human rights, opens two opportunities. First, human rights can be promoted by liberalizing the internal practices of states. Second, there is an opportunity to circumvent the decolonization deal of sovereign equality for all by reviving the 'standard of civilization', by declaring some states, or at least their governments, not fit for membership. As always, who does such declaring is a crucial issue: an authorized collective body such as the UN Security Council, or some self-declared standard-bearers such as the mooted 'League of Democracies'? As human rights becomes more influential within international society, it probably cannot avoid resurrecting something like the 'standard of civilization', albeit now doing so within a universal international society rather than being about the unequal relations between insiders and outsiders. Arguments about what human rights are, and what responsibilities and obligations states have towards them both within, and more especially outside, their borders, are not going to be resolved soon. This limited movement is nevertheless a gain for solidarism, even though the emergence of human rights as an institution of international society looks as if it might be a long and turbulent story like that of the emergence of the market. But, that said, there can be no doubt that human equality is now widely and deeply accepted as an institution of international society, providing a stable foundation on which the evolution of human rights can be built.

Democracy

Like human rights, and quite closely associated with it, democracy is an emergent but still hotly contested institution of international society. It is the counterpoint to the demise of dynasticism in the sense that both represent primary institutions that define the legitimate form of government within the state members of 'civilized' international society. But democracy has not yet acquired the general legitimacy that dynasticism once had as the norm for government, nor has it been as widely successful as nationalism in the role of legitimizing politics. Democracy promotion has nevertheless achieved some legitimacy within international society, and this is reflected in the practices and policies of a lot of IGOs (Stivachtis 2006: 102; Clark 2009c: 563, 568–9). As well as conditionalities for membership and/or access based on democratic values, many INGOs have achieved limited official standing within IGOs (Clark 1995; Clark 2007: 189–93) and increasingly play significant roles in the promotion of solidarist values, from environmentalism through human rights to restraints on war. Mayall (2000a: 86; 2000b: 64–8) argues that, even though democracy is far from universal, democratic values such as human rights, representative government and the rule of law have become influential, perhaps even the standard of legitimacy, in international society. But democracy promotion is still essentially a Western and especially an American project (Stivachtis 2006: 103; Clark 2009c). Democracy promotion has been a longstanding part of US foreign policy dating back at least to Wilsonianism (Clark 2009c: 564–5).

After the Second World War, democracy became consolidated as a primary institution within Western international society. Democracy promotion was part of US Cold War strategy against the Soviet Union (Stivachtis 2006: 107–8), albeit accompanied by a good deal of hypocritical, if pragmatic, support for anti-Soviet dictatorships. Disagreements over policies and alignments meant that being a democracy never earned India much favour from the US during the Cold War. There was a burst of enthusiasm after 1989, when democracy seemed to defeat its last great rival and become the dominant form of government within international society (e.g., Franck 1992). This led to a largely American debate about whether to exploit the tide of history to pursue democracy promotion more aggressively by creating a League or Concert of Democracies to act towards that end and to circumvent the paralysis of the UN Security

Council (Clark 2009c). Although this idea did not, in the end, become the organizing principle for US foreign policy, it has certainly played a role in such things as the US cultivating a coalition of Asian democracies as part of its hedging strategy against the rise of China. As can be seen from China's paranoid crackdown on its own civil society in response to the Arab Spring, democracy has enough clout as an international norm to make authoritarian regimes feel existentially challenged.

Part of the impetus to promote democracy comes from the fact that it is seen as a necessary condition for both human rights and peace (Clark 2007: 153–4; 2009c: 570–1). Among its promoters there is consequently a tendency to revive 'standard of civilization' thinking by equating democracy with 'civilization' and non-democracy with 'barbarity' (Stivachtis 2006: 111). This type of thinking opens up a classic rift between the essential openness and tolerance of pluralism, with its consequent inefficiency for decision-making, and the more efficient and solidarist idea of a League or Concert of Democracies, which then re-creates a two-tier, insider/outsider structure of international society, where legitimation is sought more in democratic values than in an international consensus (Clark 2009). This kind of promotionalism, as with human rights, raised tensions not only with nonintervention but also with the problem that the social conditions necessary to sustain democracy and human rights as a 'standard of civilization' simply do not exist in many parts of the world (Mayall 2000a: 81120).

Even although it is still contested and emergent as an institution, democracy has come far enough to count as a firm development towards solidarism in international society.

Environmental stewardship

Like human rights, environmental stewardship is at best still only emergent as an institution of international society. It is unclear how much normative leverage it has acquired, but this could change quickly if some crisis created a more unified opinion about priorities. It rose to consciousness later than human rights, and it has been more a pragmatic response to observed problems than a fundamental and longstanding question of political philosophy. Since the 1970s, it too has acquired a host of international conferences, conventions, treaties and protocols and also some standing in international law. And, as with human rights, there is both much diplomatic engagement by non-state actors and a big question about how much of this is just rhetorical posturing and how much substantive commitment. As with the right to food, even if there is agreement about the problem, there is large scope for legitimate disagreement about what should be done. And since, even more so than the right to food, environmental stewardship has potentially enormous implications for how the global economy is run, these disagreements have been deep. There is also still disagreement about whether or not the problem exists, though this could change in the face of a suitably grave and obvious crisis. Environmental stewardship probably now registers as a primary institution, but more within a logic of coexistence than with the force of a joint project.

There is now beginning to be a body of English School writing on this institution. Bull (1977: 293–5) has a brief passage in which he argues that disagreement about environmental problems is intrinsic to the issues concerned and would be present whether the political order was an interstate society or not. He acknowledges that the interstate society is unlikely to be able to tackle such global issues fully, but he maintains that it is the best place to start. Interestingly, he came quite close to a state-centric solidarist position, arguing that a greater global environmental consciousness at the level of world society might best be constructed through initial measures of cooperation by states. Reus-Smit (1996) hints at the emergence of a green moral purpose of the state, and Linklater (Linklater and Suganami 2006: 218–19, 269; Linklater 2011b) sees environmental damage as part of his harm project (discussed in chapter 8). Hurrell (2007b: 216–36) follows on from Bull, emphasizing the inescapable role of states both as part of the problem and as part of the solution, and charting the way in which environmental issues have pushed forward non-state actors and the process of global governance. He adds to this mix the need for environmentalists to pitch their normative ('one world') case to the pluralist multiculturalism of world society ('many worlds').

Jackson (1996b, 2000: 170–8) is in no doubt that environmental stewardship is a solidarist institution, and, to the extent that it continues to emerge as an institution of international society, this will strengthen the solidarist position. Interestingly, he goes out of his way to distinguish environmental stewardship from human rights cosmopolitanism by attributing to it a distinct logic of 'custodial responsibility for the planet' (ibid.: 177). This raises an issue familiar from debates about environmental security as to whether the referent object is the environment itself, as Jackson implies, or the capacity of the environment to sustain existing and desired levels of human civilization. If the environment itself is the referent object, then Jackson is correct. But if the environment is a means to the sustainability of human life and civilization, then his separate logic is more questionable. The 'life and civilization' logic would open a link between environmental stewardship and human rights, in which the right to a liveable environment is constructed as a human right. From that perspective, the emergence of environmental stewardship as an institution of international society might be more a derivative of human rights than an entirely new social concept. There are also synergies with development, both because development depends on a sustainable environment and because dealing with environmental issues almost certainly requires the resources generated by higher levels of development. Arcadian solutions to the pressure that humankind places on the environment raise the problem of what to do with the several billion people whose food supplies depend on industrial agriculture.

Paterson (2005) is concerned mainly to critique the thinness of the English School's writing on this topic and the dogged state-centrism of the approach of Bull, Jackson and Hurrell, as well as to establish a Marxist critique of the state and international society. Yet in the process he suggests that there has indeed been considerable development of state-centric solidarism on this issue. Hurrell and Sengupta's (2012) empirical analysis of global climate politics could be read as supporting this, given the erosion of a clear North–South divide on environmental politics and its replacement by a limited amount of convergence of interest and outlook.

Falkner (2012) follows Jackson in seeing environmental stewardship as a value in itself. He focuses on the greening of international society, tracing the first glimmerings back to before the First World War but the main developments arising from the 1960s. He tracks the rise of environmental norms within international society, citing the 1972 Stockholm Conference and the Rio Summit of 1992 as particular landmarks. He shows how environmental norms have interacted with, and changed the substance of, other primary institutions such as sovereignty, international law and the market. His process-tracing approach is reminiscent of Mayall's (1990) study of nationalism, and how its emergence changed the meaning and practices of sovereignty, territoriality and war. Falkner concludes that environmental stewardship is still only an emergent primary institution. Rhetorical acceptance is much ahead of practical policies, which in turn are probably inadequate in the face of the problems. But, for all these shortcomings, there is a clear case that environmental stewardship is now established as a legitimate basis for moral claims in international society (see also Palmujoki 2013).

The review of these fourteen primary institutions suggests that there can be no doubt that solidarists have not just a necessary normative perspective but also a significant empirical story to tell. In social structural terms, the evolution of international society remains as dynamic and as contested as it has always been, but the general drift favours solidarism, most obviously, but not only, in state-centric form.

CONCLUSIONS TO PART III

This part started from the idea that the pluralist/solidarist debate was not about irreconcilable opposites but reflected a normative tension that was an enduring and necessary feature of thinking in terms of international and world society. Chapter 6 teased out the essence of the pluralist position in the works of its leading proponents. Chapter 7 interrogated the pluralist position in terms of a distinctive set of primary institutions, looking at these in the historical context of their emergence. Chapter 8 reviewed the solidarist literature, distinguishing between cosmopolitan and state-centric understandings of solidarism and arguing that, for the most part, its advocates are studiously moderate in their approach and fully aware of the constraints of the interstate society. Chapter 9 extended the historical story of primary institutions, contending that the practices within many ostensibly pluralist institutions have evolved in solidarist directions (war, international law, diplomacy, colonialism, dynasticism) and that more purely solidarist institutions are emergent (human rights, development, democracy, environmental stewardship). Non-state actors are playing a significant role in the normative development of international society. In a structural sense, international society is, from the very beginning, persistently and highly dynamic. Some old institutions die, new ones arise, and many of those that endure are internally transformed by changing principles of legitimation and changing practices.

The theoretical debates about pluralism and solidarism and the empirical analysis of the evolving normative structure of international society point strongly to a complex blending and interplay of elements from both sides. There is now room for thinking that, in many ways, the market, multilateralism and the host of secondary institutions associated with them have taken over from war, the balance of power and their derivatives as the institutions that shape how sovereignty and territoriality are understood. Pluralism and solidarism are neither conceptually nor in practice, necessarily or even probably, mutually exclusive positions. The basic arrangement of international society continues to reflect pluralist norms rather than cosmopolitan ones, but state-centric solidarism is quite strongly in play across many primary institutions. Mayall (2000a: 25) was correct to point out that the end of the Cold War reduced the need for coexistence and opened the way to a more solidarist international society. But so far his fears that excessive solidarism will destabilize international society have not been borne out. It is true, as Clark (2005: 26–8) warns, that solidarist international societies can tend to narrow the range of rightful membership by stiffening the criteria for entry. That was the point of the 'standard of civilization' and remains the point of contemporary proposals for a League of Democracies. Clark sees this as having been a growing problem since the First and Second world wars (ibid.: 109–29, 173–89), and it is clear from the discussion of human rights and democracy that such dynamics are powerfully in play. Yet it is also clear that there have been many changes, sometimes quite profound and widespread, towards more solidarist practices in what constitutes rightful behaviour. This is true from imperialism/colonialism and war, through the economy, to human rights and, in a modest way, environmental stewardship. There have also been solidarist changes in diplomacy and communication, with non-state actors having become much more engaged as a legitimate part of the process.

On top of these changes in interstate society, there are also very significant changes in world society. Up to a century ago, relatively few people thought of themselves as members of the human race in any meaningful way. Empire was common, outright slavery only recently pushed to the margins, unequal status among humans routine on grounds of class, caste, race or gender, and the idea of a common humanity very marginal except within some religious traditions. Few people knew much or cared much about what was happening in other parts of the planet. Now many more people do know at least something about what goes on elsewhere, and up to a point care about it, even if very unevenly and in ways heavily shaped by the skewed patterns of media attention. For the past half century there has been a general acceptance that all humans are equal, even if this is still violated in practice in many ways and places. This has fed a growing demand for rights. People everywhere now understand that they are embedded in a single global economy (like it or not), and up to a point that they are also embedded in a single global culture and a single global environment (again, like it or not). Things such as nationalism, the market, popular music and football, not to mention Facebook, Twitter and Google, are very widely shared understandings and practices. These developments provide the substance for the increased interplay between interstate society and world society. Potentially they contribute to the stability of international society by embedding ideas not just in state elites but in the minds of the peoples as well.

Hurrell (2007b: 1–21, 287–98) is thus quite right both to see this as mixed-actor, multi-sector international society in which the operation of power and norms are deeply entangled and to argue that the pluralist vision in any pure sense simply cannot work in today's world. Pluralism is neither intellectually nor historically a free-standing, singular position. Intellectually, it is chained to solidarism by the endless permutations of the dilemma between order and justice. Historically, it has perhaps never been present as a pure or static practice. When history is closest to the pluralist model, there are not only always big changes and evolutions going on but also other things happening which are not pluralist. And, as has been shown in chapters 7 and 9, the historical unfolding of the primary institutions of international society reveals a powerful dynamic of ongoing change and evolution and, within that, both the growth of tensions and contradictions among the elements of the pluralist package and an increasing array of solidarist practices and institutions. Bellamy (2005: 292) rightly argues that there is a 'need to think much more carefully about how different types of solidarism emerge', and I hope the analysis in these chapters at least begins to answer that call.

Like Hurrell, Armstrong (1998) also seems correct with his idea of 'social states' as being in continuous negotiation with international society about interplay between their own identities and the institutions of international society. Thus, Vincent's (1978: 37; 1986: 150–2; 1992: 253–61) vision of a 'world society', in which states have somewhat converged and transnational actors and individuals all have rights in relation to each other, is, in a modest way, coming into being. But Williams's (2005) caution that, contrary to the hopes of some solidarists, world society is more thoroughly and deeply fragmented and diverse, and therefore more embeddedly pluralist, than international society is also highly relevant. There isn't a ready-made cosmopolitan alternative to the states-system, but there is increasing interplay and in some ways merger between the different pluralisms in the interstate and world society domains.

These conclusions reinforce Reus-Smit's (2002: 502–5) argument that the underlying assumptions of pluralism are untenable as seen from a constructivist perspective. Its sharp separation of interstate society from global civil society is simply not sustainable empirically, as subsequently shown by Clark's (2007) study of 'world society' influences on the norms of interstate society from the anti-slavery movement onwards. Neither is the idea of international society as a practical association, because the actual practice of international society requires a significant degree of shared identity in the form of the criteria for legitimate membership. That in turn undermines the simplification of Jackson's 'situational ethics', which may be part of what is going on but cannot function without some prior moral decisions about what responsibilities states have beyond their borders. Pluralism cannot by itself represent the normative character of international society. It cannot detach itself from natural law, which was dominant for much of its formative historical process. It cannot be just about the 'is' rather than the 'ought', because the 'is' is not static but in seemingly permanent evolution. And it cannot be just about order because, as the impact of nationalism makes clear, the natural evolution of international society is continuously changing the moral foundations of order.

10 ONGOING DEBATES AND EMERGENT AGENDAS

The previous chapters have sketched out both what the English School is and what it has done. They have set out the main concepts, questions, debates and lines of research and shown the ongoing dynamism of the English School's 'great conversation' for more than half a century. This final chapter turns forward from the past and the present to the future. It looks first at the traditional, and in some cases perennial, debates that will remain a continuing core feature of the English School literature. It then turns to some newer debates that seem likely to become part of this core, and finally it touches on one emergent agenda that might become a new site for the further development of English School thinking.

Traditional debates

There are four well-established mainstream debates that are likely to remain central to the English School conversation: about the expansion story; between the pluralist and solidarist normative perspectives; about methods; and about the distinction between international system and international society. The first three of these have been largely covered in the preceding chapters, and I will only sum up here. The fourth has been touched upon at various points above but gets a fuller account here.

The expansion story

As set out in chapter 5, this core English School story dates back to British Committee days. It is in many ways the source not only for the distinctiveness of the English School from other approaches to IR, and for the concept of primary institutions, but also for much of the pluralist/solidarist debate. Given this centrality, not to mention the intrinsic interest of the project, it is not surprising that the expansion story remains a lively part of the literature. The original telling was broadly pluralist, with Mayall making the initial critique on the basis of nationalism and the market. He looked to put the story into a broader perspective, and more needs to be done to link the changes in international society during the nineteenth century to the general impact of the revolutions of modernity. More recently, the emphasis has been on postcolonial revisions to the expansion story, bringing in more non-Western voices, perspectives and experiences. One part of this has aimed at building up the West–non-West encounter as a two-way story, in the process dissolving some of the force of that distinction. Another part has aimed at being more open and explicit about the institution of imperialism/colonialism and the role of coercion and inequality in the making of contemporary international society. Such revisions are important not only in getting the story right but also in how the story plays to its contemporary global audience. The expansion story is in some ways the flagship of the English School. It provides a distinctive picture of how the world came to be as it is and to have the problems that it has. Initially this story was constructed by and for a Western (mainly European) audience. Increasingly it speaks to a global audience, much of which was very differently positioned from Europe in the expansion process. As the English School 'goes global' (Y. Zhang 2014), all of those involved will want, and should be encouraged, to put their own histories into the story. Asians are already retelling their side of the encounter, and there is more to do there. Interestingly, the Americas generally and the US in particular are still only weakly represented in how the expansion story is told. Yet they played a crucial role in the early part of the expansion from European to Western, not only increasing the size of international society but also changing some of its institutions. This part of the story needs to be filled in. It is a safe bet that the debates about it will remain vigorous for a long time.

The pluralist/solidarist debate

The pluralist/solidarist debate, covered extensively in Part III, is the normative heart of the English School's conversation. It provides the basic framing for the perennial and permanently necessary discussion of how order and justice relate to each other in an ever changing global system, which is one of the great strengths and attractions of the English School's societal approach to IR. This debate will therefore remain a core feature of the School's conversation. As it has done in the past, it will continually adapt to new events and circumstances such as those created by the global war on terrorism and the rise of concerns about environmental harm. Because it has the rich history of the expansion story (itself continuously expanding) to draw on, this debate can usefully deploy older concepts, such as *the standard of civilization* and *raison de système*, to interrogate and critique new ones, such as human rights and conditionality. As noted at several places in preceding chapters, English School authors have already made this link, illustrating the advantage of keeping a long historical perspective in play when thinking about IR. The pluralist/solidarist debate is not about one or the other winning or both agreeing to some bland compromise. It is about sustaining a creative tension in thinking normatively about the endlessly unfolding and changing problematique of how to get the best mix of order and justice under any given circumstances. I hope the clarifying distinction between cosmopolitan and state-centric solidarism made in chapter 8 might remove some unnecessary heat from this debate by making clear that there is more common ground than is at first apparent. But essential normative tensions will always remain and need to be argued over, both in themselves and in their applications.

Methods

The English School's debate about methods goes back to the British Committee discussions and Bull's (in)famous defence of the classical approach against US-led behaviouralism and scientific methods. As discussed in chapter 3, the English School's complacency about methodological pluralism has been attacked as mere conceptual sloppiness, and the methods debate has been reopened by Cornelia Navari. Because of its commitment to a holistic approach to thinking about IR, the English School is both methodologically and substantively distinct from realism, liberalism, Marxism and constructivism. Its blending of normative and historical structural elements enables it not only to address the most pressing problems of the day but also to investigate deeper questions about the structure and evolution of international systems and societies. Its strong historical commitment makes it more open to the postcolonial influences than the more ideologically committed IR theories, and this equips it well to deal with a culturally and materially more polycentric world. This capacity explains both why the English School has flourished during recent decades and why it is, and will be, increasingly popular as IR becomes less of 'an American social science' and more a globally distributed activity reflecting local as well as Western roots. Given that IR as a whole tends to evolve when new methods (or even just new methodological fashions) arise, it seems reasonable to expect this debate to be ongoing.

The international system/international society distinction

The drawing of a clear distinction between international system and international society goes right back to the debates within the British Committee and is foundational to the English School's three traditions. Vigezzi (2005: 83, 93, 292–6) features it as the British Committee's major contribution to IR theory and the key difference from the system-oriented IR theory developing in the US. Like much else in English School theory, this distinction, or at least the strong formulation of it, originates with Bull (1977: 3–20; see also Gills 1989: 106–9; Stivachtis 2010). Bull and Watson's (1984b: 1) definition that embodies it is widely cited within the English School:

> a group of states (or, more generally, a group of independent political communities) which not merely form a system, in the sense that the behaviour of each is a necessary factor in the calculations of the others, but also have established by dialogue and consent common rules and institutions for the conduct of their relations, and recognise their common interest in maintaining these arrangements.

System in this definition is basically about physical interaction and calculation, while society is about the structuring of interaction through shared rules, norms and institutions.

Yet, despite its foundational quality, the system/society distinction has for long been contested. The grounds for this challenge are that one can cover most or perhaps all of the ground claimed by physical system theories from within a social structural theory, whereas the reverse move is not possible. The key to such an interpretation is the high degree of overlap between physical and social systems. All human social interaction presupposes the existence of physical interaction of some sort, and physical interaction without social content is, if not quite impossible, at least rather rare and marginal in human affairs (de Almeida 2001). Berridge (1980: 86–7) was an early critic of Bull for separating system and society. Wight (1991: 39) leans in this direction: 'it might be argued cogently that at any given moment the greater part of the totality of international relationships reposes on custom rather than force.' Much more forcefully, James (1993) demonstrates in detail that Bull's distinction between the two is shot through with ambiguities and difficulties, leading him to the conclusion that international system is a meaningless idea and that international society is the key concept. As noted in chapter 4, Jackson (2000: 113–16) interprets Bull's 'system' as representing not a physical but a social (i.e., Hobbesian) interpretation to cover the domain of realism. Adam Watson (1987, 1990), though being a party to Bull's distinction, concludes definitively that 'no international system as defined by Bull has operated without some regulatory rules and institutions' (Watson 1987: 151–2). Buzan (2004: 98–108) makes a call for the English School to drop the idea of international system and to focus instead on constructing a typology of international societies that will cover the Hobbesian side of international relations. He argues (ibid.: 100) that

> If all human interaction is in some sense social and rule-bound, then what results is not a distinction between international systems and international societies, but a spectrum of international societies ranging from weak, or thin, or poorly developed, or conflictual, to strong, or thick or well developed, or cooperative.

This idea that society goes all the way down is supported by Williams (2010a).

Despite this assault, the idea of international system still has firm defenders. Little (2005) defends Bull's distinction against James's attack, though he does leave the door open to resolution in a typology of international societies. He deploys a similar defence against Buzan's call for the dropping of international system, while again leaving open the door to a typology of international societies (Little 2009: 81–7; 2011). Dunne (2008: 276–9) also argues against the dropping of international system.

It is fair to say that the English School remains divided on this question. It has been so for a long time, and so this debate is likely to continue. The rift is similar to that between 'all the way down' constructivists and those allowing at least some 'rump materialism'. This points to an epistemological divide that is likely to remain durable. In the case of the English School, however, this question might well be pursued in terms of a debate about types of international society, on which more in the next section.

Newer debates

In addition to these long-established debates, there are three newer ones that in various ways grow out of the traditional debates but have taken, or are taking, distinctive forms of their own. They are about primary institutions, types of international society, and regional international societies and the meaning of 'global level' international society. At the end of Part II, I raised two questions:

1 How are primary institutions to be theorized? Are they just empirically observed, or is there some principle of differentiation, whether functional or something else, that can be used to put bookends around the possible set?
2 Is it possible to create comprehensive taxonomies of types of international society? If it is, do we need the concept of international system that has been an important part of the English School's classical triad, or does the system element reduce to a mere rump of interaction capacity?

Now that chapters 7 and 9 have given a fuller picture of the primary institutions in play in contemporary Western-global international society, we are in a better position to consider these questions. I will address the issue of how to theorize primary institutions in the next subsection and that of taxonomies in the one following that. The question about the system/society distinction has already been covered.

Primary institutions

Primary institutions were defined in chapter 2 and have played throughout subsequent chapters. The theoretical discussion of them in the conclusions to Part II noted that they were the key both to thinking about the structure and evolution of international societies and to differentiating regional international societies from the Western-global one and each other. They also played a significant role both in comparing international societies and in constructing typologies of them. The discussion of the pluralist/solidarist debate in Part III was framed by primary institutions in two ways. First, the basic division in the debate was set up in terms of tensions between different primary institutions, particularly the pluralist emphasis on sovereignty and nonintervention as the key to international order and the solidarist concern with human rights as necessary to justice and legitimacy. Second, the actual evolution of contemporary international society was set up in empirical terms of how its primary institutions have emerged and evolved over the past five centuries, and how that story plays into pluralist and solidarist characterizations of international society. This discussion of primary institutions has been based almost entirely on what has been said about them in the English School literature. That literature is itself based on either empirical observation of such institutions at work in historical and present-day international societies and/or normative promotion of (or opposition to) the strengthening of primary institutions thought to be desirable, such as human rights or environmental stewardship. There are justified objections that this approach lacks rigour and is open to the selection biases of authors (Finnemore 2001; Wilson 2012). In Part III I nevertheless treated this empirical approach to primary institutions as unproblematic for two reasons: first, in order to survey the English School literature on this topic and, second, to flesh out both the pluralist–solidarist debate and the evolving social structure of international society.

But the question remains: can primary institutions be theorized and, if so, how? It is tempting to follow Bull (1977: 53–7), whose conception of society comes out of a kind of sociological functionalism in which all human societies must be founded on three understandings: about security against violence, observance of agreements, and rules about property rights. It is quite easy to start fitting the primary institutions of international society into this functional template:

- security against violence: nonintervention, balance of power, war (rules of), great power management, human rights;
- observance of agreements: diplomacy, international law;
- property rights: territoriality, sovereignty, colonialism, nationalism, dynasticism.

Functional logic is also implicit in the legitimacy framing from Clark and others discussed in chapter 7. This emphasizes rightful membership and rightful conduct and focuses on how pluralist and solidarist understandings differ on these. Given their tolerance for cultural and political diversity, pluralists have looser criteria for both membership and rightful conduct. Solidarists defend tighter definitions of 'standards of civilization' and promote more rule-bound social structures across a wider range of issues. They therefore necessarily have tighter criteria for both membership and rightful conduct.

Buzan (2004: 187–90), with the particular needs of second-order societies in mind, adds two more categories to Bull's three: membership (sovereignty, dynasticism, democracy) and authoritative communication (diplomacy). Donnelly (2006: 11–12) is working on an approach to primary institutions based on six functions: making rules, regulating conflicts, regulating the use of force, regulating ownership and exchange, communicating and interacting, and aggregating interests and power (i.e., enabling collective action). Schouenborg (2011) critiques these schemes and tries to construct a functional set that is tied less to modernity. Buzan and Albert have pushed the functional line a little further by trying to think about primary institutions in the light of functional differentiation theory.[1] This posits three types of differentiation: segmentary (like units), stratificatory (hierarchically ordered) and functional (where subsystems are defined by the coherence of particular types of activity). This too provides a way of ordering primary institutions: nationalism, territoriality and sovereignty are clearly segmentary; great power management, hegemony, colonialism, human inequality and dynasticism are clearly stratificatory; and international law, diplomacy, the market and environmental stewardship are clearly functional.

Such functional approaches are useful in at least two ways. First, they provide schemes for grouping institutions into clusters of like kind. Second, they provide a template that can be applied to historical cases in order to look for their primary institutions. But what they do not, and probably cannot, do is to provide any bookends that might define or limit the whole set of possible primary institutions. In this regard, primary institutions are in the same boat as sectors and function systems. As Stichweh (2013) says of the latter:

> A theory looking for synthetic processes of system formation knows no inherent limits to the number of function systems it will be able to describe. It only needs an abstract catalogue of (necessary) constituents of any function system and can do historical analyses on the basis of such a catalogue of constituents which in itself has a provisional status. It can be enlarged and corrected on the basis of new analytical insights or from new insights won in historical studies about individual function systems.

In other words, there can be no fixed set of primary institutions (or sectors, or function systems) because they are emergent from the complex processes of human society. Human societies can be, and have been, almost endlessly inventive about the social forms and structures that they generate. To date, human societies have exhibited astounding diversity over time and place, and there is no reason at all to think that everything that could be invented has been.

If the set of primary institutions is potentially infinite, then empirical identification is the only way of determining what such institutions exist in any given case. Functional and comparative approaches can help with this but don't determine it. It is not clear that a comprehensive set of functions can be generated that would not itself fall victim to the infinite creativity of human societies, and, even within any of the functional categories listed above, the possible institutions that might address each function is itself probably infinite. Relying on empirical identification means that how primary institutions are defined becomes crucial to the coherence of the collective enterprise, and this remains a problem for English School theory. The classical English School literature is pretty unclear about defining primary institutions (see the critique in Buzan 2004: 167–76). Holsti (2004: 18–24) has taken a lead by seeking an operational definition that offers three fairly precise criteria for identifying primary institutions:

- the existence of patterned, recurrent practices;
- the existence of coherent sets of ideas/beliefs that frame these practices and make them purposive;
- the presence of norms, rules and etiquettes that both prescribe and proscribe legitimate behaviour.

Buzan (2004: 167) opts for a more general definition:

- that they are relatively fundamental and durable practices that are evolved more than designed; and
- that they are constitutive of actors and their patterns of legitimate activity in relation to each other.

Some others are also working on this problem. Wilson (2012) offers a method for identifying primary institutions through the perceptions of diplomats and statespersons. Navari is convening a project to look at whether the constitutional documents of IGOs can be used as an empirical source for identifying the primary institutions on which the secondary ones rest. And, as mentioned at the end of chapter 3, the opening to practice theory seems to offer another approach to the problem of identifying primary institutions. The potentiality of this is indicated by the fact that both of the attempted definitions of primary institutions just cited refer to practices.

Given the centrality of primary institutions to the English School's work, this is an area in which more work urgently needs to be done. Holsti's approach is a useful formalization of the definition but leads him, controversially, to drop two of the classic primary institutions – the balance of power and great power management – that are central to much English School literature. Buzan's approach highlights some essential features, but it is too general to give a clear enough answer to the question of how we know whether something is a primary institution or not. Wilson's approach could provide a clear line of evidence, but it is open to the critique that what practitioners see in their view from the coal-face of international relations may not actually give a fair representation of what primary institutions are in play. Mining the constitutional documents of IGOs might well tell us something useful about the primary institutions of modern international society, but it will be of no help as a method for premodern international societies that did not have secondary institutions. And almost nothing has been done to think about whether or how the concept of primary institutions can or should be applied to world society.

In the absence of a clear, or at least clearer, definition of primary institutions and some degree of consensus about it, it is difficult to come to

agreement about how to understand the evolution of international societies, and how to differentiate contemporaneous regional international societies from each other and from the Western-global one. The waters are also
muddied in considering whether or not various things should be considered as primary institutions. Is hegemony an institution for at least
parts of contemporary international society, as argued by Wight, Watson,
Simpson and Clark? Should development be considered a contemporary
institution and the successor to imperialism/colonialism, given the fre-
quency with which it turns up in the constitutional documents of IGOs?
And, while human equality is pretty much universally accepted as a
primary institution, how do we understand human rights, democracy and
environmental stewardship? They are strongest in the Western core, but
not accepted universally even there, and are much more contested
globally.

Part of the definitional question about primary institutions needs to take
into account who should recognize and practise them. Is it only state elites,
or also wider elites, and even in some sense the people as a whole? As
Gaskarth (2012) also argues, primary institutions cannot be reproduced
without practitioners socially equipped to make them work. As discussed
earlier in relation to Wendt (1999), it makes a difference to the stability
and durability of any social structure both how (consent/belief, calculation,
coercion), and how widely, primary institutions are internalized. Practice
theory may have something to offer here. In contemporary international
society, for example, sovereignty, territoriality, nonintervention, diplomacy, international law, great power management, nationalism, self-
determination (not all versions), popular sovereignty and equality of
people(s) are all pretty deeply internalized and not widely or deeply contested as either principles or practices at the level of state elites. Particular
instances or applications may excite controversy – for example, resent-
ments of great power management or opposition to some self-determination bids based on cultural nationalism. But the basic institutions of pluralist
interstate society have wide support among states, and pretty wide support
among peoples and non-state actors (NSAs). Most liberation movements
seek sovereignty. Most NSAs, especially economic ones, want and need a
stable legal framework. Although these institutions were originally imposed
coercively by the West, it is far from clear that they are now held in place
primarily by Western power and influence. Even if Western power declined,
it does not seem unreasonable to think that most of these pluralist institutions would remain in place, as too might the modest level of commitment
to environmental stewardship.

The same cannot yet be said for some of the solidarist elements of
contemporary international society. Should the backing for human rights,

R2P and humanitarian intervention by the West weaken, it remains an open question how much standing they would retain as global institutions, even though they would retain strong constituencies of interstate support both regionally and more widely in the transnational and interhuman domains. At the global interstate level they are perhaps held in place more by calculation and coercion than by belief or doxa. Whether the same is true of the market and its derivatives is an interesting, important and difficult question. While many states support the market out of belief, many others adhere to it because of calculation or soft forms of coercion. One does not see much of gunboats being sent in to open markets as was done during colonial times, but, for most periphery states, access to aid, loans and markets is frequently made conditional on compliance with market rules.

It is probably the case that primary institutions cannot be theorized in the sense of being derived from some general principles. Nor can the possible set be delimited in any abstract or general way. Functional approaches to primary institutions offer some insight, some classificatory leverage, and a useful template for conducting comparative studies. But the empirical approach seems likely to remain the principal line of understanding for primary institutions, and for that to progress the English School needs to work more on the criteria for identifying and defining them. Given the centrality of this concept to English School theory, both structural and normative, and the ever unfolding landscape of primary institutions in practice, this is certain to remain a core subject of discussion.

Types of international society

That international societies can and do come in different forms is inherent to the comparative historical work of Watson and Wight discussed in chapter 4. It is intrinsic both to the debates between pluralists and solidarists and to the idea of a variable set of primary institutions. Functional approaches also frame the basis for differentiating types of international society, as does Wendt's (1992) famous proposition that 'anarchy is what states make of it'. The basis for a typology of international societies is thus inherent in the whole English School canon. Despite this, it has not until recently become a focus for debate. Nobody has really taken up Wight's typological initiative, and the comparative historical work of Wight and Watson has somehow failed to inspire any tidy-minded taxonomists to derive a general scheme from it. Perhaps Linklater's project on harm conventions will reopen this debate. Most of the English School's discussion has been about the evolution of contemporary international society, both empirically and aspirationally, and not much interest has been shown in either theoretical or empirical cases of international society rooted outside the modern Western tradition.

A key impetus for this new interest is that a typology of international societies is one way of addressing, and possibly resolving, the differences within the English School about the standing of international system as something distinct from international society, a physical logic beyond the social one. If a typology of international societies can incorporate much or all of what is now discussed as 'international system', then the need for the system concept disappears. Buzan (2004: 190–5; see above in Conclusions to Part III) argues for exactly that in setting out four types of international society: power political, coexistence, cooperative and convergence. In this reasoning, the key question is not about the distinction between physical and social systems but about how any physical-social system is structured. What is the dominant type of interaction? What are the dominant units? What is the distribution of capability? What is the interaction capacity of the system? What type of social structure is it, and how is it maintained? It is important to note that this move does not take the physical out of the analysis altogether. Physical elements such as the distribution of power and the nature of interaction capacity remain central to the analysis of all social systems. What changes is that the physical aspect ceases to provide the principal basis for distinguishing one type of international system from another. Instead of thinking in a frame of two basic forms (international systems and international societies), this move pushes one inexorably down the path of seeking a classification scheme for a spectrum of types of international society.

Quite what that spectrum should look like remains an open question, as does the issue of whether it is a good idea or not to ditch the concept of system. Buzan's scheme is probably too West-centric, or perhaps just too simple. It does suggest how the system logic could be covered by power-political institutions, but it may well have difficulty encompassing both non-Western cases such as the classical Chinese tribute system or the social structure of the classical Islamic world. There is a need to move away from the tyranny of liberal forms of international society in English School thinking, perhaps by returning to the comparative historical work of Wight and Watson, or by examining the international society logics of other ideologies such as fascism and communism. As already hinted at in preceding chapters, the English School has begun to open up at least the beginnings of a distinction in the European case between dynastic and modern forms of international society. This type of thinking needs to be pushed further and extended to other types of international society both within and beyond the West.

Regional international societies and the meaning of 'global level' international society

This new debate was reviewed at the end of chapter 4. The classical English School accounts of contemporary international society largely submerged the regional level in their concern with the development and problems of global-level international society. With the 'rise of the rest' and the relative decline of Western power and influence, there is good reason to expect that interest in regional international society will increase. This will be so partly because regions are likely to become more important within the overall global scheme of things, and because universalist Western values will be more subject to cultural challenge. Western-global international society incorporates an array of peripheral regional international societies that are in varying degrees of integration with, subordination to, and alienation from the Western core. Often, as most obviously in East Asia, the degree of coherence (or not) of the regional international society is directly connected to agreement or disagreement over whether the local states feel more integrated with or more alienated from the Western core. Although much common ground will remain at the global level on things such as nationalism, human equality, sovereignty, diplomacy and, up to a point, international law and the market, it is reasonable to expect that regions will want to differentiate themselves according to their own cultural and political dispositions. The degree of this differentiation, and whether it is regionally coherent or not, will vary a lot from place to place and will be the subject of local contestation. The EU can be seen as a leader in this process of regional differentiation, even though it is part of the core.

In this way, thinking about regional international society, or putting the global-level international society into core–periphery perspective, raises necessary questions about how the structure of global-level international society should be understood. I have used the term *Western-global international society* in order to move away from any easy assumption that global-level international society represents some kind of coherent model based on like units. As the whole English School concern with decolonization and the 'revolt against the West' indicates, it does not. Postcolonial states are often quite different types of construct from the states in their former metropoles, a difference highlighted by differentiations such as that of Cooper (1996) into postmodern, modern and premodern states. Even the thin commonality of sovereign equality is questioned by the persistence, and legitimacy, of hegemony that has been a recurrent theme in the preceding chapters. Yet there is sufficient differentiation within the periphery to make a simple binary core–periphery model equally inadequate. The regional differences within the periphery – between Africa and Asia, or Latin America and the Middle East – are easily large enough to suggest that the most accurate model for global-level international society is neither a like-units nor a core–periphery one, but a core-plus-regions one. This too has its difficulties because the (in)coherence of regions varies a lot. But it has the merit of deconstructing a too simple and too homogeneous assumption about what global-level international society means. It strips away the assumption of equality by making clear that the consequences of the monocentric model by which the global level was made have left a legacy that remains strong. This, in turn, largely solves, or at least puts into clear perspective, the problem of hegemony versus sovereign equality that has bedevilled English School thinking.

It seems therefore a good bet that, as debates about regional international society become more prominent within the English School, so too will debates about the overall nature and structure of international society at the global level.

A possible emerging agenda? international society and international security[2]

The 'English School' and 'International Security Studies' are names seldom found in the same sentence. Relatively few within the English School have explicitly addressed the international security agenda, and the concept of security does not play much of a role in English School thinking.[3] Yet there is a substantial English School literature about security, and the English School can be used as a general theoretical framing for thinking about international security comparable with realism and liberalism and Marxism. Realism and Marxism see a world of enemies and rivals running on a logic of survival, coercion, calculation, relative gains and inevitable conflict. Liberalism sees a world of rivals and friends running on a logic of calculation, belief, absolute gains and the possibility of peace. The English School agrees with Wendt (1999) in allowing enemies, rivals and friends and, running on a logic of coercion, calculation and belief. In this sense, it incorporates both the realist and liberal framings and contextualizes them in a range of possible types of international society.

The spectrum of types of international society can be set up in various ways. But, even just using Buzan's four general types, it is immediately apparent that what type of international society one is in has huge consequences for what the agenda of international security will look like. Life within a power-political international society will be extremely different from life in a cooperative or convergence one. The classical English School view of coexistence international societies, like the realist one, stresses great powers, war and the balance of power as key institutions of the social order. But in cooperative and convergence international societies of almost any conceivable sort, war and the balance of power will be respectively marginalized or nearly eliminated as institutions. This does not, of course, mean that such societies have no security agenda. As one can see from the contemporary practice of the EU or the liberal international economic order, security concerns move away from the traditional military ones towards economic, societal and environmental ones and the human security agenda.

If international society is conceived of as a social structure, then it has inside/outside qualities, and this points to at least three novel lines for thinking about international security.

1 What are the security consequences for insiders of being included within the particular set of primary institutions that defines any international society?
2 What are the security consequences for outsiders of being excluded from international society?
3 Can international society itself become a referent object of security?

This is how the English School *could* be used as a comprehensive approach to international security, and there is a substantial literature that already goes in this direction.

The security consequences of international society for insiders

The primary institutions of international society are the key social framework within which the processes of securitization occur. It makes a difference whether the dominant institutions are, say, dynasticism, human inequality and suzerainty, or popular sovereignty, human equality and nationalism. Likewise, the possibilities for securitization are shaped by whether the dominant economic institution is mercantilism or the market. Some institutions have an obvious major impact on what the agenda of international security will look like (e.g., sovereignty, territoriality, colonialism, war, the balance of power, human inequality, nationalism, the market, environmental stewardship). Will it be a security agenda arising from classic military-political competition among states, or one centred more around interdependence issues such as economy, environment and/ or identity?

The classical literature had little to say on the question of how overall social structures might impact on the likely agendas of international security. The discussion of types of international society, which would give leverage on it, is still fairly new. But one can also look at individual primary institutions of international society and their security consequences. The exemplar here is Mayall's (1990) discussions of how the rise of nationalism and the market during the nineteenth century as new institutions of international society not only changed the nature of international politics and security in themselves but also transformed the practices associated with other institutions such as war and territoriality. There has been no systematic attempt to relate the whole possible range of English School institutions to security issues, though this would be a valuable thing to do. What there has been is quite a lot of work on some institutions but not much on others. Much of this work parallels discussions in International Security Studies, though little of it was done with an international security audience in mind. The English School has devoted a lot of discussion to war,[4] and there is a body of work specifically on the laws of war by Adam Roberts (Roberts and Guelff 2000; Roberts 2004, 2006). There has also been substantial English School work on the balance of power[5] and great power management (Bull 1977; Brown 2004; Little 2006). Although the security dilemma is not considered to be an institution of international society, there have been English School reflections on that as well.[6]

The other big debates in the English School that relate to International Security Studies are those on intervention and human rights, which can be read as close to human security. The English School discussion of human rights is partly a general one about the tensions between human rights and sovereignty in relation to international order (Bull 1977, 1984b; Vincent 1986; Hurrell 2007b: 143–64) and partly a more particular one about the emergence (or not) of human rights as a norm or institution of international society. There is a lot of analysis of (non)intervention generally[7] and humanitarian intervention in particular.[8] In considering this question, Williams (2004) makes the case for linking the more radical concerns with human rights in the English School to the emancipatory themes of Critical Security Studies in order to create a more revolutionist English School approach to security. Morris (2004) and Nardin (2004) address the related, but more general, question of how the structure of international society defines the legimacy (or not) of the use of force.

The security consequences of international society for outsiders

Insiders have to live with the security consequences of the prevailing institutions and character of international society. Outsiders have the problem of not being recognized as equals, or possibly not being recognized at all. Think of the era of European (or Roman, or Persian, or Chinese) imperialism, with the world divided into the civilized, barbarian and savage and with few or sometimes no restraints on the 'civilized' from subordinating or even exterminating the 'lesser breeds'. Even in these post-imperial times, a few days in Taipei quickly reveals how non-recognition poses real security problems for outsiders. The English School view of inside/outside relating to membership of international society provides a framing for International Security Studies that makes much more sense for constructivist, feminist and Copenhagen School approaches, and puts the traditionalist, military-political approach into a wider context within which one can see whether its assumptions are appropriate or not.

The only systematic general attempt to think through the security consequences of being inside or outside international society is by Buzan (1996). This remains a pretty preliminary exercise, but it did attempt to map out both the specific character of the spectrum of international societies on a sector by sector basis and the possible security implications of these for insiders and outsiders. There has been no specific attempt to follow it up, though work by both Buzan (2004, 2010b) and Holsti (2004) can be read partly along those lines. Nevertheless, one of the big stories of the English School – that of the expansion of an initially European international society to global scale – is essentially about insiders and outsiders, and much of it is about the coercive imposition of European values and institutions.[9] As noted in chapter 5, there are many studies in this literature of the encounters between, on the one hand, well-armed Europeans (and later Americans) not hesitant to use force to impose their values and, on the other, a variety of non-Western cultures (mainly Japan, China, the Ottoman Empire, Thailand) forced to come to terms with the new Western order. These encounters, with their stories of unequal treaties and threats of occupation, give a stark insight into the problems of being either outside international society or else in a second and inferior tier of it in relation to some core.

In a global international society, of course, all are to some degree insiders, and the idea of outsiders becomes much more relative than it was during the 'expansion' story, when in and out could be pretty clearly drawn. When outsider status is relative, and contingent on one's placement in a differentiated international society (e.g., core or periphery), Wendt's (1999: 247–50) opinion that social structures can be held in place by coercion, calculation and/or belief is one useful way of approaching the idea of outsiders in contemporary international society. Where a particular institution is either contested or held in place mainly by coercion, that could be seen as marking a form of outsider status.

International society as a referent object of security

If one puts the inside and outside perspectives together, then the institutions of international society, both individually and collectively, can become the referent objects of security. Since the institutions of international society constitute both the players and the game, threats to those institutions affect both the units and the social order. One of the logics behind the 'war on terrorism' is that violence-wielding outfits such as al-Qaeda threaten the institution of sovereignty. The global market easily becomes a referent object when there are threats to the rules on trade and finance on which its operation rests (Buzan et al. 1998: 95–117).

This line of thinking features either the international social order as a whole (Bull 1977: 18) or individual primary institutions as the referent objects for security. It plays to the English School's focus on social structures and contrasts with the realist's inclination to privilege the state as the central referent object for all security studies. The Copenhagen School has applied its securitization theory to show how the primary (e.g., sovereignty, market) and secondary (e.g., WTO, UN) institutions of international society can be referent objects for securitization in their own right (Buzan et al. 1998). It has also featured regional security in a way that could easily be linked to the discussion of regional international society in preceding chapters.

The English School thus has much to offer to International Security Studies, but it needs to be considerably more proactive than it has been in making this clear to the community of International Security Studies scholars. For their part, some of the International Security Studies community need to open their eyes to the importance of international society in framing and shaping the agenda of international security.

· Conclusions

The account of the English School given in this book portrays a well-developed and intellectually lively approach to thinking about international relations. It has been going strong for half a century and has been successfully transferred not only across several generations but also across oceans and continents to all countries where the study of international relations is taken seriously. The English School offers an impressive body of literature containing a number of classic works and has developed several lines of well-structured and durable debate. That said, there is still huge scope within it for original work on many topics. There are many gaps in the expansion story to be filled in, and there is much room for expanding work on comparative international society, both historical and regional. The debate about system and society is far from over, and the possible development of an English School approach to Security Studies and the incorporation of international political economy into international society thinking are opportunities waiting to be seized. Both the theorizing and the historical accounting of primary institutions and legitimacy are still in their infancy. The range and variety of possibilities for new work is part of what has made the English School attractive to successive generations of scholars. Subsequent generations of writers are steadily improving the stories, and correcting the distortions and absences, that were part of the legacy of the founding fathers on such things as imperialism/colonialism and hegemony. In the process they are building an ever stronger English School historical account and theoretical framing.

By establishing an approach that is distinctive from other mainstream theories, the English School has earned its place in the IR canon. It offers concepts (international society, primary institutions) and debates (pluralism/solidarism) that are not available through other approaches to IR. Its openness to normative debate offers a well-structured, and partly non-zero-sum, approach to the moral analysis of international relations that contrasts with the moral sterility of neorealism, neoliberalism and a surprising amount of constructivism. It offers a holistic approach that goes some way to overcoming the chronic fragmentation of IR as a discipline. It holds out better linkages to world history, international law and historical sociology than other mainstream IR theories. And some of its debates, most obviously that about system/society and that about the social structure of world politics, have ramifications for the whole discipline of IR.

Although it does offer some limited capacity to generate hypotheses, and to predict the likely direction of the evolution of international society, the English School is never going to satisfy those who hold that positivism is the only acceptable form of knowledge in IR. It is not alone in that and has no need to apologize for it. But it does have a need to sharpen up its concepts and methods and, while some good progress has been made along these lines, there is still more to do.

The English School's attractiveness rests largely on its merits and on its ability to offer distinctive and holistic ways of thinking about international relations. Yet there is no denying that some part of its appeal has been simply that it is conspicuously not an American IR theory. Since its founding, IR has been a peculiar discipline in the extent of its narrow cultural placement. It has been predominantly a discipline of the Anglosphere, with the vast bulk of its literature and journals located in the US and Britain as a fairly distant second. This has created a certain tension because of the fact of US primacy in world politics running in close parallel with the development of IR as a discipline. Since Britain has been number two in the development of IR, there is a certain justice in the otherwise inappropriate label of 'English School'. Now, however, as the discipline builds up in China, India, Latin America and elsewhere, IR is at last beginning to become more genuinely global. The English School can claim some credit for leading the way in this. It has been, and will continue to be, part of the process of bringing the discipline of IR itself into better alignment with the global nature of its subject matter.

NOTES

Chapter 1   The Evolution of the English School

1   On the British Committee and its members, see Dunne 1998: 89–135; Suganami 2003; Vigezzi 2005; Cochran 2009; Epp 2010.

2   For example: Howard 1976; Bull 1977a, 1984a; Gong 1984a; Wight 1977, 1979, 1991; Vincent 1986; Watson 1992, 1997, 2007.

3   Donelan 1978; Mayall 1982; Navari 1991. See also Navari 2009, 7–8.

4   For further assessment of Butterfields's work, see Thompson 1980; Coll 1985; Epp 1991; Dunne 1998: 71–88; Katano 1998; Hall 2002; Sharp 2003; Zhou 2005; Schweizer and Sharp 2007.

5   For further assessment of Bull's work, see Miller and Vincent 1990; Der Derian 1996; Dunne and Wheeler 1996; Kingsbury 1996; Dunne 1998: 136–60; Wheeler and Dunne 1998; Alderson and Hurrell 2000; Hurrell 2002c; Guo 2005; Vigezzi 2005; Little and Williams 2006; Williams 2010b; Ayson 2012.

6   For further assessment of Watson's work, see Wæver 1996; Buzan and Little 2009.

7   For further assessment of Wight's work, see Bull 1976; Porter 1978, 2007; Nicholson 1981, 1982; Jackson 1990b, 2008; Epp 1996; Dunne 1998; Weber 1998; Thomas 2001; Hall 2003, 2006b; Chiaruzzi 2008.

8   For further assessment of Manning's work, see James 1973; Suganami 2001a; Wilson 2004; Long 2005; Aalberts 2010.

9   James 1963; Mackinnon 1966; Butterfield and Wight 1966; Howard 1966; Bull 1972, 1977a; Manning 1972; Armstrong 1977; Bull 1977a; Suganami 1982; Palliser 1984.

10   Bull 1971, 1977a, 1984a; Butterfield 1972; James 1973; Brewin 1978; Vincent 1975, 1988, 1990; Miller and Vincent 1990; Suganami 1989.

11   Bull et al. 1990; Fawn and Larkins 1996; Finnemore 1996; Mapel and Nardin 1998; Roberson 1998.

12   James 1986; Suganami 1989; Mayall 1990; Armstrong 1993; Watson 1997; Linklater 1998; Stivachtis 1998; Y. Zhang 1998; Dunne and Wheeler 1999.

13   For further assessment of Buzan's work, see Little 1995; Adler 2005; Dunne 2005; Miao and Qin 2005; Williams 2010a, 2011; Schouenborg 2011.

14   Suganami 1983; Grader 1988; Wilson 1989; Cutler, 1991; Evans and Wilson 1992; Shaw 1992; Wæver 1992; Buzan 1993; Brown 1995a; Dunne 1995b; Little 1995; Linklater 1996a; Epp 1998; Wæver 1998; Little 2000; Makinda 2000; Buzan 2001; Hall 2001; Suganami 2002, 2003; de Almeida 2003; Jones 2003; Little 2003; Manners 2003; Neumann 2003; Y. Zhang 2003; Young 2005.

15   Vincent 1988; Miller and Vincent 1990; Wheeler 1992; Dunne and Wheeler 1996; Wheeler and Dunne 1998; Alderson and Hurrell 2000; Little and Williams 2006; Williams 2010b.

16   Foot et al. 2003; Bellamy 2005; Schweizer and Sharp 2007; Navari 2009; Navari and Green 2014.

17   Buzan and Little 2000; Jackson 2000; Mayall 2000a; Wheeler 2000; Keene 2002; Bain 2003; Keal 2003; Buzan 2004; Holsti 2004; Clark 2005; Vigezzi 2005; Hall 2006b; Linklater and Suganami 2006; Clark 2007; Hurrell 2007b; Little 2007a; Suzuki 2009; Clark 2011.

18   Riemer and Stivachtis 2002; Hurrell 2007a, 2007b; Buzan and Gonzalez-Pelaez 2009; Stivachtis 2010; Merke 2011; Buzan and Zhang 2014.

19   Pang 1996; Shi 2000; Y. Zhang 2003; Ren 2003; Callahan 2004a, 2004b; Fang 2004; Xu 2005; Wang 2007; X. Zhang 2010.

20   A much fuller listing of English School works from these three countries can be found in the bibliography at www.leeds.ac.uk/polis/englishschool/.

Chapter 2   Key Concepts

1   Wight's meaning of 'rationalism' is about a philosophical disposition. It has nothing to do with the current mainstream IR meaning about rational choice theory. Unless otherwise specified, all uses of the term in this book will follow Wight's meaning.

2   For a more complex genealogical view on society, see Roshchin 2013.

3   I am grateful to Ole Wæver for this latter point.

4   The framing of the three traditions is, like much IR theory, essentially state-centric, thereby making the location of transnational organizations problematic. To the limited extent that such things are discussed within the English School, they tend to be put into the world society segment (e.g., Clark 2007).

5   Primary institutions originally evolve in some place and time. After that, they can be imposed upon, or adopted by, others, as was the case with sovereignty, nationalism and territoriality during the expansion of Western international society to global scale. I am grateful to Mutsumi Hirano for this point.

6   One could add to this set *raison de famille*, as the logic of dynastic systems preceding *raison d'état* (Green 2013).

7   I am grateful to Hidemi Suganami for this formulation.

8   For example: Rengger 1992; Brown 1995b, 1998; Halliday 1992; Linklater 1998; Jackson 2000; Roshchin 2013.

Chapter 3   Theories and Methodologies

1   Little 1995, 1998, 2000; Jackson 2000, 2009; Linklater and Suganami 2006: 81–116; Navari 2009, 2010.
2   Buzan 2004; Clark 2005, 2007; Linklater and Suganami 2006; Hurrell 2007b.
3   Buzan 2004; Holsti 2004; Albert and Buzan 2011; Wilson 2012.
4   To avoid confusion with the normative meaning of pluralism I will use the term 'eclectic' when referring to the English School's approach to method and theory.
5   For further assessment of Vincent's work, see Neumann 1997; Dunne 1998: 161–80; Fu 2005; Gonzalez-Pelaez and Buzan 2003; Gonzalez-Pelaez 2005; Linklater 2011a; Rengger 2011; Reus-Smit 2011b; Welsh 2011.
6   On the Hobbesian analogy, see also Bull 1966c; Navari 1982; Suganami 1989; Yurdusev 2006. For critique of some English School interpretations of Hobbes, see Malcolm 2002.
7   Carr's perspective was doubly anti-liberal, on realist and Marxist grounds, both of which stressed the inevitability of conflict.
8   I am grateful to Cornelia Navari for this formulation.
9   Bull 1984b; Vincent 1986; Wheeler 2000; Linklater 1998, 2011b; Linklater and Suganami 2006: 117ff.
10   Keohane 1988; Hurrell 1993; Evans and Wilson 1992; Buzan 1993; Dunne 1995b: 140–3; Wæver 1998: 109–12; Alderson and Hurrell 2000.
11   Reus-Smit 2002: 499–502; 2005: 82–4; 2009: 58–9. See also Dunne 2008: 279–82.

Introduction to Part II

1   On the general issue of bringing IR and world history together, see Gills 1989; Little 1994, 2005; Osiander 2001; Hobson and Lawson 2008. More specifically, on the relationship between the English School and history, see Weber 1998; Keene 2008.
2   Republican ideas are of course much older. See Deudney 2007.

Chapter 4   International Society in World History

1   Some of the discussion in this subsection is drawn from Buzan and Little (2009).
2   Watson 1990, 1992; Buzan and Little 1996, 2009; Wæver 1996.
3   This argument has an obvious resonance with hegemonic stability theory, but I am not aware than anyone has connected the two.
4   This figure is simplified because it omits suzerainty and dominion. Watson locates hegemony and dominion on either side of the pendulum's resting

point. However, this figure is in line with Watson's view of hegemony representing the norm position in international relations.

5   Ayoob 1999; Y. Zhang 2001; Buzan and Gonzalez-Pelaez 2009; F. Zhang 2009; Suzuki 2009; Quayle 2013; Buzan and Zhang 2014.

Chapter 5   The Expansion of European International Society

1   Wight 1977: 115–22; Naff 1984; Gong 1984a: 106–19; Yurdusev 2009.
2   Gong 1984a: 136–63, 1984b; Y. Zhang 1991, 2001; X. Zhang 2011b.
3   This discussion perhaps confuses hegemony and primacy, with Watson's general line actually being more about primacy. See Clark (2009a, 2011) for discussion of the difference.
4   Interaction capacity refers to the amount of transportation, communication and organizational capacity within the system, and how much in the way of information, goods and people can be moved over what distances, at what speeds, and at what cost. See Buzan and Little 2000: 80–4.
5   Jones 2007; Simpson 2004; Little 2007b; Fabry 2010.

Conclusions to Part II

1   See also Williams 2011; Adler 2005; Dunne 2005; Schouenborg 2011.

Introduction to Part III

1   Bull 1984b; Vincent 1986; Dunne and Wheeler 1996; Linklater 1998; Wheeler and Dunne 1998; Knudsen 1999; Wheeler 2000; Mayall 2000a; Jackson 2000.
2   See, e.g., Brown 1995a, 1995b, 1998; Mapel and Nardin 1998; Rengger 2011.
3   See, e.g., Bull 1981; Bull et al. 1990; Hurrell 1996; Keene 2005; Kingsbury 2002; Vincent 1984a; Wight 2004.
4   See Linklater and Suganami 2006: 238–9, 243–4, for an interesting attempt to list the practical characteristics of pluralist and solidarist positions.
5   I am grateful to Molly Cochran for this point.
6   Mayall 2000a; Bain 2003, 2007a; Hurrell 2007b; for overviews, see Cochran 2009; Bain 2010.

Chapter 7   Pluralism in Historical Perspective

1   Thereafter, European history largely drops out of IR theory and becomes the self-containing story of the European Union. The English School follows this lead and has paid almost no attention to the EU despite its being the major empirical case of a solidarist international society.
2   De Almeida (2006) argues that Wight's misconstruction of the mediaeval to modern transition, in which he staged the mediaeval order as cosmopolitan, goes a long way to explain why so many in the classical English School,

including Bull, ended up wrongly seeing cosmopolitanism as a revolutionist alternative to the society of states rather than as something that exists within and through the society of states.

3 It might be argued that this placing is wrong. Bull's three basic elements apply to any type of society. They are thus prior to the choice of constitutional normative principle. That choice sets the terms in which the three elements will be interpreted. For a states-system rules of coexistence are the starting point for international society, but for empires or cosmopolitan communities these elements of society would take different forms. I am grateful to Will Bain for pointing this out.

4 Holsti 1991: 36, 39; Reus-Smit 1999: 87–9; Clark 2005: 51–70; Navari 2007.

5 The English School is of course not alone in discussing sovereignty as a key principle constituting the international system/society. See, for example, Keohane 1995; Krasner 1999; Onuf 2002.

6 Armstrong 1977; Bull 1977a: 162–83; Watson 1982; Palliser 1984; Wight 1991: 141; Watson 1992; Reus-Smit 1999; Jackson 2000; Hall 2002, 2006a; Neumann 2001, 2003; Sharp 2003.

7 James 1963; Mackinnon 1966; Manning 1972; Bull 1972, 1977a: 127–61; Suganami 1982; Watson 1992; Armstrong 2006.

8 Holsti 1991: 71–89; Watson 1992: 198–213; Clark 2005: 71–84; Keene 2013.

9 I am grateful to Tim Dunne for this point.

10 Gong 1984a: 90–3; Donnelly 1998; Jackson 2000: 287–93; Keene 2002: 122–3, 147–8; Gong, 2002; Clark 2007: 183; Bowden 2009: locs. 2289–322.

11 In our post-Holocaust times, it is quite difficult for contemporary readers to appreciate just how normal and 'scientific' this discourse of racism was during the nineteenth century. Anyone wanting to taste the flavour of it should look at Taylor (1840), with its talk of the Caucasian as the 'highest variety of the human species' (p. 17) and the possibility of 'breeding out the taint' of inferior types by interbreeding with Caucasian stock (p. 19), though many were against this, fearing the opposite effect and the degrading of the human stock by such miscegenation.

Chapter 8   Classical Solidarism and its Successors

1 Arguably, that kind of 'offensive solidarism' would fall outside the English School's requirement for collective legitimation of practices.

2 This cuts close to Bull's (1977a: 243–8) idea of an 'ideologically homogenous' system, which, because he is thinking globally rather than regionally, he dismisses as unlikely to arise.

3 Vincent 1978. See also Wheeler 1992; Linklater and Suganami 2006: 56–74; Reus-Smit 2011b; Linklater 2011a; Welsh 2011.

4 Interestingly, Yan (2011) makes a similar argument based on his reading of classical Chinese political philosophy.

Chapter 9   Solidarism in Historical Perspective

1 Good liberals will of course argue that promoting the market is in the long run a way of promoting human rights because the operation of the market requires that individuals be empowered and have some rights and freedoms.
2 Watson 1992: 299–309, 319–25; 1997; Gong 1984a: 7–21; Clark 1989; Kingsbury 1999; Hurrell 2007b: 13, 35–6, 63–5, 71, 111–14; Buzan 2010a.

Chapter 10   Ongoing Debates and Emergent Agendas

1 Buzan and Albert 2010, 2011. See also Donnelly 2009, 2012; Albert et al. 2013.
2 This subsection draws heavily on Buzan 2010b.
3 One exception being Bellamy and McDonald 2004.
4 Howard 1966; Bull 1977a; Draper 1990; Holsti 1991, 1996, 2004; Windsor 1991; Best 1994; Hassner 1994; Song 2005; Jones 2006.
5 Butterfield 1966; Wight 1966c; Bull 1977a; Hobson and Seabrooke 2001; Kingsbury 2002; Little 2006, 2007a, 2007b.
6 Butterfield 1951; Hurrell 2007b; Booth and Wheeler 2008; Wheeler 2013.
7 Vincent 1974; Little 1975; Bull 1984c; Roberts 1993, 1996, 1999, 2006; Vincent and Wilson 1993; Makinda 1997, 1998; Mayall 1998; Cronin 2002; Buzan 2004.
8 Wheeler 1992, 2000; Knudsen 1996, 1999; Wheeler and Morris 1996; Williams 1999; Ayoob 2001; Brown 2002; Bellamy 2003; Wu 2006.
9 Bull and Watson 1984a; Gong 1984a; Y. Zhang 1991; Keene 2002; Keal 2003; Suzuki 2005, 2009.

REFERENCES

Aalberts, Tanja E. (2010) 'Playing the Game of Sovereign States: Charles Manning's Constructivism *avant-la-lettre*', *European Journal of International Relations*, 16:2, 247–68.

Abulafia, D. (2008) *The Discovery of Mankind: Atlantic Encounters in the Age of Columbus*, New Haven, CT: Yale University Press.

Acharya, Amitav (2008) '"The Expansion of International Society" Revisited', unpublished paper, University of Bristol, 12 pp.

Adler, Emanuel (2005) 'Barry Buzan's Use of Constructivism to Reconstruct the English School: "Not All the Way Down"', *Millennium*, 34:1, 171–82.

Adler, Emanuel (2008) 'The Spread of Security Communities: Communities of Practice, Self-Restraint, and NATO's Post-Cold War Transformation', *European Journal of International Relations*, 14:2, 195–230.

Albert, Mathias, and Barry Buzan (2011) 'Securitization, Sectors and Functional Differentiation', *Security Dialogue*, 42:4–5, 413–25.

Albert, Mathias, Barry Buzan and Michael Zürn (eds) (2013) *Social Differentiation as IR Theory: Segmentation, Stratification, and Functional Differentiation in World Politics*, Cambridge: Cambridge University Press.

Alderson, Kai, and Andrew Hurrell (eds) (2000) *Hedley Bull on International Society*, London: Macmillan.

Alexandrowicz, C. H. (1967) *An Introduction to the History of the Law of Nations in the East Indies: 16th, 17th, and 18th Centuries*, Oxford: Clarendon Press.

Alexandrowicz, C. H. (1973) *The European–African Confrontation: A Study in Treaty Making*, Leiden: A. E. Sijthoff.

Armstrong, David (1977) *Revolutionary Diplomacy: The United Front Doctrine and Chinese Foreign Policy*, Berkeley and Los Angeles: University of California Press.

Armstrong, David (1993) *Revolution and World Order*, Oxford: Clarendon Press.

Armstrong, David (1998) 'Globalization and the Social State', *Review of International Studies*, 24:4, 461–78.

Armstrong, David (1999) 'Law, Justice and the Idea of a World Society', *International Affairs* 75:3, 643–53.

Armstrong, David (2006) 'The Nature of Law in an Anarchical Society', in Richard Little and John Williams (eds), *The Anarchical Society in a Globalized World*, Basingstoke: Palgrave, 121–40.

Ayoob, Mohammed (1999) 'From Regional System to Regional Society: Exploring Key Variables in the Construction of Regional Order', *Australian Journal of International Affairs*, 53:3, 247–60.

Ayoob, Mohammed (2001) 'Humanitarian Intervention and International Society', *Global Governance*, 7:3, 225–30.

Ayson, Robert (2012) *Hedley Bull and the Accommodation of Power*, Basingstoke: Palgrave Macmillan.

Bain, William (2003) *Between Anarchy and Society: Trusteeship and the Obligations of Power*, Oxford: Oxford University Press.

Bain, William (2007a) 'One Order, Two Laws: Recovering the "Normative" in English School Theory', *Review of International Studies*, 33, 557–75.

Bain, William (2007b) 'Are There Any Lessons of History? The English School and the Activity of Being an Historian', *International Politics*, 44:5, 513–30.

Bain, William (2009) 'The English School and the Activity of Being an Historian', in Cornelia Navari (ed.), *Theorising International Society: English School Methods*, Basingstoke: Palgrave, 148–66.

Bain, William (2010) 'The Pluralist–Solidarist Debate in the English School', in Robert A. Denemark (ed.), *International Studies Encyclopedia*, Chichester: Wiley-Blackwell.

Barkin, J. Samuel (1998) 'The Evolution of the Constitution of Sovereignty and the Emergence of Human Rights Norms', *Millennium*, 27:2, 229–52.

Beeson, Mark, and Shaun Breslin (2014) 'Regional and Global Forces in East Asia's Economic Engagement with International Society', in Barry Buzan and Yongjin Zhang (eds), *International Society and the Contest Over 'East Asia'*, Cambridge: Cambridge University Press.

Bellamy, Alex J. (2003) 'Humanitarian Responsibilities and Interventionist Claims in International Society', *Review of International Studies*, 29:3, 321–40.

Bellamy, Alex J. (ed.) (2005) *International Society and its Critics*, Oxford: Oxford University Press.

Bellamy, Alex J., and Matt McDonald (2004) 'Securing International Society: Towards an English School Discourse of Security', *Australian Journal of Political Science*, 39:2, 307–30.

Bentley, Jerry H. (1993) *Old World Encounters: Cross-Cultural Contacts and Exchanges in Pre-Modern Times*, Oxford: Oxford University Press.

Benton, L. (2002) *Law and Colonial Cultures: Legal Regimes in World History*, Cambridge: Cambridge University Press.

Berridge, Geoffrey (1980) 'The Political Theory and Institutional History of States-Systems', *British Journal of International Studies*, 6:1, 82–92.

Best, Geoffrey (1994) *War and Law since 1945*, Oxford: Clarendon Press.

Blanchard, Eric M. (2011) 'Why Is There No Gender in the English School?', *Review of International Studies*, 37:2, 855–79.

Booth, Ken, and Nicholas Wheeler (2008) *The Security Dilemma: Anarchy, Society and Community in World Politics*, Basingstoke: Palgrave.

Bowden, Brett (2009) *The Empire of Civilization: The Evolution of an Imperial Idea*, Chicago: University of Chicago Press, Kindle edn.

Bowden, Brett, and Leonard Seabrooke (eds) (2006) *Global Standards of Market Civilization*, Abingdon: Routledge.

Bozeman, Ada (1984) 'The International Order in a Multicultural World', in Hedley Bull and Adam Watson (eds), *The Expansion of International Society*, Oxford: Oxford University Press, 387–406.

Branch, Jordan (2012) '"Colonial Reflection" and Territoriality: The Peripheral Origins of Sovereign Statehood', *European Journal of International Relations*, 18:2, 277–97.

Brewin, Christopher (1978) 'Justice in International Relations', in Michael Donelan (ed.), *The Reason of States: A Study in International Political Theory*, London: Allen & Unwin.

Brewin, Christopher (1982) 'Sovereignty', in James Mayall (ed.), *The Community of States: A Study in International Political Theory*, London: Allen & Unwin, 34–48.

Brown, Chris (1995a) 'International Theory and International Society: The Viability of the Middle Way', *Review of International Studies*, 21:2, 183–96.

Brown, Chris (1995b) 'International Political Theory and the Idea of World Community', in Ken Booth and Steve Smith (eds), *International Relations Theory Today*, Cambridge: Polity, 90–109.

Brown, Chris (1998) 'Contractarian Thought and the Constitution of International Society Perspective', in David R. Mapel and Terry Nardin (eds), *International Society: Diverse Ethical Perspectives*, Princeton NJ: Princeton University Press, ch. 8.

Brown, Chris (2001) 'World Society and the English School: An "International Society" Perspective on World Society', *European Journal of International Relations*, 7:4, 423–41.

Brown, Chris (2002) 'Intervention and the Westphalian Order', in Richard Norman and Alexander Moseley (eds), *Human Rights and Military Intervention*, Aldershot: Ashgate.

Brown, Chris (2004) 'Do Great Powers Have Great Responsibilities? Great Powers and Moral Agency', *Global Society*, 18:1, 5–19.

Bull, Hedley (1966a) 'International Theory: The Case for the Classical Approach', *World Politics*, 18:3, 361–77.

Bull, Hedley (1966b) 'The Grotian Conception of International Society', in Herbert Butterfield and Martin Wight (eds), *Diplomatic Investigations*, London: Allen & Unwin, 50–73.

Bull, Hedley (1966c) 'Society and Anarchy in International Relations', in Herbert Butterfield and Martin Wight (eds), *Diplomatic Investigations*, London: Allen & Unwin, 35–50.

Bull, Hedley (1971) 'Order vs. Justice in International Society', *Political Studies*, 19:3, 269–83.

Bull, Hedley (1972) 'International Law and International Order', review essay, *International Organization*, 26.3, 583–8.

Bull, Hedley (1976) 'Martin Wight and the Theory of IR', *British Journal of International Studies*, 2:2, 101–16.

Bull, Hedley (1977) *The Anarchical Society: A Study of Order in World Politics*, London: Macmillan.

Bull, Hedley (1979) 'Natural Law and International Relations', *British Journal of International Studies*, 5:2, 171–81.

Bull, Hedley (1980) 'The Great Irresponsibles? The United States, the Soviet Union and World Order', *International Journal*, 35:3, 437–47.

Bull, Hedley (1981) 'Hobbes and the International Anarchy', *Social Research*, 48:4, 717–38.

Bull, Hedley (1982) 'Civilian Power Europe: A Contradiction in Terms', *Journal of Common Market Studies*, 21:1, 149–64.

Bull, Hedley (1984a) 'The Revolt against the West', in Hedley Bull and Adam Watson (eds), *The Expansion of International Society*, Oxford: Oxford University Press, 217–28.

Bull, Hedley (1984b) *Justice in International Relations*, Waterloo, Ontario: University of Waterloo.

Bull, Hedley (ed.) (1984c) *Intervention in World Politics*, Oxford: Clarendon Press.

Bull, Hedley (1990) 'The Importance of Grotius in the Study of International Relations', in Hedley Bull, Benedict Kingsbury and Adam Roberts (eds), *Hugo Grotius and International Relations*, Oxford: Clarendon Press, 65–93.

Bull, Hedley (1991) 'Martin Wight and the Theory of International Relations', in M. Wight, *International Theory: The Three Traditions*, Leicester: Leicester University Press/Royal Institute of International Affairs, ix–xxiii.

Bull, Hedley, and Adam Watson (eds) (1984a) *The Expansion of International Society*, Oxford: Oxford University Press.

Bull, Hedley, and Adam Watson (1984b) 'Introduction', in Hedley Bull and Adam Watson, (eds), *The Expansion of International Society*, Oxford: Oxford University Press, 1–9.

Bull, Hedley, and Adam Watson (1984c) 'Conclusion', in Hedley Bull and Adam Watson, (eds) *The Expansion of International Society*, Oxford: Oxford University Press, 425–35.

Bull, Hedley, Benedict Kingsbury and Adam Roberts (eds) (1990) *Hugo Grotius and International Relations*, Oxford: Clarendon Press.

Burton, John W. (1972) *World Society*, Cambridge: Cambridge University Press.

Butler, Peter F. (1978) 'Legitimacy in a States-System', in Michael Donelan (ed.), *The Reason of States: A Study in International Political Theory*, London: Allen & Unwin.

Butterfield, Herbert (1951) *History and Human Relations*, London: Collins.

Butterfield, Herbert (1966) 'The Balance of Power', in Herbert Butterfield and Martin Wight (eds), *Diplomatic Investigations*, London: Allen & Unwin.

Butterfield, Herbert (1972) 'Morality and an International Order', in B. Porter (ed.), *The Aberystwyth Papers: International Politics, 1919–1969*, London: Oxford University Press.

Butterfield, Herbert, and Martin Wight (eds) (1966) *Diplomatic Investigations*, London: Allen & Unwin.

Buzan, Barry (1993) 'From International System to International Society: Structural Realism and Regime Theory Meet the English School', *International Organization*, 47:3, 327–52.

Buzan, Barry (1996) 'International Society and International Security', in Rick Fawn and Jeremy Larkins (eds), *International Society after the Cold War*, London: Macmillan.

Buzan, Barry (2001) 'The English School: An Underexploited Resource in IR', *Review of International Studies*, 27:3, 471–88 [and see discussion in Forum on the English school, 465–513].

Buzan, Barry (2004) *From International to World Society? English School Theory and the Social Structure of Globalisation*, Cambridge: Cambridge University Press.

Buzan, Barry (2005) 'International Political Economy and Globalization', in Alex J. Bellamy (ed.), *International Society and its Critics*, Oxford: Oxford University Press, ch. 6.

Buzan, Barry (2007 [1991]) *People, States and Fear*, Colchester: ECPR Press.

Buzan, Barry (2008) 'A Leader without Followers? The United States in World Politics after Bush', *International Politics*, 45:5, 554–70.

Buzan, Barry (2010a) 'Culture and International Society', *International Affairs*, 86:1, 1–25.

Buzan, Barry (2010b) 'The English School and International Security', in Myriam Dunn Cavelty and Victor Mauer (eds), *The Routledge Companion to Security Studies*, London: Routledge.

Buzan, Barry (2011) 'A World Order without Superpowers: Decentered Globalism', *International Relations*, 25:1, 1–23.

Buzan, Barry, and Mathias Albert (2010) 'Differentiation: A Sociological Approach to International Relations Theory', *European Journal of International Relations*, 16:3, 315–37.

Buzan, Barry, and Mathias Albert (2011) 'Securitization, Sectors and Functional Differentiation', *Security Dialogue*, special issue, 42:4–5, 413–25.

Buzan, Barry, and Ana Gonzalez-Pelaez (eds) (2009) *International Society and the Middle East: English School Theory at the Regional Level*, Basingstoke: Palgrave.

Buzan, Barry, and George Lawson (2012) 'Rethinking Benchmark Dates in International Relations', *European Journal of International Relations*, doi: 10.1177/1354066112454553.

Buzan, Barry, and George Lawson (2013) 'The Global Transformation: The Nineteenth Century and the Making of Modern International Relations', *International Studies Quarterly*, 57:3, 620–34.

Buzan, Barry, and George Lawson (2014) 'Capitalism and the Emergent World Order', *International Affairs*, 90:1, 71–91.

Buzan, Barry, and George Lawson (forthcoming) *The Global Transformation*, Cambridge: Cambridge University Press.

Buzan, Barry, and Richard Little (1994) 'The Idea of International System: Theory Meets History', *International Political Science Review*, 15:3, 231–56.

Buzan, Barry, and Richard Little (1996) 'Reconceptualizing Anarchy: Structural Realism Meets World History', *European Journal of International Relations*, 2:4, 403–38.

Buzan, Barry, and Richard Little (2000) *International Systems in World History: Remaking the Study of International Relations*, Oxford: Oxford University Press.

Buzan, Barry, and Richard Little (2009) 'Introduction to the 2009 Reissue', in Adam Watson, *The Evolution of International Society*, London: Routledge, ix–xxxv.

Buzan, Barry, and Richard Little (2010) 'The Historical Expansion of International Society', in Robert A. Denemark (ed.), *International Studies Encyclopedia*, Chichester: Wiley-Blackwell.

Buzan, Barry, and Yongjin Zhang (eds) (2014) *International Society and the Contest Over 'East Asia'*, Cambridge: Cambridge University Press.

Buzan, Barry, Ole Wæver and Jaap de Wilde (1998) *Security: A New Framework for Analysis*, Boulder, CO: Lynne Rienner.

Callahan, William A. (2004a) 'Nationalizing International Theory: The Emergence of the "English School" and "IR Theory with Chinese Characteristics"', *World Economic and Politics*, 6, 49–54 [in Chinese].

Callahan, William A. (2004b) 'Nationalizing International Theory: Race, Class and the English School', *Global Society*, 18:4, 305–23.

Carr, E. H. (1946) *The Twenty Years Crisis*, 2nd edn, London: Macmillan.

Carvalho, Benjamin de, Halvard Leira and John Hobson (2011) 'The Big Bangs of IR: The Myths That Your Teachers Still Tell You about 1648 and 1919', *Millennium*, 39:3, 735–58.

Chiaruzzi, Michele (2008) *Politica di potenza nell'età del Leviatano : La teoria internazionale di Martin Wight* [*Power politics in the age of Leviathan: The international theory of Martin Wight*], Bologna: il Mulino.

Clark, Ann Marie (1995) 'Non-Governmental Organizations and their Influence on International Society', *Journal of International Affairs*, 48:2, 507–25.

Clark, Ian (1989) *The Hierarchy of States: Reform and Resistance in the International Order*, Cambridge: Cambridge University Press.

Clark, Ian (2005) *Legitimacy in International Society*, Oxford: Oxford University Press.

Clark, Ian (2007) *International Legitimacy and World Society*, Oxford: Oxford University Press.

Clark, Ian (2009a) 'Towards an English School Theory of Hegemony', *European Journal of International Relations*, 15:2, 203–28.

Clark, Ian (2009b) 'Bringing Hegemony Back In: The United States and International Order', *International Affairs*, 85:1, 23–36.

Clark, Ian (2009c) 'Democracy in International Society: Promotion or Exclusion?', *Millennium*, 37:3, 563–81.

Clark, Ian (2011) *Hegemony in International Society*, Oxford: Oxford University Press.

Clark, Ian (2013) *The Vulnerable in International Society*, Oxford: Oxford University Press.

Cochran, Molly (2008) 'The Ethics of the English School', in Christian Reus-Smit and Duncan Snidal (eds), *The Oxford Handbook of International Relations*, Oxford: Oxford University Press, 286–97.

Cochran, Molly (2009) 'Charting the Ethics of the English School: What "Good" is There in a Middle-Ground Ethics?', *International Studies Quarterly*, 53:1, 203–25.

Cohen, Raymond, and Raymond Westbrook (eds) (2000) *Amarna Diplomacy: The Beginnings of International Relations*, Baltimore: Johns Hopkins University Press.

Coll, A. (1985) *The Wisdom of Statecraft: Sir Herbert Butterfield and the Philosophy of International Politics*, Durham, NC: Duke University Press.

Cooper, Robert (1996) *The Postmodern State and the World Order*. London: Demos.

Copeland, Dale C. (2003) 'A Realist Critique of the English School', *Review of International Studies*, 29:3, 427–41.

Cronin, Bruce (1999) *Community under Anarchy: Transnational Identity and the Evolution of Cooperation*, New York: Columbia University Press.

Cronin, Bruce (2002) 'Multilateral Intervention and the International Community', in Michael Keren and Donald A. Sylvan (eds), *International Intervention: Sovereignty vs. Responsibility*, London: Frank Cass, 147–65.

Cronin, Bruce (2003) *Institutions for the Common Good: International Protection Regimes in International Society*, Cambridge: Cambridge University Press.

Cutler, Claire A. (1991) 'The "Grotian Tradition" in International Relations', *Review of International Studies*, 17:1, 41–65.

Darwin, John (2012) *Unfinished Empire: The Global Expansion of Britain*, London: Allen Lane.

de Almeida, João Marques (2001) 'The Origins of Modern International Society and the Myth of the State of Nature: A Critique', paper presented to the ECPR Pan-European International Relations Conference, University of Kent, September, 39 pp.

de Almeida, João Marques (2003) 'Challenging Realism by Returning to History: The British Committee's Contribution to IR Forty Years On', *International Relations*, 17:3, 273–302.

de Almeida, João M. (2006) 'Hedley Bull, "Embedded Cosmopolitanism", and the Pluralist–Solidarist Debate', in Richard Little and John Williams (eds), *The Anarchical Society in a Globalized World*, Basingstoke: Palgrave, 51–72.

Der Derian, James (1988) 'Introducing Philosophical Traditions in International Relations', *Millennium*, 17:2, 189–93.

Der Derian, James (1992) *Antidiplomacy: Spies, Terror, Speed and War*, Oxford: Blackwell.

Der Derian, James (ed.) (1994) *Critical Investigations*, London: Macmillan.

Der Derian, James (1996) 'Hedley Bull and the Idea of Diplomatic Culture', in Rick Fawn and Jeremy Larkins (eds), *International Society after the Cold War*, London: Macmillan.

Deudney, Daniel H. (2007) *Bounding Power*, Princeton, NJ: Princeton University Press.

Diez, Thomas, and Richard Whitman (2002) 'Analysing European Integration, Reflecting on the English School: Scenarios for an Encounter', *Journal of Common Market Studies*, 40:1, 43–67.

Donelan, Michael (ed.) (1978) *The Reason of States*, London: Allen & Unwin.

Donnelly, Jack (1998) 'Human Rights: A New Standard of Civilization?' *International Affairs*, 74:1, 1–23.

Donnelly, Jack (2006) 'The Constitutional Structure of International Societies', unpublished paper, 23 pp., http://mysite.du.edu/~jdonnell/papers.htm (accessed 18 November 2012).

Donnelly, Jack (2009) 'Rethinking Political Structures: From "Ordering Principles" to "Vertical Differentiation" – and Beyond', *International Theory*, 1:1, 49–86.

Donnelly, Jack (2012) 'The Differentiation of International Societies: An Approach to Structural International Theory', *European Journal of International Relations*, 18:1, 151–76.

Dore, R. (1984) 'Unity and Diversity in Contemporary World Culture', in Hedley Bull and Adam Watson (eds), *The Expansion of International Society*, Oxford: Oxford University Press, 407–24.

Draper, G. I. A. D. (1990) 'Grotius' Place in the Development of Legal Ideas about War', in Hedley Bull, Benedict Kingsbury and Adam Roberts (eds), *Hugo Grotius and International Relations*, Oxford: Clarendon Press.

Dunne, Tim (1995a) 'The Social Construction of International Society', *European Journal of International Relations*, 1:3, 367–89.

Dunne, Tim (1995b) 'International Society – Theoretical Promises Fulfilled?', *Cooperation and Conflict*, 30:2, 125–54.

Dunne, Tim (1997) 'Colonial Encounters in International Relations: Reading Wight, Writing Australia', *Australian Journal of International Affairs*, 51:3, 309–23.

Dunne, Tim (1998) *Inventing International Society: A History of the English School*, London: Macmillan.

Dunne, Tim (2001a) 'New Thinking on International Society', *British Journal of Politics and International Relations*, 3:2, 223–44.

Dunne, Tim (2001b) 'International Society', unpublished MS presented at the English School workshop, Bristol, June, 109 pp.

Dunne, Tim (2003) 'Society and Hierarchy in International Relations', *International Relations*, 17:3, 303–20.

Dunne, Tim (2005) 'System, State and Society: How Does it all Hang Together?', *Millennium*, 34:1, 157–70.

Dunne, Tim (2008) 'The English School', in Chris Reut-Smit and Duncan Snidal (eds), *The Oxford Handbook of International Relations*, Oxford: Oxford University Press, 267–85.

Dunne, Tim, and Nicholas Wheeler (1996) 'Hedley Bull's Pluralism of the Intellect and Solidarism of the Will', *International Affairs*, 72:1, 91–107.

Dunne, Tim, and Nicholas Wheeler (1999) *Human Rights in Global Politics*, Cambridge: Cambridge University Press.

Dunne, Tim, and Nicholas Wheeler (2004) ' "We the Peoples": Contending Discourses of Security in Human Rights Theory and Practice', *International Relations*, 18:1, 9–23.

Englehart, Neil A. (2010) 'Representing Civilization: Solidarism, Ornamentalism, and Siam's Entry into International Society', *European Journal of International Relations*, 16:3, 417–39.

Epp, Roger (1991) *The 'Augustinian Moment' in International Politics: Niebuhr, Butterfield, Wight and the Reclaiming of a Tradition*, International Politics Research Occasional Paper no.10, Aberystwyth: University College of Wales, Department of International Politics.

Epp, Roger (1996) 'Martin Wight: International Relations as Realm of Persuasion', in F. A. Beer and R. Hariman (eds), *Post-Realism: The Rhetorical Turn in International Relations*, East Lansing: Michigan State University Press.

Epp, Roger (1998) 'The English School on the Frontiers of International Relations', *Review of International Studies*, 24:5, 47–63 [special issue].

Epp, Roger (2010) 'The British Committee on the Theory of International Politics and Central Figures in the English School', in Robert A. Denemark (ed.), *International Studies Encyclopedia*, Chichester: Wiley-Blackwell.

Evans, Tony, and Peter Wilson (1992) 'Regime Theory and the English School of International Relations: A Comparison', *Millennium*, 21:3, 329–51.

Fabry, M. (2010) *Recognizing States: International Society and the Establishment of New States since 1776*, Oxford: Oxford University Press.

Falkner, Robert (2012) 'Global Environmentalism and the Greening of International Society', *International Affairs*, 88:3, 503–22.

Fang Changpin (2004) 'The English School and Mainstream Constructivism: A Comparative Analysis', *World Economics and Politics*, 12: 34–8.

Fawn, Rick and Jeremy Larkins (eds) (1996) *International Society after the Cold War*, London: Macmillan.

Ferguson, Niall (2004) *Empire: How Britain Made the Modern World*, London: Penguin.

Fidler, David (2000) 'A Kinder, Gentler System of Capitulations? International Law, Structural Adjustment Policies, and the Standard of Liberal, Globalized Civilization', *Texas International Law Journal*, 35:3, 387–413.

Finnemore, Martha (1996) *National Interests in International Society*, Ithaca, NY: Cornell University Press.

Finnemore, Martha (2001) 'Exporting the English School', *Review of International Studies*, 27:3, 509–13.

Foot, Rosemary (2006) 'Chinese Strategies in a US-Hegemonic Global Order: Accommodating and Hedging', *International Affairs*, 82:1, 77–94.

Foot, Rosemary, John Gaddis and Andrew Hurrell (eds) (2003) *Order and Justice in International Relations*, Oxford: Oxford University Press.

Franck, Thomas M. (1992) 'The Emerging Right to Democratic Governance', *American Journal of International Law*, 86:1, 46–91.

Fu Qiuxiang (2005) 'International Society from Pluralism to Solidarism: Brief Analysis on the Theory of International Society of Vincent', *Studies of International Politics*, 4: 59–66.

Gaskarth, Jamie (2012) 'The Virtues in International Society', *European Journal of International Relations*, 18:3, 431–53.

Gellner, Ernest (1992) 'Nationalism Reconsidered and E. H. Carr', *Review of International Studies*, 18:4, 286–93.

Gills, Barry (1989) 'International Relations Theory and the Processes of World History: Three Approaches', in Hugh C. Dyer and Leon Mangasarian (eds), *The Study of International Relations: The State of the Art*, London: Macmillan, ch. 6.

Gilpin, Robert (1981) *War & Change in World Politics*, Cambridge: Cambridge University Press.

Gong, Gerritt W. (1984a) *The Standard of 'Civilization' in International Society*, Oxford: Clarendon Press.

Gong, Gerritt W. (1984b) 'China's Entry into International Society', in Hedley Bull and Adam Watson (eds), *The Expansion of International Society*, Oxford: Oxford University Press, 171–83.

Gong, Gerrit W. (2002) 'Standards of Civilization Today', in Mehdi Mozaffari (ed.), *Globalization and Civilizations*, London: Routledge, 77–96.

Gonzalez-Pelaez, Ana (2005) *Human Rights and World Trade*, London: Routledge.

Gonzalez-Pelaez, Ana, and Barry Buzan (2003) 'A Viable Project of Solidarism? The Neglected Contributions of John Vincent's Basic Rights Initiative', *International Relations*, 17:3, 321–39.

Grader, Sheila (1988) 'The English School of International Relations: Evidence and Evaluation', *Review of International Studies*, 14:1, 29–44.

Green, Daniel (2013) 'Not 1648, but How About 1689? Early Modern Europe after the 1680s and a Model of the "Eighteenth Century European System"', paper presented at the European International Studies Association conference, Warsaw, 18–21 September.

Griffiths, Martin (1992) 'Order and International Society: The Real Realism?', *Review of International Studies*, 18:3, 217–40.

Guo, Guanqiao (2005) 'A Study of Hedley Bull's Theory of International Society', *Chinese Journal of European Studies*, 4, 19–33.

Hall, Ian (2001) 'Still the English Patient? Closures and Inventions in the English School' (and reply from Buzan and Little), *International Affairs*, 77:4, 931–46.

Hall, Ian (2002) 'History, Christianity and Diplomacy: Sir Herbert Butterfield and International Relations', *Review of International Studies*, 28:4, 719–36.

Hall, Ian (2003) 'Challenge and Response: The Lasting Engagement of Arnold J. Toynbee and Martin Wight', *International Relations*, 17:3, 389–404.

Hall, Ian (2006a) 'Diplomacy, Anti-Diplomacy and International Society', in Richard Little and John Williams (eds), *The Anarchical Society in a Globalized World*, Basingstoke: Palgrave Macmillan, 144–61.

Hall, Ian (2006b) *The International Thought of Martin Wight*, Basingstoke: Palgrave Macmillan.

Halliday, Fred (1992) 'International Society as Homogeneity: Burke, Marx, Fukuyama', *Millennium*, 21:3, 435–61.

Halliday, Fred (1994) *Rethinking International Relations*, Basingstoke: Macmillan.

Halliday, Fred (1999) *Revolution and World Politics: The Rise and Fall of the Sixth Great Power*, Basingstoke: Macmillan.

Halliday, Fred (2009) 'The Middle East and Conceptions of "International Society"', in Barry Buzan and Ana Gonzalez-Pelaez (eds), *International Society and the Middle East: English School Theory at the Regional Level*, Basingstoke: Palgrave, 1–23.

Hannaford, Ivan (1996) *Race: The History of an Idea in the West*, Baltimore: Johns Hopkins University Press.

Hassner, Pierre (1994) 'Beyond the Three Traditions: The Philosophy of War and Peace in Historical Perspective', *International Affairs*, 70:4, 737–56.

Heeren, A. H. L. (1834) *A Manual of the History of the Political System of Europe and its Colonies, from its Formation at the Close of the Fifteenth Century, to its Re-establishment upon the Fall of Napoleon*, trans. D. A. Talboys, Oxford.

Henderson, Conway W. (2001) 'Investigating International Society', *Global Society*, 15:4, 415–23.

Hill, Chris (1996) 'World Opinion and the Empire of Circumstance', *International Affairs*, 72:1, 109–31.

Hjorth, Ronnie (2011) 'Equality in the Theory of International Society: Kelsen, Rawls and the English School', *Review of International Studies*, 37:5, 2585–602.

Hobsbawm, Eric (1962) *The Age of Revolution 1789–1848*, London: Abacus.

Hobsbawm, Eric (1975) *The Age of Capital 1848–1875*, London: Abacus.

Hobsbawm, Eric (1990) *Nations and Nationalism since 1780: Programme, Myth, Reality*, Cambridge: Cambridge University Press.

Hobson, John M. (2004) *The Eastern Origins of Western Civilisation*, Cambridge: Cambridge University Press.

Hobson, John M. (2012) *The Eurocentric Conception of World Politics: Western International Theory 1760–2010*, Cambridge: Cambridge University Press, Kindle edn.

Hobson, John M., and George Lawson (2008) 'What is History in International Relations?', *Millennium*, 37:2, 415–35.

Hobson, John M., and Leonard Seabrooke (2001) 'Reimagining Weber: Constructing International Society and the Social Balance of Power', *European Journal of International Relations*, 7:2, 239–74.

Holsti, Kalevi J. (1991) *Peace and War: Armed Conflicts and International Order 1648–1989*, Cambridge: Cambridge University Press.

Holsti, Kalevi J. (1996) *The State, War and the State of War*, Cambridge: Cambridge University Press.

Holsti, Kalevi J. (2004) *Taming the Sovereigns: Institutional Change in International Politics*, Cambridge: Cambridge University Press.

Holsti, Kalevi J. (2009) 'Theorising the Causes of Order: Hedley Bull's *The Anarchical Society*', in Cornelia Navari (ed.), *Theorising International Society: English School Methods*, Basingstoke: Palgrave, 125–47.

Hosoya, Yuuichi (1998) 'The English School and the Theory of the International Politics', *Journal of Law and Political Studies* [Keio University], 37, 237–80 [in Japanese].

Howard, Michael (1966) 'War as an Instrument of Policy', in Herbert Butterfield and Martin Wight (eds), *Diplomatic Investigations*, London: Allen & Unwin.

Howard, Michael (1976) *War in European History*, Oxford: Oxford University Press.

Howard, Michael (1984) 'The Military Factor in European Expansion', in Hedley Bull and Adam Watson (eds), *The Expansion of International Society*, Oxford: Oxford University Press, 33–42.

Hui, Victoria Tin-bor (2005) *War and State Formation in Ancient China and Early Modern Europe*, New York: Cambridge University Press.

Hurrell, Andrew (1993) 'International Society and the Study of Regimes: A Reflective Approach', in Volker Rittberger (ed.), *Regime Theory and International Relations*, Oxford: Clarendon Press, 49–72.

Hurrell, Andrew (1995) 'Regionalism in Theoretical Perspective', in Louise Fawcett and Andrew Hurrell (eds), *Regionalism in World Politics*, Oxford: Oxford University Press, 37–73.

Hurrell, Andrew (1996) 'Vattel: Pluralism and its Limits', in Ian Clark and Iver Neumann (eds), *Classical Theories of International Relations*, Basingstoke: Macmillan.

Hurrell, Andrew (2001) 'Keeping History, Law and Political Philosophy Firmly within the English School', *Review of International Studies*, 27:3, 489–94.

Hurrell, Andrew (2002a) ' "There Are No Rules" (George W. Bush): International Order after September 11', *International Relations*, 16:2, 185–204.

Hurrell, Andrew (2002b) 'Norms and Ethics in International Relations', in Walter Carlsnaes, Thomas Risse and Beth A. Simmons (eds), *Handbook of International Relations*, London: Sage, 137–54.

Hurrell, Andrew (2002c) 'Foreword to the Third Edition: *The Anarchical Society* 25 Years On', in Hedley Bull, *The Anarchical Society*, Basingstoke: Palgrave, vii–xxiii.

Hurrell, Andrew (2007a) 'One World? Many Worlds? The Place of Regions in the Study of International Society', *International Affairs*, 83:1, 127–46.

Hurrell, Andrew (2007b) *On Global Order: Power, Values and the Constitution of International Society*, Oxford: Oxford University Press.

Hurrell, Andrew, and Louise Fawcett (1995) 'Regionalism and International Order', in Louise Fawcett and Andrew Hurrell (eds), *Regionalism in World Politics*, Oxford: Oxford University Press, 309–27.

Hurrell, Andrew, and Sandeep Sengupta (2012) 'Emerging Powers, North–South Relations and Global Climate Politics', *International Affairs*, 88:3, 463–84.

Ikeda, Josuke (2009) 'Prudence, Justice, and Emancipation: Ethical Perspectives of the English School and its Implication to World Political Theory', *Ritsumeikan Kokusai Chiiki Kenkyu*, 29, 69–83 [in Japanese].

Ikenberry, John G., and Anne-Marie Slaughter (2006) *Forging a World of Liberty under Law: US National Security in the 21st Century*, Princeton, NJ: Woodrow Wilson School of Public and International Affairs, Princeton University.

Jackson, Robert H. (1990a) *Quasi-States, Sovereignty, International Relations and the Third World*, Cambridge: Cambridge University Press.

Jackson, Robert H. (1990b) 'Martin Wight, International Theory and the Good Life', *Millennium*, 19:2, 261–72.

Jackson, Robert H. (1992) 'Pluralism in International Political Theory', *Review of International Studies*, 18:3, 271–81.

Jackson, Robert H. (1996a) 'Is There a Classical International Theory?', in S. Smith, K. Booth and M. Zalewski, *International Theory: Positivism and Beyond*, Cambridge: Cambridge University Press, 203–18.

Jackson, Robert H. (1996b) 'Can International Society Be Green?', in Rick Fawn and Jeremy Larkins (eds), *International Society after the Cold War*, London: Macmillan, 172–92.

Jackson, Robert H. (2000) *The Global Covenant: Human Conduct in a World of States*, Oxford: Oxford University Press.

Jackson, Robert H. (2008) 'From Colonialism to Theology: Encounters with Martin Wight's International Thought', *International Affairs*, 84:2, 351–64.

Jackson, Robert H. (2009) 'International Relations as a Craft Discipline', in Cornelia Navari (ed.), *Theorising International Society: English School Methods*, Basingstoke: Palgrave, 21–38.

James, Alan (1963) 'The Role of International Law in the Study of International Relations', *Political Studies*, 11:2, 212–15.

James, Alan (ed.) (1973) *The Bases of International Order: Essays in the Honour of C. A. W. Manning*, London: Oxford University Press.

James, Alan (1978) 'International Society', *British Journal of International Studies*, 4:2, 91–106.

James, Alan (1984) 'Sovereignty: Ground Rule or Gibberish?', *Review of International Studies*, 10:1, 1–18.

James, Alan (1986) *Sovereign Statehood: The Basis of International Society*, London: Allen & Unwin.

James, Alan (1989) 'The Realism of Realism: The State and the Study of International Relations', *Review of International Studies*, 15:3, 215–29.

James, Alan (1992) 'The Equality of States: Contemporary Manifestations of an Ancient Doctrine' *Review of International Studies*, 18:4, 377–91.

James, Alan (1993) 'System or Society', *Review of International Studies*, 19:3, 269–88.

James, Alan (1999) 'The Practice of Sovereign Statehood in Contemporary International Society', *Political Studies*, 47:3, 457–73.

Jeffery, Renée (2006) 'Hersch Lauterpacht, the Realist Challenge and the "Grotian Tradition" in 20th-Century International Relations', *European Journal of International Relations*, 12:2, 223–50.

Jones, Charles A. (2003) 'Christian Realism and the Foundations of the English School', *International Relations*, 17:3, 371–87.

Jones, Charles A. (2006) 'War in the Twenty-First Century: An Institution in Crisis', in Richard Little and John Williams (eds), *The Anarchical Society in a Globalized World*, Basingstoke: Palgrave, 162–88.

Jones, Charles A. (2007) *American Civilization*, London: Institute for the Study of the Americas.

Jones, Roy E. (1981) 'The English School of International Relations: A Case for Closure', *Review of International Studies*, 7:1, 1–13.

Kadorcan, Burak (2012) 'Military Competition and the Emergence of Nationalism: Putting the Logic of Political Survival into Historical Context', *International Studies Review*, 14:3, 401–28.

Katano, Atsuhiko (1998) 'Herbert Butterfield's Arguments about War: Focusing on His Remark of "War for Righteousness"', *Chuo Law Review* [Chuo University], 105:1, 111–28 [in Japanese].

Kayaoglu, T. (2010) *Legal Imperialism: Sovereignty and Extraterritoriality in Japan, the Ottoman Empire, and China*, Cambridge: Cambridge University Press.

Keal, Paul (1995) 'Just Backward Children: International Law and the Conquest of the Non-European Peoples', *Australian Journal of International Affairs*, 49:2, 191–206.

Keal, Paul (2003) *European Conquest and the Rights of Indigenous Peoples: The Moral Backwardness of International Society*, Cambridge: Cambridge University Press.

Kedourie, E. (1984) 'A New International Disorder', in Hedley Bull and Adam Watson (eds), *The Expansion of International Society*, Oxford: Oxford University Press, 347–56.

Keene, Edward (2002) *Beyond the Anarchical Society: Grotius, Colonialism and Order in World Politics*, Cambridge: Cambridge University Press.

Keene, Edward (2005) *International Political Thought: A Historical Introduction*, Cambridge: Polity.

Keene, Edward (2007) 'A Case Study of the Construction of International Hierarchy: British Treaty-Making against the Slave Trade in the Early Nineteenth Century', *International Organization*, 61:2, 311–39.

Keene, Edward (2008) 'The English School and British Historians', *Millennium*, 37:2, 381–93.

Keene, Edward (2013) 'The Naming of Powers', *Cooperation and Conflict*, 48:2, 268–82.

Keens-Soper, Maurice (1978) 'The Practice of a States-System', in Michael Donelan (ed.), *The Reason of States: A Study in International Political Theory*, London: Allen & Unwin, 25–44.

Kennedy, Paul (1989) *The Rise and Fall of the Great Powers*, London: Fontana.

Keohane, Robert O. (1988) 'International Institutions: Two Approaches', *International Studies Quarterly*, 32:4, 379–96.

Keohane, Robert O. (1995) 'Hobbes' Dilemma and Institutional Change in World Politics: Sovereignty in International Society', in Hans-Henrik Holm and Georg Sørensen (eds), *Whose World Order*, Boulder, CO: Westview Press, 165–86.

Kingsbury, Benedict (1996) 'Grotius, Law and Moral Scepticism: Theory and Practice in the Thought of Hedley Bull', in Ian Clark and Iver Neumann (eds), *Classical Theories of International Relations*, Basingstoke: Macmillan.

Kingsbury, Benedict (1999) 'Sovereignty and Inequality', in Andrew Hurrell and Ngaire Woods (eds), *Inequality, Globalization, and World Politics*, Oxford: Oxford University Press, 66–94.

Kingsbury, Benedict (2002) 'Legal Positivism as Normative Politics: International Society, Balance of Power and Lassa Oppenheim's Positive International Law', *European Journal of International Law*, 13:2, 401–36.

Knudsen, Tonny Brems (1996) 'Humanitarian Intervention Revisited: Post-Cold War Responses to Classical Problems', *International Peacekeeping*, 3:4, 146–65.

Knudsen, Tonny Brems (2009) *Humanitarian Intervention and International Society: Contemporary Manifestations of an Explosive Doctrine*, Abingdon: Routledge.

Krasner, Stephen (1999) *Sovereignty: Organized Hypocrisy*, Princeton, NJ: Princeton University Press.

Kratochwil, Friedrich, and John Gerard Ruggie (1986) 'International Organisation: A State of the Art on an Art of the State', *International Organization*, 40:4, 753–75.

Kupchan, Charles A. (1998) 'After Pax Americana: Benign Power, Regional Integration, and the Sources of Stable Multipolarity', *International Security*, 23:2, 40–79.

Kupchan, Charles A. (2002) *The End of the American Era: US Foreign Policy and the Geopolitics of the Twenty-First Century*, New York: Alfred Knopf.

Kupchan, Charles A. (2012) *No One's World*, New York: Oxford University Press.

Lach, Donald F. (1965, 1970, 1993) *Asia in the Making of Europe*, Vols. 1–3, Chicago: University of Chicago Press.

Linklater, Andrew (1981) 'Men and Citizens in International Relations', *Review of International Studies*, 7:1, 23–37.

Linklater, Andrew (1990) *Beyond Realism and Marxism: Critical Theory and International Relations*, London: Macmillan.

Linklater, Andrew (1996a) 'Rationalism', in Scott Burchill, Andrew Linklater, et al., *Theories of International Relations*, London: Macmillan.

Linklater, Andrew (1996b) 'Citizenship and Sovereignty in the Post-Westphalian State', *European Journal of International Relations*, 2:1, 77–103.

Linklater, Andrew (1998) *The Transformation of Political Community*, Cambridge: Polity.

Linklater, Andrew (2010) 'Global Civilizing Processes and the Ambiguities of Human Interconnectedness', *European Journal of International Relations*, 16:2, 155–78.

Linklater, Andrew (2011a) 'Prudence and Principle in International Society: Reflections on Vincent's Approach to Human rights', *International Affairs*, 87:5, 1179–92.

Linklater, Andrew (2011b) *The Problem of Harm in World Politics: Theoretical Investigations*, Cambridge: Cambridge University Press.

Linklater, Andrew, and Hidemi Suganami (2006) *The English School of International Relations: A Contemporary Reassessment*, Cambridge: Cambridge University Press.

Little, Richard (1975) *Intervention: External Involvement in Civil Wars*, London: Martin Robertson.

Little, Richard (1994) 'International Relations and Large-Scale Historical Change', in A. J. R. Groom and Margot Light (eds), *Contemporary International Relations: A Guide to Theory*, London: Pinter.

Little, Richard (1995) 'Neorealism and the English School: A Methodological, Ontological and Theoretical Reassessment', *European Journal of International Relations*, 1:1, 9–34.

Little, Richard (1998) 'International System, from International to World Society? A Re-evaluation of the English School', in B. A. Roberson (ed.), *International Society and the Development of International Relations Theory*, London: Pinter.

Little, Richard (2000) 'The English School's Contribution to the Study of International Relations', *European Journal of International Relations*, 6:3, 395–422.

Little, Richard (2003) 'The English school vs. American Realism: A Meeting of Minds or Divided by a Common Language?', *Review of International Studies*, 29:3, 443–60.

Little, Richard (2005) 'The English School and World History', in Alex J. Bellamy (ed.), *International Society and its Critics*, Oxford: Oxford University Press, 45–63.

Little, Richard (2006) 'The Balance of Power and Great Power Management', in Richard Little and John Williams (eds), *The Anarchical Society in a Globalized World*, Basingstoke: Palgrave, 97–120.

Little, Richard (2007a) *The Balance of Power in International Relations: Metaphors, Myths and Models*, Cambridge: Cambridge University Press.

Little, Richard (2007b) 'British Neutrality versus Offshore Balancing in the American Civil War: The English School Strikes Back', *Security Studies*, 16:1, 68–95.

Little, Richard (2008a) 'International Relations Theory from a Former Hegemon', in Christian Reus-Smit and Duncan Snidal (eds), *The Oxford Handbook of International Relations*, Oxford: Oxford University Press, 675–87.

Little, Richard (2008b) *The Expansion of the International Society in Heeren's Account of the European States-System*, SPAIS Working Paper no. 07-08, University of Bristol, School of Sociology, Politics, and International Studies, 20pp.

Little, Richard (2009) 'History, Theory and Methodological Pluralism in the English School', in Cornelia Navari (ed.), *Theorising International Society: English School Methods*, Basingstoke: Palgrave, 78–103.

Little, Richard (2011) 'Britain's Response to the Spanish Civil War: Investigating the Implications of foregrounding Practice for English School Thinking', in

Emanuel Adler and Vincent Pouliot (eds), *International Practices*, Cambridge: Cambridge University Press, 174–99.

Little, Richard (2013) 'Eurocentrism, World History, Meta-Narratives and the Meeting of International Societies', in Shogo Suzuki, Yongjin Zhang and Joel Quirk (eds), *International Orders in the Early Modern World: Before the Rise of the West*, London: Routledge.

Little, Richard, and John Williams (eds) (2006) *The Anarchical Society in a Globalized World*, Basingstoke: Palgrave.

Long, David (2005) 'C. A. W. Manning and the Discipline of International Relations', *Round Table*, 94:1, 77–96.

Louis, W. R. (1984) 'The Era of the Mandates System and the Non-European World', in Hedley Bull and Adam Watson (eds), *The Expansion of International Society*, Oxford: Oxford University Press, 201–13.

Luard, Evan (1976) *Types of International Society*, London: Macmillan.

Luard, Evan (1990) *International Society*, London: Macmillan.

McKeown, A. (2003) 'Review of Lauren Benton Law and Colonial Cultures', *Journal of World History*, 14:2, 259–61.

Mackinnon, D. (1966) 'Natural Law', in Herbert Butterfield and Martin Wight (eds), *Diplomatic Investigations*, London: Allen & Unwin.

Makinda, Samuel (1997) 'International Law and Security: Exploring a Symbiotic Relationship', *Australian Journal of International Affairs*, 51:3, 325–38.

Makinda, Samuel (1998) 'The United Nations and State Sovereignty: Mechanism for Managing International Security', *Australian Journal of Political Science*, 33:1, 101–15.

Makinda, Samuel (2000) 'International Society and Eclecticism in IR Theory', *Cooperation and Conflict*, 35:2, 205–16.

Malcolm, Noel (2002) 'Hobbes's Theory of International Relations', in *Aspects of Hobbes*, Oxford: Clarendon Press, 432–56.

Manners, Ian (2003) 'The Missing Tradition of the ES: Including Nietzschean Relativism and World Imagination in Extranational Studies', *Millennium*, 32:2, 241–64.

Manning, C. A. W. (1962) *The Nature of International Society*, London: Macmillan.

Manning, C. A. W. (1972) 'The Legal Framework in a World of Change', in Brian Porter (ed.), *The Aberystwyth Papers: International Politics 1919–1969*, London: Oxford University Press.

Mapel, David R., and Terry Nardin (eds) (1998) *International Society: Diverse Ethical Perspectives*, Princeton, NJ: Princeton University Press.

March, James G., and Johan P. Olsen (1998) 'The Institutional Dynamics of International Political Orders', *International Organization*, 52:4, 943–69.

Mason, Andrew, and Nicholas J. Wheeler (1996) 'Realist Objections to Humanitarian Intervention', in Barry Holden (ed.), *The Ethical Dimensions of Global Change*, London: Macmillan.

Mayall, James (ed.) (1982) *The Community of States: A Study in International Political Theory*, London: Allen & Unwin.

Mayall, James (1984) 'Reflections on the "New" Economic Nationalism', *Review of International Studies*, 10:4, 313–21.

Mayall, James (1989) '1789 and the Liberal Theory of International Society', *Review of International Studies*, 15:4, 297–307.

Mayall, James (1990) *Nationalism and International Society*, Cambridge: Cambridge University Press.

Mayall, James (1998) 'Intervention in International Society: Theory and Practice in Contemporary Perspective', in B. A. Roberson (ed.), *International Society and the Development of International Relations Theory*, London: Pinter.

Mayall, James (2000a) *World Politics: Progress and its Limits*, Cambridge: Polity.

Mayall, James (2000b) 'Democracy and International Society', *International Affairs*, 76:1, 61–75.

Mazrui, Ali (1984) 'Africa Entrapped: Between the Protestant Ethic and the Legacy of Westphalia', in Hedley Bull and Adam Watson (eds), *The Expansion of International Society*, Oxford: Oxford University Press, 289–308.

Mearsheimer, John (2005) 'E. H. Carr vs. Idealism: The Battle Rages On', *International Relations*, 19:2, 139–52.

Mendelsohn, Barak (2009) 'English School, American Style: Testing the Preservation-Seeking Quality of the International Society', *European Journal of International Relations*, 15:2, 291–318.

Merke, Federico (2011) 'The Primary Institutions of Latin American Regional Interstate Society', Paper for IDEAS Latin America Programme, LSE, 27 January, 38pp.

Meyer, John W., John Boli, George M. Thomas and Francisco O. Ramirez (1997) 'World Society and the Nation-State', *American Journal of Sociology*, 103:1, 144–81.

Miao, Hongni, and Qin, Zhilai (2005) 'Barry Buzan's Remaking of the English School', *Chinese Journal of European Studies*, no. 4, 34–47.

Miller, J. D. B., and Vincent, John (eds) (1990) *Order and Violence: Hedley Bull and International Relations*, Oxford: Clarendon Press.

Mitrani, Mor (2013) 'Global Civil Society and International Society: Compete or Complete?', *Alternatives: Global, Local, Political*, 38:2, 172–88.

Modelski, George (1987) *Long Cycles in World Politics*, Seattle: University of Washington Press.

Molloy, Sean (2003) 'The Realist Logic of International Society', *Cooperation and Conflict*, 38:2, 83–99.

Morris, Justin (2004) 'Normative Innovation and the Great Powers', in Alex J. Bellamy (ed.), *International Society and its Critics*, Oxford: Oxford University Press, 247–63.

Morris, Justin (2005) 'Normative Innovation and the Great Powers', in Alex J. Bellamy (ed.), *International Society and its Critics*, Oxford: Oxford University Press, 265–82.

Naff, T. (1984) 'The Ottoman Empire and the European States System', in Hedley Bull and Adam Watson (eds), *The Expansion of International Society*, Oxford: Oxford University Press, 143–69.

Nardin, Terry (1983) *Law, Morality, and the Relations of States*, Princeton, NJ: Princeton University Press.

Nardin, Terry (1998) 'Legal Positivism as a Theory of International Society', in David R. Mapel and Terry Nardin (eds), *International Society: Diverse Ethical Perspectives*, Princeton, NJ: Princeton University Press, 17–35.

Nardin, Terry (2004) 'Justice and Coercion', in Alex J. Bellamy (ed.), *International Society and its Critics*, Oxford: Oxford University Press, ch. 14.

Nau, Henry R. (2001) 'Why "The Rise and Fall of the Great Powers" was Wrong', *Review of International Studies*, 27:4, 579–92.

Navari, Cornelia (1982) 'Hobbes and the "Hobbesian Tradition" in International Thought', *Millennium*, 11:3, 203–22.

Navari, Cornelia (ed.) (1991) *The Condition of States*, Buckingham: Open University Press.

Navari, Cornelia (2000) *Internationalism and the State in the Twentieth Century*, London: Routledge.

Navari, Cornelia (2007) 'States and State Systems: Democratic, Westphalian or Both?', *Review of International Studies*, 33:4, 577–95.

Navari, Cornelia (2009) *Theorising International Society: English School Methods*, Basingstoke: Palgrave.

Navari, Cornelia (2010) 'English School Methodology', in Robert A. Denemark (ed.), *International Studies Encyclopedia*, Chichester: Wiley-Blackwell.

Navari, Cornelia (2011) 'The Concept of Practice in the English School', *European Journal of International Relations*, 17:4, 611–30.

Navari, Cornelia, and Daniel Green (eds) (2014) *Guide to the English School in International Studies*, Chichester: Wiley-Blackwell.

Neumann, Iver B. (1997) 'R. J. Vincent', in Iver B. Neumann and Ole Waever (eds), *The Future of International Relations: Masters in the Making?* London: Routledge.

Neumann, Iver B. (2001) 'The English School and the Practices of World Society', *Review of International Studies*, 27:3, 503–7.

Neumann, Iver B. (2002) 'Returning Practice to the Linguistic Turn: The Case of Diplomacy', *Millennium*, 31:3, 627–51.

Neumann, Iver B. (2003) 'The English School on Diplomacy: Scholarly Promise Unfulfilled', *International Relations*, 17:3, 341–69.

Neumann, Iver B. (2011) 'Entry into International Society Reconceptualised: The Case of Russia', *Review of International Studies*, 37:2, 463–84.

Neumann, Iver B., and Jennifer Welsh (1991) 'The Other in European Self-Definition: An Addendum to the Literature on International Society', *Review of International Studies*, 17:4, 327–48.

Nicholson, Michael (1981) 'The Enigma of Martin Wight', *Review of International Studies*, 7:1, 15–22.

Nicholson, Michael (1982) 'Martin Wight: Enigma or Error', *Review of International Studies*, 8:2, 125–8.

O'Brien, P. (1984) 'Europe in the World Economy', in Hedley Bull and Adam Watson (eds), *The Expansion of International Society*, Oxford: Oxford University Press, 43–60.

O'Hagan, J. (2005) 'The Question of Culture', in Alex J. Bellamy (ed.), *International Society and its Critics*, Oxford: Oxford University Press, 209–28.

O'Neill, R., and Vincent, R. J. (eds) (1990) *The West and the Third World: Essays in Honour of J. D. B. Miller*, Basingstoke: Macmillan.

Onuf, Nicholas (2002) 'Institutions, Intentions and International Relations', *Review of International Studies*, 28:2, 211–28.

Onuma, Yasuaki (2000) 'When Was the Law of International Society Born? An Inquiry of the History of International Law from an Intercivilizational Perspective', *Journal of the History of International Law*, 2, 1–66.

Osiander, Andreas (1994) *The State System of Europe 1640–1990: Peacemaking and the Conditions of International Stability*, Oxford: Clarendon Press.

Osiander, Andreas (2001) 'History and International Relations Theory', in Anja V. Hartmann and Beatrice Heuser (eds), *War, Peace and World Orders in European History*, London: Routledge, 14–24.

Palliser, Michael (1984) 'Diplomacy Today', in Hedley Bull and Adam Watson (eds), *The Expansion of International Society*, Oxford: Oxford University Press.

Palmujoki, Eero (2013) 'Fragmentation and Diversification of Climate Change Governance in International Society', *International Relations*, 27:2, 180–201.

Pang, Zhongying (1996) 'Guoji Shehui Lilun yu Guoji Guanxi de Yingguo Xuepai' ['The Theory of International Society and the English School in International Relations'], *Europe*, 2, 32–40.

Paterson, Matthew (2005) 'Global Environmental Governance', in Alex J. Bellamy (ed.), *International Society and its Critics*, Oxford: Oxford University Press, ch. 8.

Pejcinovic, Lacy (2013) *War in International Society*, Abingdon: Routledge.

Phillips, Andrew (2012) 'Saving Civilization from Empire: Belligerency, Pacifism and the Two Faces of Civilization during the Second Opium War', *European Journal of International Relations*, 18:1, 5–27.

Porter, Brian (ed.) (1972) *The Aberystwyth Papers: International Politics 1919–1969*, London: Oxford University Press.

Porter, Brian (1978) 'Patterns of Thought and Practice: Martin Wight's "International Theory"', in M. Donelan (ed.), *The Reasons of States*, London: Allen & Unwin.

Porter, Brian (1982) 'Nationalism', in James Mayall (ed.), *The Community of States: A Study in International Political Theory*, London: Allen & Unwin.

Porter, Brian (2007) 'The International Political Thought of Martin Wight', *International Affairs*, 83:4, 783–9.

Pouliot, Vincent (2008) 'The Logic of Practicality: A Theory of Practice of Security Communities', *International Organization*, 62:2, 257–88.

Qin, Yaqing (2005) 'Core Problematic of International Relations Theory and the Construction of a Chinese School', *Social Sciences in China*, no. 3, 165–76.

Quayle, Linda (2013) *Southeast Asia and the English School of International Relations: A Region-Theory Dialogue*, Basingstoke: Palgrave Macmillan.

Ralph, Jason (2005) 'International Society, the International Criminal Court and American Foreign Policy', *Review of International Studies*, 31:1, 27–44.

Ralph, Jason (2010) 'War as an Institution of International Hierarchy: Carl Schmitt's Theory of the Partisan and Contemporary US Practice', *Millennium*, 39:2, 279–98.

Rana, A. P. (1993) 'The New Northern Concert of Powers in a World of Multiple Interdependencies', in K. Ajuha, H. Coppens and H. van der Wusten (eds), *Regime Transformation and Global Realignments*, New Delhi: Sage.

Ren, Xiao (2003) 'Learn from the English School', *World Economics and Politics*, 7.

Rengger, Nicholas (1992) 'A City Which Sustains All Things? Communitarianism and International Society', *Millennium*, 21:3, 353–69.

Rengger, Nicholas (2011) 'The World Turned Upside Down: Human Rights in International Relations after 25 Years', *International Affairs*, 87:5, 1159–78.

Reus-Smit, Christian (1996) 'The Normative Structure of International Society', in Fen Osler Hampson and Judith Reppy (eds), *Earthly Goods: Environmental Change and Social Justice*, Ithaca, NY: Cornell University Press, 96–121.

Reus-Smit, Christian (1997) 'The Constitutional Structure of International Society and the Nature of Fundamental Institutions', *International Organization*, 51:4, 555–89.

Reus-Smit, Christian (1999) *The Moral Purpose of the State*, Princeton, NJ: Princeton University Press.

Reus-Smit, Christian (2001) 'Human Rights and the Social Construction of Sovereignty', *Review of International Studies*, 27:4, 519–38.

Reus-Smit, Christian (2002) 'Imagining Society: Constructivism and the English School', *British Journal of Politics and International Relations*, 4:3 487–509.

Reus-Smit, Christian (2005) 'The Constructivist Challenge after September 11', in Alex J. Bellamy (ed.), *International Society and its Critics*, Oxford: Oxford University Press, ch. 4.

Reus-Smit, Christian (2009) 'Constructivism and the English School', in Cornelia Navari, (ed.), *Theorising International Society: English School Methods*, Basingstoke: Palgrave, 58–77.

Reus-Smit, Christian (2011a) 'Struggles for Individual Rights and the Expansion of the International System', *International Organization*, 65:2, 207–42.

Reus-Smit, Christian (2011b) 'Human Rights in a Global Ecumene', *International Affairs*, 87:5, 1205–18.

Riemer, Andrea K., and Yannis A. Stivachtis (eds) (2002) *Understanding EU's Mediterranean Enlargement: The English School and the Expansion of Regional International Societies*, Frankfurt: Peter Lang.

Roberson, Barbara A. (ed.) (1998) *International Society and the Development of International Relations Theory*, London: Pinter; rev. edn, London and New York: Continuum, 2002.

Roberson, Barbara A. (2009) 'Law, Power and the Expansion of International Society', in Cornelia Navari (ed.), *Theorising International Society: English School Methods*, Basingstoke: Palgrave, 189–208.

Roberts, Adam (1991) 'Foreword', in Martin Wight, *International Theory: The Three Traditions*, Leicester: Leicester University Press/Royal Institute of International Affairs, xxiv–xxvii.

Roberts, Adam (1992) 'Evan Luard as a Writer on International Affairs', *Review of International Studies*, 18:1, 63–73.

Roberts, Adam (1993) 'Humanitarian War: Military Intervention and Human Rights', *International Affairs*, 69:3, 429–49.

Roberts, Adam (1996) *Humanitarian Action in War*, Adelphi Paper 305, London: IISS.

Roberts, Adam (1999) 'NATO's "Humanitarian War" over Kosovo', *Survival*, 41:3, 102–23.

Roberts, Adam (2004) 'The Laws of War', in Audrey Kurth Cronin and James M. Ludes (eds), *Attacking Terrorism: Elements of a Grand Strategy*, Washington, DC: Georgetown University Press, 186–219.

Roberts, Adam (2006) 'Transformative Military Occupation: Applying the Laws of War and Human Rights', *American Journal of International Law*, 100:3, 580–622.

Roberts, Adam, and Richard Guelff (2000) *Documents on the Laws of War*, 3rd edn, Oxford: Oxford University Press.

Röling, B. V. A. (1990) 'Are Grotius' Ideas Obsolete in an Expanded World?', in Hedley Bull, Benedict Kingsbury and Adam Roberts (eds), *Hugo Grotius and International Relations*, Oxford: Clarendon Press, 281–99.

Roshchin, Evgeny (2013) '(Un)Natural and Contractual International Society: A Conceptual Inquiry', *European Journal of International Relations*, 19:2, 257–79.

Rosenberg, Justin (1994) *The Empire of Civil Society*, London: Verso.

Ruggie, John Gerard (1982) 'International Regimes, Transactions and Change: Embedded Liberalism in the Postwar Economic Order', *International Organization*, 36:2, 379–415.

Ruggie, John Gerard (1986) 'Continuity and Transformation in the World Polity', in Robert O. Keohane (ed.), *Neorealism and its Critics*, New York: Columbia University Press, 131–57.

Ruggie, John Gerard (1993) 'Territoriality and Beyond: Problematizing Modernity in International Relations', *International Organization*, 47:1, 139–74.

Schouenborg, Laust (2011) 'A New Institutionalism? The English School as International Sociological Theory', *International Relations*, 25:1, 26–44.

Schouenborg, Laust (2012) 'Exploring Westphalia's Blind Spots: Exceptionalism Meets the English School', *Geopolitics*, 17:1, 130–52.

Schwarzenberger, Georg (1951) *Power Politics: A Study of International Society*, London: Stevens & Sons.

Schweizer, Karl, and Paul Sharp (eds) (2007) *The International Thought of Herbert Butterfield*, Basingstoke: Palgrave.

Seth, Sanjay (2011) 'Postcolonial Theory and the Critique of International Relations', *Millennium*, 40:1, 167–83.

Sharp, Paul (2003) 'Herbert Butterfield, the English School and the Civilizing Virtues of Diplomacy', *International Affairs*, 79:4, 855–78.

Shaw, Martin (1992) 'Global Society and Global Responsibility: The Theoretical, Historical and Political Limits of "International Society"', *Millennium*, 21:3,

421–34; repr. in Rick Fawn and Jeremy Larkins (eds), *International Society after the Cold War*, London: Macmillan, 1996.

Shi, Yinghong (2000) 'Xiandai Guoji Shehui Gongtong Jiazhi Guannian – Cong Jidujiao Guoji Shehui dao Dangdai Quanqiu Guoji Shehui' [Common Values in Modern International Society – From the Christian International Society to Contemporary Global International Society], *International Forum*, no. 1, 4–9.

Shin, Wookhee (2008) 'In Pursuit of East Asian International Theory', *Journal of World Politics*, 29:2, 63–88 [in Korean].

Simpson, Gerry (2004) *Great Powers and Outlaw States: Unequal Sovereigns in the International Legal Order*, Cambridge: Cambridge University Press.

Smaje, Chris (2000) *Natural Hierarchies: The Historical Sociology of Race and Caste*, Oxford: Blackwell.

Song, Dexing (2005) 'The War Philosophy of the English School: A Grotian Interpretation', *World Economics and Politics*, 10, 26–31.

Sørensen, Georg (1999) 'Sovereignty: Change and Continuity in a Fundamental Institution', *Political Studies*, 47:3, 590–604.

Spegele, Roger (2005) 'Traditional Political Realism and the Writing of History', in Alex J. Bellamy (ed.), *International Society and its Critics*, Oxford: Oxford University Press, 97–114.

Stichweh, Rudolph (2013) 'The History and Systematics of Functional Differentiation in Sociology', in Mathias Albert, Barry Buzan and Michael Zürn (eds), *Social Differentiation as IR Theory: Segmentation, Stratification, and Functional Differentiation in World Politics*, Cambridge: Cambridge University Press, ch. 2.

Stivachtis, Yannis A. (1998) *The Enlargement of International Society: Culture versus Anarchy and Greece's Entry into International Society*, London: Macmillan.

Stivachtis, Yannis A. (2006) 'Democracy: The Highest Stage of Civilized Statehood', *Global Dialogue*, 8:3–4, 101–12.

Stivachtis, Yannis A. (2010) 'International Society: Global/Regional Dimensions and Geographic Expansion', in Robert A. Denemark (ed.), *International Studies Encyclopedia*, Chichester: Wiley-Blackwell.

Stopford, John M., Susan Strange, with John S. Henley (1991) *Rival States, Rival Firms: Competition for World Market Shares*, Cambridge: Cambridge University Press.

Suganami, Hidemi (1982) 'International Law', in James Mayall (ed.), *The Community of States: A Study in International Political Theory*, London: Allen & Unwin.

Suganami, Hidemi (1983) 'The Structure of Institutionalism: An Anatomy of British Mainstream International Relations', *International Relations*, 7, 2363–81.

Suganami, Hidemi (1984) 'Japan's Entry into International Society', in Hedley Bull and Adam Watson (eds), *The Expansion of International Society*, Oxford: Oxford University Press, 185–99.

Suganami, Hidemi (1989) *The Domestic Analogy and World Order Proposals*, Cambridge: Cambridge University Press.

Suganami, Hidemi (2001a) 'C. A. W. Manning and the Study of International Relations', *Review of International Studies*, 27:1, 91–107.

Suganami, Hidemi (2001b) 'Alexander Wendt and the English School', *Journal of International Relations and Development*, 4:4, 403–23.

Suganami, Hidemi (2002) 'The International Society Perspective on World Politics Reconsidered', *International Relations of the Asia-Pacific*, 2:1, 1–28.

Suganami, Hidemi (2003) 'British Institutionalists, or the English School, 20 Years On', *International Relations*, 17:3, 253–72.

Suganami, Hidemi (2010) 'The English School of International Relations: Historical Development', in Robert A. Denemark (ed.), *International Studies Encyclopedia*, Chichester: Wiley-Blackwell.

Suzuki, Shogo (2005) 'Japan's Socialization into Janus-Faced European International Society', *European Journal of International Relations*, 11:1, 137–64.

Suzuki, Shogo (2009) *Civilisation and Empire: China and Japan's Encounter with European International Society*, London: Routledge.

Suzuki, Shogo, Yongjin Zhang and Joel Quirk (eds) (2013) *International Orders in the Early Modern World: Before the Rise of the West*, London: Routledge.

Taylor, W. Cooke (1840) *The Natural History of Society in the Barbarous and Civilized State*, London: Brown, Green & Longmans.

Terhalle, Maximilian (2011) 'Reciprocal Socialization: Rising Powers and the West', *International Studies Perspectives*, 12:4, 341–61.

Thomas, Scott M. (2000) 'Taking Religious and Cultural Pluralism Seriously: The Global Resurgence of Religion and the Transformation of International Society', *Millennium*, 29:3, 815–41.

Thomas, Scott M. (2001) 'Faith, History and Martin Wight: The Role of Religion in the Historical Sociology of the English School of International Relations', *International Affairs*, 77:4, 905–29.

Thompson, K. W. (ed.) (1980) *Herbert Butterfield: The Ethics of History and Politics*, Washington, DC: University Press of America.

Tilly, Charles (1990) *Coercion, Capital and European States AD 990–1990*, Oxford: Blackwell.

Towns, Ann (2009) 'The Status of Women as a Standard of "Civilization"', *European Journal of International Relations*, 15:4, 681–706.

True, Jacqui (2005) 'Feminism', in Alex J. Bellamy (ed.), *International Society and its Critics*, Oxford: Oxford University Press, ch. 9.

Vigezzi, Brunello (2005) *The British Committee on the Theory of International Politics (1954–1985): The Rediscovery of History*, Milan: Edizioni Unicopli.

Vincent, R. John (1974) *Nonintervention and International Order*, Princeton, NJ: Princeton University Press.

Vincent, R. John (1975) 'The Idea of Concert and International Order', *Yearbook of World Affairs*, 31, London: Institute of World Affairs, 34–55.

Vincent, R. John (1978) 'Western Conceptions of a Universal Moral Order', *British Journal of International Studies*, 4:1, 20–46.

Vincent, R. John (1982) 'Race in International Relations', *International Affairs*, 58:4, 658–70.

Vincent, R. John (1984a), 'Edmund Burke and the Theory of International Relations', *Review of International Studies*, 10:3, 205–18.

Vincent, R. John (1984b) 'Racial Equality', in Hedley Bull and Adam Watson (eds), *The Expansion of International Society*, Oxford: Oxford University Press, 239–54.

Vincent, R. John (1986) *Human Rights and International Relations: Issues and Responses*, Cambridge: Cambridge University Press.

Vincent, R. John (1988) 'Hedley Bull and Order in International Politics', *Millennium*, 17:2, 195–213.

Vincent, R. John (1990) 'Order in International Politics', in J. D. B. Miller and R. John Vincent (eds), *Order and Violence: Hedley Bull and International Relations*, Oxford: Clarendon Press, 38–64.

Vincent, R. John (1992) 'The Idea of Rights in International Ethics', in Terry Nardin and David Mapel (eds), *Traditions of International Ethics*, Cambridge: Cambridge University Press, 250–69.

Vincent, R. John, and Peter Wilson (1993) 'Beyond Non-Intervention', in Ian Forbes and Mark Hoffman (eds), *Ethics and Intervention*, London: Macmillan.

Wæver, Ole (1992) 'International Society – Theoretical Promises Unfulfilled?', *Cooperation and Conflict*, 27:1, 97–128.

Wæver, Ole (1996) 'Europe's Three Empires: A Watsonian Interpretation of Post-Wall European Security', in Rick Fawn and Jeremy Larkins (eds), *International Society after the Cold War*, London: Macmillan, 220–60.

Wæver, Ole (1998) 'Four Meanings of International Society: A Trans-Atlantic Dialogue', in B. A. Roberson (ed.), *International Society and the Development of International Relations Theory*, London: Pinter.

Wæver, Ole (1999) *Does the English School's Via Media Equal the Contemporary Constructivist Middle Ground?*, Manchester, BISA Conference Paper, 17 pp.; available at www.polis.leeds.ac.uk/research/international-relations-security/english-school/.

Walker, R. B. J. (1993) *Inside/Outside: International Relations as Political Theory*, Cambridge: Cambridge University Press.

Waltz, Kenneth N. (1979) *Theory of International Politics*, Reading, MA: Addison-Wesley.

Wang, Jiangli, and Barry Buzan (2014) 'The English and Chinese Schools of International Relations: Comparisons and Lessons', *Chinese Journal of International Politics*.

Wang Qiu-bin (2007) 'The Northeast Asia Regional International Society: From the English School Perspective', *Jilin University Journal Social Sciences Edition*, no. 2, 59–65.

Watson, Adam (1982) *Diplomacy: The Dialogue Between States*, London: Methuen.

Watson, Adam (1984a) 'Russia and the European States System', in Hedley Bull and Adam Watson (eds), *The Expansion of International Society*, Oxford: Oxford University Press, 27–41.

Watson, Adam (1984b) 'New States in the Americas', in Hedley Bull and Adam Watson (eds), *The Expansion of International Society*, Oxford: Oxford University Press, 27–41.

Watson, Adam (1984c) 'European International Society and its Expansion', in Hedley Bull and Adam Watson (eds), *The Expansion of International Society*, Oxford: Oxford University Press, 13–32.

Watson, Adam (1987) 'Hedley Bull, State Systems and International Studies', *Review of International Studies*, 13:2, 147–53.

Watson, Adam (1990) 'Systems of States', *Review of International Studies*, 16:2, 99–109.

Watson, Adam (1992) *The Evolution of International Society*, London: Routledge.

Watson, Adam (1997) *The Limits of Independence: Relations between States in the Modern World*, London: Routledge.

Watson, Adam (2001) 'Foreword' to 'Forum on the English School', *Review of International Studies*, 27:3, 467–70.

Watson, Adam (2007) *Hegemony and History*, London: Routledge.

Weber, Cynthia (1998) 'Reading Martin Wight's "Why Is There No International Theory?" as History', *Alternatives*, 23:4, 451–69.

Weinert, Matthew S. (2011) 'Reforming the Pluralist–Solidarist Debate', *Millennium*, 40:1, 21–41.

Welsh, Jennifer M. (2011) 'A Normative Case for Pluralism: Reassessing Vincent's Views on Humanitarian Intervention', *International Affairs*, 87:5, 1193–204.

Wendt, Alexander (1992) 'Anarchy is What States Make of It: The Social Construction of Power Politics', *International Organization*, 46:2, 391–425.

Wendt, Alexander (1999) *Social Theory of International Politics*, Cambridge: Cambridge University Press.

Wheeler, Nicholas J. (1992) 'Pluralist and Solidarist Conceptions of International Society: Bull and Vincent on Humanitarian Intervention', *Millennium*, 21:3, 463–89.

Wheeler, Nicholas J. (1996) 'Guardian Angel or Global Gangster: A Review of the Ethical Claims of International Society', *Political Studies*, 44, 123–35.

Wheeler, Nicholas J. (2000) *Saving Strangers: Humanitarian Intervention in International Society*, Oxford: Oxford University Press.

Wheeler, Nicholas J. (2013) 'Investigating Diplomatic Transformations', *International Affairs*, 89:2, 477–96.

Wheeler, Nicholas J., and Tim Dunne (1998) 'Hedley Bull and the Idea of a Universal Moral Community: Fictional, Primordial or Imagined?', in B. A. Roberson (ed.), *International Society and the Development of International Relations Theory*, London: Pinter.

Wheeler, Nicholas J., and Justin Morris (1996) 'Humanitarian Intervention and State Practice at the End of the Cold War', in Rick Fawn and Jeremy Larkins (eds), *International Society after the Cold War*, London: Macmillan, 135–71.

Wight, Martin (1966a) 'Why Is There No International Theory?', in Herbert Butterfield and Martin Wight (eds), *Diplomatic Investigations*, London: Allen & Unwin, 17–34.

Wight, Martin (1966b) 'Western Values in International Relations', in Herbert Butterfield and Martin Wight (eds), *Diplomatic Investigations*, London: Allen & Unwin.

Wight, Martin (1966c) 'The Balance of Power', in Herbert Butterfield and Martin Wight (eds), *Diplomatic Investigations*, London: Allen & Unwin.

Wight, Martin (1977) *Systems of States*, ed. Hedley Bull, Leicester: Leicester University Press.

Wight, Martin (1979) *Power Politics*, ed. Hedley Bull and Carsten Holbraad, 2nd edn, London: Penguin.

Wight, Martin (1991) *International Theory: The Three Traditions*, ed. Brian Porter and Gabriele Wight, Leicester: Leicester University Press/Royal Institute of International Affairs.

Wight, Martin (2004) *Four Seminal Thinkers in International Theory: Machiavelli, Grotius, Kant and Mazzini*, Oxford: Oxford University Press.

Williams, John (1999) 'The Ethical Basis of Humanitarian Intervention, the Security Council and Yugoslavia', *International Peacekeeping*, 6:2, 1–23.

Williams, John (2002) 'Territorial Borders, Toleration and the English School', *Review of International Studies*, 28:4, 737–58.

Williams, John (2005) 'Pluralism, Solidarism and the Emergence of World Society in English School Theory', *International Relations*, 19:1, 19–38.

Williams, John (2006) 'Order and Society', in Richard Little and John Williams (eds), *The Anarchical Society in a Globalized World*, Basingstoke: Palgrave, 13–34.

Williams, John (2010a) 'The International Society – World Society Distinction', in Robert A. Denemark (ed.), *International Studies Encyclopedia*, Chichester: Wiley-Blackwell.

Williams, John (2010b) 'Hedley Bull and Just War: Missed Opportunities and Lessons to be Learned', *European Journal of International Relations*, 16:2, 179–96.

Williams, John (2011) 'Structure, Norms and Normative Theory in a Re-defined English School: Accepting Buzan's Challenge', *Review of International Studies*, 37:3, 1235–53.

Williams, Paul (2004) 'Critical Security Studies', in Alex J. Bellamy (ed.), *International Society and its Critics*, Oxford: Oxford University Press, ch. 7.

Wilson, Peter (1989) 'The English School of International Relations: A Reply to Sheila Grader', *Review of International Studies*, 15:1, 49–58.

Wilson, Peter (2004) 'Manning's Quasi-Masterpiece: *The Nature of International Society* Revisited', *Round Table*, 93:377, 755–69.

Wilson, Peter (2009) 'The English School's Approach to International Law', in Cornelia Navari (ed.), *Theorising International Society: English School Methods*, Basingstoke: Palgrave, 167–88.

Wilson, Peter (2012) 'The English School Meets the Chicago School: The Case for a Grounded Theory of International Institutions', *International Studies Review*, 14:4, 567–90.

Windsor, Philip (1978) 'The Justification of the State', in Michael Donelan (ed.), *The Reason of States: A Study in International Political Theory*, London: Allen & Unwin.

Windsor, Philip (1991) 'The State and War', in Cornelia Navari (ed.), *The Condition of States*, Buckingham: Open University Press.

Wu, Zhengyu (2006) 'John Vincent: Sovereignty, Human Rights and Humanitarian Intervention', in Zhirui Chen, Guiyin Zhou and Bin Shi (eds), *Open International Society: The English School in IR Studies*, Beijing: Peking University Press, 165–77.

Xu Yali (2005) 'Theoretical Traditions of International Relations and International Society Theory of English School', *Chinese Journal of European Studies*, no. 1, 66–75.

Yan Xuetong (2011) *Ancient Chinese Thought, Modern Chinese Power*, ed. D. Bell and Sun Zhe, trans. E. Ryden, Princeton, NJ: Princeton University Press.

Young, Oran R. (2005) 'Whither the English School?', *International Studies Review*, 7:4, 629–33.

Yurdusev, A. Nuri (2006) 'Thomas Hobbes and International Relations: From Realism to Rationalism', *Australian Journal of International Affairs*, 60:2, 305–21.

Yurdusev, A. Nuri (2009) 'The Middle East Encounter with the Expansion of European International Society', in Barry Buzan and A. Gonzalez-Pelaez (eds), *International Society and the Middle East: English School Theory at the Regional Level*, Basingstoke: Palgrave Macmillan, ch. 4.

Zacher, Mark (2001) 'The Territorial Integrity Norm: International Boundaries and the Use of Force', *International Organization*, 55:2, 215–50.

Zakaria, Fareed (2009) *The Post-American World and the Rise of the Rest*, London: Penguin.

Zarakol, Ayşe (2011) *After Defeat: How the East Learned to Live with the West*, Cambridge: Cambridge University Press.

Zhang, Feng (2009) 'Rethinking the "Tribute System": Broadening the Conceptual Horizon of Historical East Asian Politics', *Chinese Journal of International Politics*, 2:4, 545–74.

Zhang, Feng (2014) 'International Societies in Premodern East Asia: A Preliminary Framework', in Barry Buzan and Yongjin Zhang (eds), *International Society and the Contest Over 'East Asia'*, Cambridge: Cambridge University Press.

Zhang, Xiaoming (2010) *English School of International Relations: History, Theory and View on China*, Beijing: People's Press [in Chinese].

Zhang, Xiaoming (2011a) 'A Rising China and the Normative Changes in International Society', *East Asia*, 28, 235–46.

Zhang, Xiaoming (2011b) 'China in the Conception of International Society: The English School's Engagements with China', *Review of International Studies*, 37:2, 763–86.

Zhang, Yongjin (1991) 'China's Entry into International Society: Beyond the Standard of "Civilization"', *Review of International Studies*, 17:1, 3–17.

Zhang, Yongjin (1998) *China in International Society since 1949*, Basingstoke: Macmillan.

Zhang, Yongjin (2001) 'System, Empire and State in Chinese International Relations', in Michael Cox, Tim Dunne and Ken Booth (eds), *Empires, Systems and States: Great Transformations in International Politics*, Cambridge: Cambridge University Press, 43–63.

Zhang, Yongjin (2003) 'The "English School" in China: A Travelogue of Ideas and their Diffusion', *European Journal of International Relations*, 9:1, 87–114.

Zhang, Yongjin (2014) 'The "English School" Goes Global – Towards a Collinsian Sociological Account', in Cornelia Navari and Daniel Green (eds), *Guide to the English School in International Studies*, Chichester: Wiley-Blackwell.

Zhang, Yongjin, and Barry Buzan (2012) 'The Tributary System as International Society in Theory and Practice', *Chinese Journal of International Politics*, 5:1, 3–36.

Zhang Zhenjian (2004) 'Resemblance and Differences: the English School and Constructivism', *Chinese Journal of European Studies*, no. 5, 38–51 [in Chinese].

Zhou Guiyin (2005) 'Christianity, History and International Politics: A Study of Herbert Butterfield's Thought', *Chinese Journal of European Studies*, no. 4, 1–18 [in Chinese].

INDEX